The Encyclopedia of Trees: Canada and the United States

The Encyclopedia of Trees:

Canada and the United States

SAM BENVIE

KEY PORTER BOOKS

Canadian Cataloguing in Publication Data

Benvie, Sam
    The encyclopedia of trees

ISBN 1-55263-086-2

1. Trees – North America – Encyclopedias I. Title

QK110.B46 1999   582.169097   C99-931100-X

The publisher gratefully acknowledges the support of the Canada Council for the Arts and the Ontario Arts Council for its publishing program.

Canadä

We acknowledge the financial support of the Government of Canada through the Book Publishing Industry Development Program (BPIDP) for our publishing activities.

Key Porter Books Limited
70 The Esplanade
Toronto, Ontario
Canada M5E 1R2

www.keyporter.com

Electronic formatting: Heidi Palfrey
Design: Peter Maher

Printed and bound in Italy

99 00 01 02 03 6 5 4 3 2 1

To Johanna Elisabeth van Ravenswaay
and Neil Stewart Benvie, my parents.

Quercūs inter Ailanthūs

Acknowledgments

I have had tremendous support in writing this book from so many people. It is a real and lasting pleasure to be able to acknowledge them here. First and foremost, I would like to thank several people at Key Porter Books for their unflagging support: Anna Porter for her passionate desire to bring this book into being; Clare McKeon for her patience and humor in shepherding me through the lengthy process; and Marjolein Visser for her coordinating abilities, especially in the final days before going to print. I owe a debt of gratitude to the editor and reviewers of the manuscript for their diligent reading, insight, and suggestions, and to the photographers whose images give such visual substance to the book. I would also like to give special thanks to my colleagues at Ryerson Polytechnic University for their encouragement and understanding of my at times complete immersion in this project. I would lastly like to thank my family for their very special and particular support.

Contents

Introduction

One of my earliest memories is of standing on a vast emerald lawn shaded by dozens of towering American elm. The sense I had of being in a living green cathedral is not much of an exaggeration. Many people have similar memories. I was also just old enough to witness the final rapid decline and disappearance of this majestic tree from the public spaces of this continent. The experience taught me that even such wonder and beauty as they had provided could end. I have been a lover of trees ever since.

Whether in my formal studies in botany and environmental studies, or in my work in landscape design and teaching, trees have never been far out of my sight or mind. It has always been important to me to promote a positive response not just to trees themselves but also to how they and their environments are integral, mutually defining and endlessly dynamic. This environment includes not only other plants, animals, soil, and climate, but also people, in increasing numbers.

This is an ecological theme. People have a relationship to trees. We derive food and shelter from them, and use them to create a huge variety of products. We also employ them to grace our surroundings, and buffer our impact upon the land and climate. In the process, we destroy vast numbers of them, and set up conditions that favor their decline. If we are to continue to enjoy their bounty, it is necessary to know what they are, their

diversity of kind, the specific environments within which they develop and which they themselves help to shape, and how they are used by people and other animals as well.

In writing this book I intended to address in a small way this necessity. Specifically I have attempted to do several things.

The first objective of this book is to present as many tree species native to North America as are currently recognized. To some extent this is a subjective exercise; it involves defining what is meant by "tree" and what constitutes a species. These definitions are not always as easy to come by as the layperson might think or wish. Generally, as presented here, a tree is any primarily woody plant of one to several perennial stems arising from the ground and living for 20 or more years, and attaining a height of at least 10 feet (3 m). Others definitions vary somewhat from this, but not significantly so. Connected to this is the issue of distinguishing trees from shrubs. In cultivation, some species of shrubs are preferentially pruned into tree-like forms; and in nature, many woody plants straddle the conceptual boundary between shrub and tree. This book deals primarily with those woody plants that assume at maturity a tree form on optimal sites in their natural habitats. Such a distinction cannot hope to please everyone. There will be plants that some consider trees which do not appear here; equally there are some plants discussed that could be considered shrubs. On the one hand, I have felt impelled by love to include a few small trees, such as Alternate-leaved Dogwood, which are more often than not shrub-like, and conventionally treated as such. I cannot rationalize such inclusions, and make no effort to do so. Those who know such plants, or come to know them, will understand why I have succumbed to mere affection. On the other hand, academic perversity has led me to include a very few species, such as Engelmann Oak, which are often

encountered as shrubs. In these very few exceptional instances, I have felt it necessary to include these plants, in part, because they represent one end of a continuum in form of the genus to which they belong. Engelmann Oak, for instance, is one of a number of Oaks, some wholly shrubby, that are characteristic of the dry, fire-dependent chaparral habitats in California. It seems to me worthwhile highlighting this, so that the reader does not go away with the idea that all the Oaks are Mighty Trees.

The question of what constitutes a species is not cut and dried either. All life forms ultimately defy human attempts at categorization, and plants particularly so. Species are described by an authority (occasionally two people working together) who delineates the boundaries, most often features physically intrinsic to the group that separate it from all others, and set it in what is termed its phylogenetic relationship to all other plants. These boundaries are not always universally agreed to, and over time arguments are put forward for recognizing as a species a group that was formerly included as a variety or subspecies within another species. Some species in some genera are very much in contention; species in the genus *Crataegus*, the Hawthorns, are a case in point. Over time, the arguments lead, we hope, to a more thorough understanding of the group in question, and general agreement is reached as to the group's status. One of the consequences of this activity, however, is that several names will arise and be used either simultaneously or consecutively for a particular group of plants. For instance, American Basswood has in the past been known as *Tilia neglecta*, but is currently called *Tilia americana*. In some instances the confusion in species status, and hence in naming, is bewildering. It is important, however, not to consider this seeming uncertainty a "bad thing." In dealing with this situation, a useful adjunct to the species-name itself is the name of the authority who has described and named it. Such names are provided in this book, as in many others, in small letters immediately after the botanical species-name. Most often the authority name is abbreviated, but not always. The addition of the authority names flags to the reader that, in some cases, the species was formerly considered under another botanical name. The reader can then, if interested, seek additional information under the former name, also known as a synonym.

In the end this is not a book on taxonomy. Some species considered here are dealt with by others as varieties or subspecies of other species. Some authors also split single species discussed here into two or more. This is an enduring legacy of taxonomy.

The second specific objective of this book is to provide, for each tree, a brief description, supported by one or two photographs, of what the tree looks like in its most salient features, i.e. overall size, habit, trunk, crown, bark, leaf, flower, fruit and root, as far as any of these are particularly notable or useful to an interested reader. In some cases flowers are so inconspicuous as to go unnoticed, and have not been described in the same level of detail as those on trees that have highly conspicuous and showy flowers. For some trees, root structure is not well documented in the literature, or is inconsistently described; consequently, I have either not discussed it or noted the varying opinions. Keeping in mind that the book is intended to be used by non-specialists, the descriptions concentrate more on what is easily observable and understandable, rather than on the taxonomically fine features.

The third goal of the book is to describe, as briefly as possible, the natural environment of each tree, including its natural range, the various habitats within which it is usually found, the trees with which it commonly associates, the topography, in some

cases the climatic regime, and the soil types on which it is found, noting those conditions under which optimal growth occurs. I have usually provided in this description the tolerance of each species to shade and/or drought, and/or flooding, and attempted to relate this to life-span and the very broad successional/climax habitat that the species seems most often to inhabit. This information is of particular use to the avid gardener or naturalist, who realizes that the more a plant and its siting are brought into consonance, the better the plant will fare, the greater the degree of predictability in behavior and the less intervention should be required.

The fourth objective is to highlight, for each species, some of its more important and interesting uses and values, not only in landscaping, human economy and ethnobotany, but also within the context of the natural environment, i.e. in restoration, watershed management and wildlife habitat. There is an enormous amount of information available in this area. Those interested in knowing more about the specific uses of a particular tree will find an abundance of information in a simple search of the literature.

Finally, in the hope that the reader will feel moved to act upon what is presented here, several sections have been added at the end, on USDA zone hardiness, further reading, and places and organizations to contact.

I hope the reader finds some favorite native trees here, as well as discovers and rediscovers many others. Each one is worthy of consideration and praise.

How to Use This Book

Species are listed alphabetically by their Latin name (genus and species). The Latin name of the first species on a two-page spread is on the top left-hand corner of every page. The top right-hand corner lists a common name of the last species on a two-page spread.

This encyclopedia introduces genera with more than three species listed. Introductions expand on tree genus-characteristics, habitat preferences, and commercial and landscape uses. When relevant, genus introductions also outline taxonomic issues.

Many entries include a key-features table, which briefly outlines a species' more salient identification characteristics. Words in bold highlight a tree's most distinctive identifying features.

Readers might also find the following sections helpful additions to this book: a glossary, a tree-hardiness chart and accompanying hardiness-zone map, a contact list of places and organizations, an index linking Latin names with common names, suggestions for further reading, and a selection of Internet sites to visit.

Alphabetical Listing
of Trees

THE FIRS (*ABIES*)

Pine Family (*Pinaceae*)

The firs consist of over 50 species of evergreen trees, widely distributed throughout the northern hemisphere in North America, Europe and Asia, and reaching as far south as Taiwan and Central America at higher altitudes. There are nine species in North America, mostly in the mountains of the west. They are usually long-lived and shade-tolerant, and found in late successional and climax forests.

Firs are characteristically tall to very tall, conically shaped trees with strongly horizontal branches, often retained right to the ground when open-grown. Those at high altitude are often stunted by extreme environmental conditions. They generally also tend to have thin bark spotted with resin blisters when young. Unlike the spruces, which have variably four-sided, sharp-pointed needles, those of the firs are distinctly flattened with either a rounded or notched tip and not sharply pointed. They are also attached directly to the twig and leave behind a smooth, disklike scar after they drop off; the needles of spruces are attached to small pegs which remain after the needles drop making the twig rough. The needles of the firs also often have two very pronounced silvery bands on the undersides of the needles. The female cones are also distinctive, in some species strongly and attractively colored violet or purple-blue when young. They are borne on the horizontal branches, pointing up at all times, the cone scales disintegrating while on the tree to release the winged seeds, and leaving behind the upward pointing central cone-stem.

Several of the native firs are popular landscape specimen trees, and a number are economically valuable for their timber, or as Christmas trees. They are also important in their natural setting, particularly those at high elevation, since they provide cover and food for many animals, as well as controlling erosion and water movement on steep slopes.

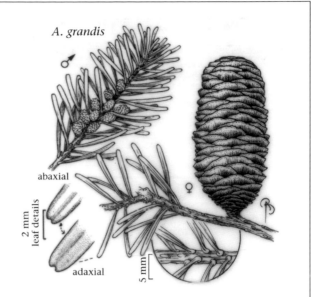

Firs typically have mature female cones pointing upward and needles attached directly to the twig.

Abies amabilis (DOUGL. ex LOUD.) DOUGL. ex FORBES
Pinaceae (Pine Family)

Pacific Silver Fir, Red Silver Fir, Amabilis Fir

Pacific silver fir is a common shade-tolerant tree of the subalpine forests of the coastal ranges of the Pacific Northwest, where it may be found growing on a variety of soils. It can attain heights of 150 ft. (46 m), and widths up to 25 ft. (8 m). It is unusual among the true firs in that the needles along the top side of the twigs point forward, not outward to the sides. Rather than silver bands on the undersides of the needles there are silver dots, which occasionally occur at the tip on the upper surface as well. The needles are very glossy dark green, and when bruised emit the wonderfully pungent odor of oranges. It has a moderately deep, wide-spreading root system that generally keeps it well anchored on slopes. Although the seed cones are large, they are not particularly notable. It may be found in pure stands, but is more likely to be mixed with other conifers.

The principal human uses of this tree are for lumber and pulp. Because of its size and pyramidal shape

Pacific silver fir is occasionally found in pure, similarly aged stands in subalpine forests.

it is also planted as a substantial ornamental in colder, moist areas. Like all firs, however, it is intolerant of air and soil pollution, and of dry, hot sites. So its appropriate landscape use must be considered with some attention to the existing environment.

Abies balsamea (L.) MILLER
Pinaceae (Pine Family)
Balsam Fir, Canada Balsam

Canada balsam is a common coniferous forest tree of northern North America from the Rockies in northern Alberta eastward to Labrador, and southward along the Appalachians into Pennsylvania. In the southern extent of its range it has a preference for higher altitudes. It is happiest on cool soils, particularly those that are acid, organic, and moist, where it attains its best growth: strongly pyramidal, shining green, reaching heights of up to 75 ft. (25 m) and widths of 25 ft. (7.5 m). It also is more shade-tolerant than other firs, especially when young, although as a consequence it has a stronger liking for moist air. At extreme altitudes and along exposed seashores (particularly in Newfoundland) where winds and sharp temperature changes are the norm, its usual form gives way to dense windswept mats of irregularly shaped, dwarf plants, called krummholz. Its developing seed cones, unlike those of some other firs, are not notable.

Balsam fir, showing typical conical habit.

Like all the true firs, Canada balsam has a smoothish bark pebbled with resin blisters, which eventually becomes scaly. The pungent resin is the source of the compound called Canada balsam, which at one time was widely used to mount samples of specimens on microscope slides. Now the resin is used in cough medicines. The tree is also harvested for lumber and pulp. On appropriate soils in cold climates it makes a good evergreen specimen plant, keeping its lower branches and pyramidal form for a long time. However, its intolerance of air and soil pollution limits its usefulness in urban environments. Its form makes it suitable for use as a Christmas tree as well, although in warm, dry interior settings it is prone to more rapid needle loss than the pines or spruces.

Abies bracteata (D. DON) D. DON ex POIT.
Pinaceae (Pine Family)
Bristlecone Fir, Santa Lucia Fir

Bristlecone fir is endemic, in small scattered stands, to the mixed evergreen forest communities of the Big Sur area of California. It is considered rare in its native habitat. The California Native Plant Society has put bristlecone fir on its watch list because of its limited distribution. It occurs on steep, gravelly ground of granite origin at elevations ranging from 700 to 5,200 ft. (215 to 1,585 m). It has a strong preference for mild climates with moist, cool summers. The young plants are shade-adapted, sensitive to desiccation and tend to scorch in the open sun. This is a fir that grows slowly to a height of 130 ft. (40 m). As a young tree it has a narrow, dense, conical habit, keeping its branches close to the ground. It is a lighter green color than most firs, although not as light as

Bristlecone fir tends to keep its branches pointing to the ground, with the tips held upward at an angle.

Colorado fir. The white bands of the needle almost cover the lower surface completely, and because the branch tips are held at an upward angle, this lightness provides an appealing visual contrast. The common name refers to the point tips of the cone scales, which give the cones a very bristly appearance.

Because of its limited distribution bristlecone fir is not considered commercially important for lumber, except perhaps as a landscape tree under suitable conditions. And although it is rare, it is abundant enough that it is not considered to be in danger of extinction.

Abies concolor (GORD. & GLEND.) LINDL. ex HILDEBR.
Pinaceae (Pine Family)
Colorado White Fir

Colorado white fir is arguably the visual equal, if not the superior, of Colorado spruce. It has the same strong pyramidal form that Colorado spruce has as a young tree. However, unlike the spruce, Colorado white fir retains the pyramidal form well into maturity. It also keeps its lower limbs, and doesn't develop the random gaps that occur on the spruce with age. Its flexible needles are flat, much longer, and rounded at the tips; they surge upward and somewhat forward along the twigs. The effect is most remarkable on younger trees, where the visual texture of the needles is as much a feature as the whitish blue-green of the foliage. Add to all this a tolerance for shade and drought not generally found among the firs, and the result is a tree of considerable landscape value. It is often planted far outside its natural range, as a specimen tree or in small groups.

The tree reaches heights of up to 160 ft. (49 m), and widths of 25 ft. (8 m) in its native habitat in the mountainous regions of the western United States. It grows on a variety of soils in small pure stands or in association with other conifers and broadleaf deciduous trees. Its seed cones, although large, are not especially notable. When bruised, the twigs and needles are pungent with a tangerine-like scent, which is especially sweet in late winter, when the sap is rising.

Young Colorado white fir, showing distinctive long blue-green needles.

Upper crown of Fraser fir, needles rising above the shoot, and upward-pointed ripened female cones.

Abies fraseri (PURSH) POIR.

Pinaceae (Pine Family)

Fraser Fir, Balsam, She-Balsam

Closely related to Balsam fir, Fraser fir is an elegant, pyramidal tree of silver-and-glossy-green foliage reaching heights of 50 ft. (15 m) and widths of about 20 ft. (6 m). It has a fairly restricted natural range, being found at elevations between 4,000 and 6,500 ft. (1,200 and 2,000 m) in the Appalachian mountains of western North Carolina, east Tennessee, and southwest Virginia. It is most often found in association with red spruce, and is tolerant, when young, of the shading of the adults of both species. The two species are locally distinguished in relation to each other. Fraser fir is called she-balsam, due to the presence of resin blisters on the smooth, thin bark of

trunk and major limbs, while the red spruce is called he-balsam because it lacks them.

Despite the restricted range, Fraser fir is widely grown, both commercially as a Christmas tree, and as an ornamental. The distinctive silver-and-green color is due to a pair of very broad bands of silvery white on the lower surfaces of the needles, which in characteristic fir fashion curve upward, exposing the silvery undersides.

Abies grandis (DOUGL. ex D. DON) LINDL.

Pinaceae (Pine Family)

Giant Fir, Lowland Fir

Giant fir is most often a native of the coastal regions of Oregon, Washington and southern British

Columbia, from low to mid altitudes. It is also found in the Rockies of Idaho, western Montana, eastern Washington and southern British Columbia. It has a preference for rainshadow areas, where it occurs on well-drained river bottoms and dry, alluvial slopes, as either an understory tree, or co-dominant with other species. It occasionally forms pure stands, and is moderately shade-tolerant. It is very aptly named, achieving on the coast a mature height of 200 ft. (61 m), although its breadth of 30 ft. (10 m) is narrow in comparison. In the Rockies, however, half this size is the norm. As a young tree, it is generally narrowly pyramidal, but with advanced maturity its spire tends to become irregularly rounded, and its crown open and high. The needles of giant fir are distinctive among the firs for being borne in

Giant fir, showing the narrow crown typical of young trees.

two very distinct horizontal rows on either side of the twig. The seed cones, while large, do not seem to produce as much seed as those of other firs. The bark of this species eventually becomes thick and scaly in flat dark, brown ridges.

The uses to which giant fir has been put are extensive. Besides its modern use as lumber and pulp, its leaves and bark were used by Native peoples for dyes, medicines, air fresheners, religious regalia and basketry. The resin from its blisters found a variety of uses, from a sealant for wood exposed to water to a cure for male baldness.

Abies lasiocarpa (HOOK.) NUTT.
Pinaceae (Pine Family)
Subalpine Fir, Alpine Fir

Subalpine fir is the smallest of the true firs native to western North America, reaching a height of about 100 ft. (30 m), and a spread of 20 ft. (6 m). It is largely a tree of the mountainous Northwest, extending north into Alaska and the Yukon and south into Arizona, growing on a variety of soils. It is rarely found near the coast, and is more often encountered at high altitude in the southern portions of its range. Although it is shade-tolerant, especially when young, southern populations that are exposed to drying wind and brighter light have evolved a thicker waxy cuticle for protection. This gives an overall silver-bluish appearance to the trees growing in these circumstances. Otherwise the needles are stiff and crowded, smelling of citron when bruised. The tree has a pleasing, dense, pyramidal form, keeping its branches right to the ground when growing in the open. At very high altitudes, however, when buffeted by strong winds, its form becomes shrubby. It is shallowly rooted but wide-spreading, and so is prone to toppling on unstable slopes or with exposure to strong wind. The resinous seed cones are not notable.

The tree is often found growing in pure stands, but may also associate with a variety of other conifers or broadleaf deciduous trees. Its most frequent uses are lumber and pulp. The silvery southern forms, however, are particularly striking as specimens or in

Subalpine fir is often found in relatively pure stands such as this.

small groups. Where hardy, they make a superior tree to the silver-blue forms of Colorado spruce. The seed is also relished by small mammals.

Abies magnifica A. MURR.
Pinaceae (Pine Family)
Red Fir, California Red Fir

With its narrow, strongly spirelike form, Red fir forms a large, distinctive tree of the northern Sierra Nevada, Coastal and Klamath mountain ranges of California; it also extends north into the Cascade Range of Oregon and extreme western Nevada. It forms pure dense forests between lower and upper montane forests, more often on north-facing slopes. Its canopy cover may be open or closed. It prefers deep, acid soils that are fertile, coarse, well-drained and moist, although it will grow on poorer soils. It is most often a dominant climax tree with high shade, frost and drought tolerance.

Unlike other firs native to North America, its needles are somewhat four-sided, reminiscent of spruce needles. Those borne along the undersides of the twigs curve strongly upward to the sides, rising above the twigs. Lines of white dots can be found on all the surfaces of the needles, which are otherwise a dark, smooth, shining green. In the wild, it reaches heights of about 200 ft. (60 m), supporting a narrow pyramidal crown on a single, often buttressed, trunk having rough fissured bark.

Red fir, growing at mid-altitude, bearing nearly ripened female cones.

The wood of red fir is used for lumber, veneer, plywood and pulp. It supports a wide variety of mammals and birds by providing nesting and protective cover, food in the form of seed, spring forage and insects. Many of these animals are sensitive, rare or endangered. It is often planted beyond its native range as a Christmas tree because of its longevity and pyramidal form.

Abies procera REHD.
Pinaceae (Pine Family)
Noble Fir

Noble fir is a large conical tree, "self-pruning," so that it develops a high, open and domed crown, up to 260 ft. (80 m) high and 60 ft. (18 m) wide. Its upward-curving needles are a bluish green, but appear silvery due to white bands appearing on all surfaces. The seed cones are unremarkable, but provide a food resource for small mammals and birds. The bark is typically resin-blistered when young, eventually becoming thick and fissured. It occurs in a maritime climate with cool summers and mild, wet winters. Noble fir grows well on a variety of soils on steep slopes, but grows best on gentle slopes and warm southern exposures. Shallow or moderately deep loams support good growth. It is the most shade-intolerant of the true firs in North America, but will persist as an understory in light shade. It is one of the first evergreen trees to colonize a disturbed site, sometimes forming pure even-aged stands and sometimes mixed with Douglas fir. Although it can be very long-lived (over 400 years), it is eventually replaced by other, more shade-tolerant species.

Often planted as an ornamental outside its range, the noble fir is also grown for its foliage use in decoration and as a Christmas tree. Although lightweight, the wood has the highest strength of the true firs, which has made it valuable in airplane construction. It is also used in light construction and pulp production.

Dense blue-green needles and nearly ripe female cones, high in the crown of a noble fir.

THE MAPLES (*ACER*)
Maple Family (*Aceraceae*)

The maples are a well-known group of trees. Worldwide there are about 125 species, mostly found in temperate East Asia. There are about a dozen species native to North America, found in a wide variety of habitats, except for the very cold and very dry. Of the North American species seven are trees at maturity in their native habitats. Two are shrublike, and the remainder

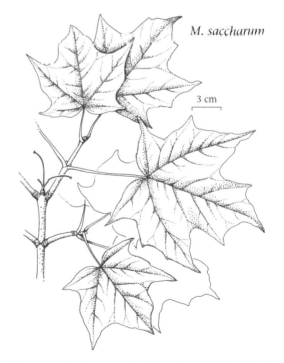

M. saccharum

3 cm

Many maples have a classic palmately lobed leaf.

may be either shrub or treelike almost equally, depending on the local conditions.

The maples have a number of characteristics in common. Their leaves and buds are borne in pairs along the stem. Branches also tend to be paired, although one is often stronger than the other. The flowers are generally inconspicuous, opening in the spring months, and are followed by very distinctive winged fruit, commonly called keys. The leaves are often palmately lobed, with three or five lobes being the most common; however, as the box elder shows, this is not a universal feature. All maples are shallow and fibrous rooted. This often presents difficulties in landscape applications, since growing anything else under a maple becomes problematic. The roots also tend to clog drainage tile.

Aside from these features, maples vary widely in almost every other respect. Some are huge and robust; others are decidedly small and delicate. Some color spectacularly in the autumn, but others just fade away. Some are hard-wooded; other soft. Some are tough in the face of pollution; others give up the ghost at even a trace. Some are adaptable to the point of invasiveness, and others are finicky about their growing circumstances, while some are in between.

The maples as a group capture our imagination and attention as few other trees do. Everyone knows at least one maple. And knowing one makes the rest easier to learn.

Rock maple usually bears deeply three-lobed leaves, as shown here.

mountains of the Pacific Northwest, where it usually matures into a small tree with a short trunk and an irregular crown reaching to about 30 ft. (10 m). In cultivation, however, it is more often encountered as a large multistemmed shrub.

It is notable primarily for its showy reddish autumn foliage, and valued as an ornamental. Its leaves are otherwise dark green and coarse, about 3 to 6 in. (7.5 to 15 cm) long, with three large, ragged-edged lobes that are sometimes divided into three leaflets. Neither its flowers, borne in drooping clusters in the spring with the emerging leaves, nor its fruit are particularly notable. It is one of the maple species in which male and female flowers appear on separate plants, so that not all trees will bear fruit. In winter its smooth, dark reddish-brown bark and slender twigs, which occasionally are purplish, give it a refined air. Older bark, however, does become rough.

Acer glabrum TORR.
Aceraceae (Maple Family)
Rock Maple, Douglas Maple, Rocky Mountain Maple

Most of the year, rock maple is an unassuming tree. It is native to moist sites, primarily along streams and rivers, in the northern Rockies and the coastal

Acer macrophyllum PURSH
Aceraceae (Maple Family)
Oregon Maple, Bigleaf Maple, Broadleaf Maple

As its other names suggest, Oregon maple is distinguished by its very large leaves, which are usually about 12 in. (30 cm) wide and almost as long. On vigorous branches and young trees, the leaves can reach 24 in. (60 cm) wide and long. On the gravelly,

Oregon maple showing its typically orange autumn color.

moist soils it prefers along the Pacific coast from California to southern British Columbia, it forms the largest native maple, reaching a height of about 100 ft. (30 m). In forested conditions it is moderately shade-tolerant and tends to form a straight trunk for at least half its height, and a narrow crown. In more open situations, it will produce a shorter trunk and a broad, rounded crown.

Although it is relatively long-lived (up to 250 years), in natural settings where it has colonized disturbed sites, it is usually replaced by conifers. It is not commonly grown ornamentally because of its large size, shallow roots and generally coarse aspect. However, in large-scale situations its bright orange or yellow autumn foliage makes it a worthy landscape tree.

Acer negundo L.

Aceraceae (Maple Family)

Box Elder, Manitoba Maple, Ash-leaf Maple

Box elder is often an object of contempt for being invasive from seed, fast-growing, weak-wooded and all too ready to establish itself where it is least wanted. Still, if it is a weed, it is because human activity has provided it with the opportunity to apply what nature has endowed it with. Its native habitat is lakeshores and stream banks, with a preference for seasonally flooded locations and disturbed sites, where it can exploit full sun and become quickly established. Before European colonization, this tree already had a wide distribution throughout the eastern United States, across the Great Plains in both the United States and Canada, and sporadically through the southern tier of states into California. Within the past two centuries it has expanded its range even more, into virtually every corner of the continent, showing a particular liking for disturbed and abandoned urban sites.

Box elder can quickly grow to about 70 ft. (21 m) high, with a generally short trunk and broad uneven crown of crooked limbs and branches. As with the majority of fast-growing, weak-wooded trees, it is short-lived, usually about 65 years. In some urban settings, its tolerance for abused, deteriorated soils makes its otherwise invasive tendencies useful, because it provides the often unofficial street and shade tree where all other trees would perform poorly, if not fail outright. On the prairie, it is valued for being a tough tree, and is used in shelter belts and for street planting.

This tree is unique among maples in having a variably, pinnately divided leaf. The first leaves to emerge in the spring and the first leaves on a seedling are usually whole leaves, vaguely three-lobed and coarsely toothed. On vigorous branches and seedlings, later leaves become increasingly pinnately divided, first three, then five, then seven and at times as many as nine leaflets being formed per leaf. On older branches and generally older trees,

Young keys on a female box elder hang from long slender stems.

be bright pink, emerging with the leaves. The female trees in flower are bland in comparison, and the flowers are followed eventually by long hanging clusters of keys which persist through the winter. The seed is extraordinarily viable and will germinate in the spring in even the most unpromising bit of damp dust or debris.

It is also worth noting that a sweet syrup can be distilled from the sap tapped in the spring, similar to that of sugar maple. Box elder syrup is generally regarded as inferior in quality, however.

Acer pensylvanicum L.
Aceraceae (Maple Family)
Striped Maple, Snakebark Maple, Moose Maple

Striped maple is a small tree of northern woods, reaching heights and breadths of about 30 ft. (9 m) in the understory where soil conditions are cool, moist, well drained and quite acidic. In cultivation, it usually reaches about 20 ft. (6 m) under similar soil conditions. However, it is often poorly sited, and ends up a rather battered-looking, uneven, large shrub. It can be badly scorched by the sun, especially on dry soil.

The most striking aspect of striped maple is its bark, which is very smooth and striped vertically in shades of green and white, all the way down the trunk. The young twigs in winter are reddish, so that at this time of year the bark effect is very attractive. Neither the pendulous flower clusters nor the keys on female trees are particularly striking. The leaves are large, with two small side lobes framing a larger middle lobe. They are bright green, changing to vivid yellow in the autumn.

The twigs are a favored winter food of moose and deer, and the trees are often established and maintained in shrubby condition by game wardens to provide browse. The inner bark was used by Native peoples for medicinal purposes: a strong infusion was used as an emetic, while a milder one was used as a gargle for sore throat.

leaves often never develop more than three leaflets. The leaves are a dull mid-green, turning at best a weak yellow in the autumn. The twigs are interesting in that they develop a pronounced gray-white bloominess in the late summer and autumn. The twigs of some trees also turn a deep purple as temperatures become colder, so that in combination with the bloominess, they appear an amethyst color in the winter. The effect can be subtly attractive when viewed against the dark foliage of evergreens.

Box elder, like rock maple, is another of the maples that has male and female flowers on separate plants. Some male trees in the spring can be quietly appealing in that the flower stems, which are long, thin and clustered, may on some individuals

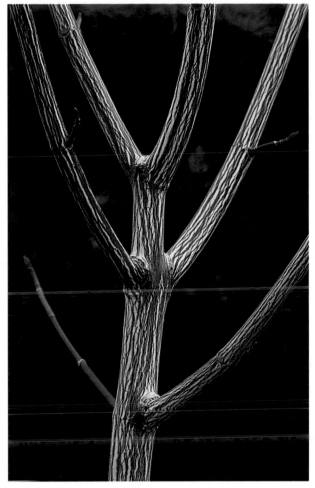

The exquisite smooth striped bark of the striped maple remains for many years, and looks very effective in winter against dark evergreens.

Acer rubrum L.

Aceraceae (Maple Family)

Red Maple, Swamp Maple, Soft Maple

Red maple is one of the most stunning forest trees in autumn color, turning a brilliant scarlet. It also has probably the most extensive natural range of any deciduous tree in eastern North America, from the Florida everglades to the mixed forests around Lake Superior. In its native habitat on cool, moist, acidic soils adjacent to swamps and marshes it reaches heights of about 80 ft. (25 m). It is also tol-

erant of other soils provided they are not alkaline or compacted, but will generally not become as large. The crown tends to be narrow and high off the ground when in the forest, but lower and more rounded when open grown. At times, there will be two or three trunks in a cluster. This tree does not perform well in dry or polluted environments or close to roads, where salt spray from traffic occurs in winter.

In addition to its fall color, red maple has scarlet flowers, which open in very late winter or early spring, before the leaves. Although they are quite small, the visual effect can be pleasing. The keys that develop after the flowers are also crimson until they are shed in mid-June, when they dry out and become

Red maple gets its name in part from its brilliant scarlet autumn foliage.

tan-colored. The leaves are usually three-lobed with fine teeth along the edges, mid-green above, and silvery-green below. The winter twigs and buds also tend toward a bright red color. Older branches, limbs and the trunk are silver-gray, the bark on the trunk eventually becoming vertically fissured into dark gray-brown ridges.

Acer saccharinum L.
Aceraceae (Maple Family)
Silver Maple, Soft Maple

Silver maple is a rapid-growing tree of eastern North America, reaching heights in excess of 100 ft. (30 m). In a forest setting its crown is high and open; in the open it generally has a shorter trunk, which develops into a number of outward-arching limbs, drooping at the tips and giving the tree an overall "vase" profile. Its preferred setting is moist, rich bottomlands near water. It is adaptable to other soils, but may not thrive in shade and alkaline conditions.

Being fairly tolerant of urban conditions, it can also be planted as a street tree, although there are drawbacks to this practice. Its roots quest after water, and can clog drainage tile and sewers. Weak-wooded and prone to rot, it tends to drop twigs and branches in storms, and its gray bark also falls off in large, long, vertical straplike pieces. Keys are produced in vast numbers, littering the ground in mid-June. Many

This young silver maple already has a dense crown, which will grow rapidly to create substantial shade.

municipalities discourage the planting of the silver maple for these reasons.

KEY FEATURES

Acer saccharum MARSH.

Form:	Large tree, narrow to round crown
Trunk:	Usually single **ascend high into crown**; straight
Bark:	Light to dark gray; fissuring to form long vertical broad ridges, lifting along the edges
Twig:	Slender, shining reddish brown; **sharply conical; dark brown buds**
Leaves:	Opposite, to 5.5" (14 cm) long & wide, palmately 5 lobed; **lobes long blunt pointed** with **few rounded teeth**
Flower:	**Yellowish green**, small, male and female together in drooping clusters with the leaves in spring
Fruit:	**Paired samaras**, each to 0.25" (0.6 cm) long, including **down-pointing wing**, green to brown shedding in autumn

This mature sugar maple shows the characteristic form and autumn color of the species.

Unlike red maple, to which it is closely related, this tree does not develop good autumn color, generally turning pale yellow-green or brownish. In summer, when breezes lift the coarsely toothed, deeply five-lobed leaves, the silver undersides will flash in contrast to the light green tops. Its flowers, appearing in late February to early April before the leaves, are individually small, but clustered, and sometimes are quite noticeable.

Acer saccharum MARSH.
Aceraceae (Maple Family)
Sugar Maple

Sugar maple, if only for its glorious autumn colors of red, orange, gold and yellow, is one of the more notable trees of North America. It is greatly prized for maple syrup and its timber as well. In eastern North America it is one of the more prevalent forest

The autumn leaves of sugar maple typically show blended colors, such as these.

trees, often found in extensive pure stands. Some authorities recognize black maple (*A. nigrum*), big-tooth maple (*A. grandidentatum*), Florida maple (*A. barbatum*) and chalk maple (*A. leucoderme*) as subspecies, while others treat these as separate species, differing in range, ecological preference, autumn color, and minor characteristics.

In its forest setting, sugar maple reaches a height of about 120 ft. (35 m). In cultivation, however, the maximum size is much less, about 70 ft. (20 m). Grown in the open, along roads, between fields and in parks, it forms a dense, oval canopy. The winter silhouette of a mature tree has considerable visual appeal. The trunk develops into one to three major ascending limbs that give the tree, when leafless, a sense of almost eager vitality. The rugged, mid-gray bark is highly variable in its texture, ranging from scales to vertical ridges and wide plates deeply furrowed.

The leaves emerge in May, hard on the heels of the small, clustered, yellow-green flowers, and quickly expand to the classic five-lobed maple-leaf shape. Its foliage is often confused with the introduced Norway maple. But a simple test will distinguish the two. If a broken leaf-stem exudes milky sap, the tree is a Norway maple. The flowers are followed by clusters of keys. These ripen in late summer and early autumn, and are easily identified as sugar maple keys by their rounded green body.

Sugar maple prefers moist, well-drained, fertile, slightly acid soils, over limestone bedrock. In cultivation these same preferences apply, although there is some tolerance of neutral or slightly alkaline soils. It also has a high susceptibility to damage from air- and water-borne pollutants. Consequently, it is not a suitable tree for highly urban or pollution-prone environments. But in extensive areas away from roads, especially in the company of other trees, sugar maple performs very well.

THE BUCKEYES (*AESCULUS*)
Horsechestnut and Buckeye Family
(*Hippocastanaceae*)

Of the approximately 13 species of horse-chestnuts and buckeyes found throughout the world, six are native to North America, and of these, five are trees. The remaining species are native to southeastern Europe and Asia. All exhibit a strong preference for moist soils. They are also fairly long-lived and shade-tolerant particularly as saplings. Rarely found in pure stands of any size, the buckeyes of North America normally characterize climax forest types, although on marginal sites they are typically displaced.

Although two species can exhibit shrublike form (California buckeye and red buckeye), the North American buckeyes are generally small to large trees having coarse, stout branches and large terminal buds. Their leaves are borne oppositely and are palmately compound, usually with long leafstalks. Autumn colors can be highly attractive, particularly on Ohio buckeye. Flowers are always borne in many-flowered, upright clusters in the late spring, and are fairly showy white, yellow or red. Many are as impressive in flower as the horsechestnut (*Aesculus hippocastanum*), which is native to the Balkans. The fruit is a large, dry capsule, in some species somewhat pear-shaped and in others somewhat spiny. It splits open in the autumn to release one to three large brown, smooth, shiny seeds, reminiscent of a chestnut.

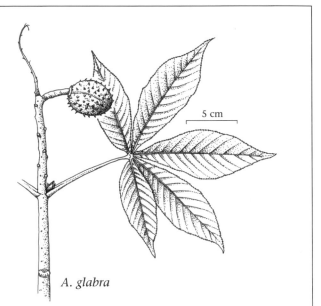

5 cm

A. glabra

The leaves of buckeyes are palmately divided. The fruit, which is often spiny, splits open to release large seeds.

The buckeyes are prized as landscape shade trees, as well as for their attractive flowers and often good fall color. They generally perform well, not being overly prone to insect pests or diseases when stressed by drought. In this regard they are superior to the horsechestnut. They have been hybridized with one another and with the horsechestnut to produce some notable landscape trees. The wood is not of much commercial importance, and the foliage and fruit are poisonous to people and animals. Native peoples used to crush the nuts of various species to poison fish for easy catching.

Aesculus californica (SPACH) NUTT.
Hippocastanaceae (Horsechestnut Family)
California Buckeye

California buckeye, a small deciduous tree, is endemic to California, being found in the Klamath, Coastal and Cascade ranges, as well as the foothills of the Sierra Nevada. If not burned back by forest fire, it can reach a height of 23 ft. (7 m). The palmately divided leaves reach about 6 in. (15 cm) in size. The white flowers, although individually small, are borne in fairly conspicuous panicles about 8 in. (20 cm) long. The pear-shaped, smooth fruit is light brown containing up to six (but usually one) fairly large glossy brown seeds. California buckeye is found in Mediterranean-type climates with cool, moist winters and hot dry summers. It can be found along waterways and on dry slopes in a variety of habitats, showing a preference for well-drained loamy soils. Scattered individuals grow as large shrubs in grasslands prone to fire, regenerating from the stump or root crown. It is also occurs in mixed evergreen forest as an understory shrub, as well as in chaparral and mixed oak communities. It is dominant in the habitat bearing its name: the California buckeye woodlands.

California buckeye has a wide variety of uses. Although it is poisonous in all its parts, cattle and wildlife are known to browse on it. The Native peoples of California used the seed as a food staple after leaching out the poison. Crushed seeds were also submerged in streams to stupefy fish for easy catching. Considered a pest species in rangeland, California buckeye is nonetheless used as an ornamental tree in landscaping. Bees pollinate the flowers, but are susceptible to poisoning by both pollen and nectar. There are also reports of people being poisoned by honey made from flowers of this tree.

Aesculus flava SOLAND.
Hippocastanaceae (Horsechestnut Family)
Yellow Buckeye, Sweet Buckeye

The largest of the native buckeyes, yellow buckeye tops out at 90 ft. (27 m), with an upright, oval form. Its leaves are similar to those of Ohio buckeye (q.v.), but somewhat larger, dark green above, yellow-green

California buckeye is often encountered as an isolated specimen; this one is growing in grassland.

Soft yellow flowers develop on yellow buckeye after the leaves have emerged.

and sometimes hairy below, with the leaflets occasionally tending to be widest closer to the tips. The autumn color is a delightful pumpkin orange. The flowers are yellow, barely tinged with green, in fairly showy terminal upright panicles, borne before the leaves. The fruit is a smooth light brown capsule opening in autumn along two or three lines to reveal two large chestnut-brown seeds. The bark is initially thin, smooth and beige-gray, but develops into large smooth flat plates with an interesting combination of brown and gray. Yellow buckeye has a more limited range than the Ohio buckeye, from southwestern Pennsylvania south to northern Alabama and Georgia and north to southern Illinois. It has a strong preference for the rich, moist, deep soils of river bottoms and lower mountain slopes, and is found in mixed association with other forest hardwoods.

Yellow buckeye is poisonous in all its parts. However, Native peoples used to roast the seeds, then leach them in water to remove the poison, thus obtaining a nutritious food. The wood has much the same uses as Ohio buckeye. Because it lacks the rank odor of Ohio buckeye, is less prone to leaf diseases, and has outstanding autumn foliage, yellow buckeye is arguably a better landscape tree, where space, climate, soil and water permit its use.

Painted buckeye has rich red autumn foliage.

Aesculus georgiana SARG.
Hippocastanaceae (Horsechestnut Family)
Painted Buckeye, Georgia Buckeye, Dwarf Buckeye

Found on moist and well-drained soil in the understory of mixed forests and along streambanks, painted buckeye has a range that covers the Piedmont of the southern Appalachians from southeast Virginia to northeast Alabama and then northward into northeast Tennessee. It is a small deciduous tree, growing to about 25 ft. (8 m), but it can also be found as a large shrub. It has typical, palmately compound buckeye leaves consisting of usually five narrowly elliptical, finely toothed leaflets. They are yellow-green above, green below, and usually hairy underneath as well. Flowers are borne in typical buckeye fashion in erect panicles to 6 in. (15 cm), and are usually bright yellow with a touch of red in the flower interior. On occasion some plants have reddish flowers. The fruit is a spineless light brown capsule containing up to three large, shiny, brown seeds. The bark is thin when young and gray-brown, but with age becomes scaly.

In all its parts, painted buckeye is highly toxic, and may be fatal if eaten. It contains a number of toxic principles that cause muscular weakness, paralysis, vomiting, diarrhea, stupor and depression. Nonetheless, it is cultivated as a small flowering tree or large shrub.

Aesculus glabra WILLD.
Hippocastanaceae (Horsechestnut Family)
Ohio Buckeye, Fetid Buckeye

A stately, round-crowned tree reaching heights of 70 ft. (21 m), Ohio buckeye is commonly found in mixed hardwood forests on moist rich soils along river bottoms but it may also be encountered on drier mountain slopes. Occasionally it forms a thicket shrub along streambanks. Its range extends from western Pennsylvania south to central Alabama, west to southeastern Oklahoma, and north into central Iowa. The palmately divided leaves are fairly large, composed of five or seven elliptical leaflets, yellow-green above, paler and somewhat hairy below. The autumn tints are generally a consistent warm orange-yellow. The relatively small, yellow-green flowers emerge in upright clusters at the ends of stout branches before the leaves in the spring. They have a distinctly unpleasant odor, and are not as showy as those of the introduced, closely related horsechestnut. The fruit, which ripens in late summer or autumn, is a spiny, light brown capsule, which splits open along two or three lines to release up to five large chestnut-brown seeds. The bark is ash-gray and smooth, becoming fissured and platy with age.

In addition to the flowers, both leaves and bark have an unpleasant odor when bruised or crushed, and all parts of the tree are poisonous. Despite this, the bark was once used in folk medicines, and pioneers carried the seeds in their pockets to fend off rheumatism. The wood is used for cabinetry, flooring, and a variety of other purposes. Ohio buckeye is the state tree of Ohio, and is used in landscaping as a shade tree and for the showy autumn foliage.

Aesculus pavia L.
Hippocastanaceae (Horsechestnut Family)
Red Buckeye, Scarlet Buckeye, Firecracker Plant

Red buckeye varies from a small, irregularly crowned tree of about 25 ft. (8 m) to a large shrub. It has a preference for the light shade and moist soils of a mixed forest understory, along streams or swamps and in floodplains. It ranges along the Atlantic coast from southeast North Carolina to northern Florida, then westward to central Texas. It penetrates inland along the Mississippi to southern Illinois. Its palmately divided leaves are composed of (usually) five narrowly elliptical leaflets, which are dark green and nearly hairless above, and dull green below. The lower leaf surfaces are often covered in dense whitish hair. The flowers are borne in narrow, terminal panicles of about 8 in. (200 cm) in length. They tend

Ohio buckeye usually has an oval to rounded crown.

Red buckeye is valued as a small ornamental tree with brilliant red flowers.

to be very showy, and bright red, although they may also verge on yellow. The fruit is a smooth, light brown capsule that splits open to release up to three large shiny brown seeds. The bark is usually a light gray-brown and smooth.

Painted buckeye is widely used in landscaping for its brilliant red flower color. It has been hybridized with other trees in the genus to produce a number of larger trees with reddish flowers, most notable ruby red horsechestnut. Native peoples crushed the poisonous seeds or branches to stun fish in streams and lakes for easy catching. The pioneers used the root gum as a substitute for soap, and the inner bark was used in various medicinal remedies.

THE ALDERS (*ALNUS*)
Birch Family (*Betulaceae*)

Largely native to the north temperate regions of the world, the alders comprise some 35 species of trees and shrubs. Of these about seven to ten are natives of North America. Depending on the authority cited, varieties of some species are treated as separate species. Only three of these species reliably form good trees, and all are prone to shrublike growth when browsed by animals or growing on marginal sites. The alders are fairly adaptable to soil but show a strong affinity for wet to moist soils. They are short-lived, fairly shade-intolerant, and are noted for invading sites disturbed by logging or fire, particularly wherever bare mineral soils are exposed. They are also notable for forming relationships between their roots and soil bacteria that convert atmospheric nitrogen into a form usable by the trees. They are consequently important for improving soil fertility for the forest plant communities which replace them.

Often thicket-forming as very large shrubs, alders become small trees under more controlled conditions. They are characteristically slender-trunked with simple, oval, toothed leaves borne alternately along slender twigs. The flowers are individually tiny, without petals, the males gathered together in pendulous catkins that are somewhat attractive in mid-spring when they expand to release pollen. The female flowers are gathered together in much smaller, green upright clusters and are usually barely noticeable. The whole cluster matures as a unit into a woody, brown, persistent, conelike structure which releases small winged seeds in the autumn.

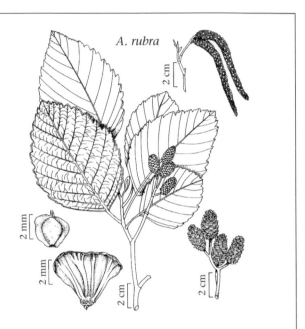

A. rubra

The long male catkins of alders are notable in spring, while the woody, conelike fruit are visible in the autumn and winter.

Except for red alder, which is commercially important for its wood, alders generally have very limited timber value. They are not highly valued as landscape amenity trees because of their short life span, invasive tendencies, and generally coarse visual appearance. They are all important, however, in restoration projects, especially of wetlands and riparian habitats. They are also used as nurse crops for improving soil texture and fertility for longer-lived, economically valuable tree species. In addition, many species of mammals and birds exploit groves of alder for cover, food and nesting. Both the common and botanical names derive from the same root-word as the word *yellow*, which is the color of the wood of most species when exposed to air.

Alnus rhombifolia NUTT.

Betulaceae (Birch Family)

White Alder

Restricted to riparian woodland communities along river systems draining into the Pacific, white alder has nonetheless an extensive range, from Baja California to the extreme south of British Columbia and inland into Idaho along the Snake and Clearwater Rivers. It is usually a multistemmed small to medium tree attaining heights of 80 ft. (25 m), although it can be highly variable, between 16 and 115 ft. (5 to 35 m), depending on the local environment. On young trees the bark is smooth and light gray, verging on white. Older trees display reddish platy bark. The leaves are a dark green above, lighter below, doubly toothed along the edges, reaching about 4 in. (10 cm) long. Their shape is angularly ovoid. In the extreme south of its range, white alder retains its leaves year-round, but elsewhere sheds

Although not often used as an amenity tree, white alder is fast-growing, and fine-textured.

them before the onset of winter. Flowers and fruits are typically alderlike, and wind-dependent.

White alder has limited commercial use, mostly as firewood. However, ecologically it is very important in a number of ways. It stabilizes stream banks in which water runs year-round, and establishes itself well from seed on moist, mineral soils exposed after flooding. It also develops vegetatively from root suckers. While the leaves and tender twigs are not much browsed by wildlife, the seed is an important food source for a number of birds, which also nest in its branches. In fact, more species of birds in California breed in the riparian habitats dominated by white alder than in any other. For these reasons, it is now being used extensively to revegetate disturbed riparian areas.

Alnus rubra BONG.

Betulaceae (Birch Family)

Red Alder, Oregon Alder, Western Alder

Confined to within 100 miles (165 km) of the Pacific Coast, from southeast Alaska to southern California, red alder was in precolonial times primarily restricted to streams and wet areas. Since then settlement activities in humid coastal climates have exposed mineral soils, which favor red alder colonization. It occurs on a variety of soils, but achieves its best growth on well-drained and sandy loams. On disturbed sites, where sunlight reaches exposed mineral soils, red alder rapidly takes hold, and through a symbiotic root association with a soil bacterium, fixes atmospheric nitrogen into a form absorbable by plants. As the trees grow they shade the soil and prevent further new growth of red alder seedlings. However, light and nutritional conditions are then ideal for the shade-tolerant seedlings of coniferous trees, which grow as an understory. Red alder is short-lived; after about 60 or 70 years, it is replaced by understory coniferous trees. In riparian habitats, however, red alder populations tend to persist and co-dominate with other deciduous trees, especially in drier regions of its range.

Red alder is shallow-rooted and generally forms a single trunk, growing to about 100 ft. (30 m). Its

Red alder often occurs in dense even-aged stands such as this one.

bark is mottled gray-white, often covered with green moss. Leaves are dark green above, lighter below, toothed and generally oval in shape. Flowers and fruits are typically alderlike.

The uses of red alder are extensive. It is considered the most important commercial hardwood in the Pacific Northwest, and is used in furniture, cabinetry and a wide variety of other articles, including veneers, plywood and utensils. Red alder is also useful for erosion control on steep slopes. The twigs and leaves are a source of winter food for wildlife and the seeds are eaten by a variety of birds. A red dye extracted from the inner bark was used by Native peoples to dye baskets and fish-nets in order to make them invisible to fish. They also ate the inner bark, and used a solution made from it as medicine. It has been shown to have antibiotic properties and to contain salicin, a compound related to aspirin. Coals of red alder are regarded as the best for smoking salmon.

Alnus rugosa (DUROI) SPRENG.
Betulaceae (Birch Family)
Speckled Alder, Tag Alder, Gray Alder

A deciduous large shrub to small tree found on moist soils, speckled alder is often the principal understory plant of coniferous or mixed forests. It is mostly found in the northern half of the Great Lakes Basin region and along the St. Lawrence River, extending northwest to British Columbia and the Yukon and southeast at higher elevations into Virginia and Maryland. As a tree, speckled alder tops out at 30 ft. (9 m). However, its preference is for growing in clump-like groups to about 20 ft. (6 m). It is a coarse tree, although the 4 in. (10 cm) yellow-brown male catkins in the spring are a welcome harbinger of warmer weather. The female flowers and fruit are typically alderlike. The trunk rarely exceeds about 6 in. (15 cm) in diameter and has a thin, smooth, grayish bark with conspicuous buff-orange lenticels. The oval leaves are coarsely textured, with rough, uneven edges, dull dark green above and pale gray-green below, opening after the flowers.

Speckled alder develops a coarse, twiggy crown and is occasionally single-stemmed.

Speckled alder has some potential economic value, but is even more significant for its environmental importance. Its roots form a symbiotic relationship with a soil bacterium, converting atmospheric nitrogen into a form usable by plants. Being short-lived, it has potential for improving soil nutrition for other, more valuable, timber crops. Given its adaptability to different soils and its preference for moist sites it has increasingly been used in watershed management and restoration. It is a valuable source of forage and habitat for wildlife. It was used by Native peoples and settlers for a variety of medicinal purposes, and as fuel. The wood has potential for kraft pulp and chipboard. The stems may also be harvested on a three- to five-year cycle, making the commercial growing of speckled alder a possibility.

Amelanchier arborea (MICHX. f.)

Rosaceae (Rose Family)

Downy Serviceberry, Shadblow

The common name of this tree refers to the white hairs covering the emerging leaves in the spring, an adaptation trapping warmer air near the tender growth on frosty spring nights. Downy serviceberry grows from Newfoundland south to northwestern Florida, then northwest to eastern Oklahoma and north to Minnesota. It prefers moist to somewhat dry, slightly acidic soils in the understory of hardwood forests, along forest edges and in hedgerows. It flowers in dense, upright clusters at the tips of branches in spring, just before the leaves emerge. Individually, the flowers are small and white, occasionally tinged pink, but collectively the effect is substantial. The small, dark blue to purple fruits are shaped like very tiny apples, at times dry and flavorless, ripening in June and early July. The oval leaves are finely toothed, 4 in. (10 cm) long, and half as wide. They are light green tinged very slightly with pink when they first open, but become a mid matte-green above and lighter below. Autumn color ranges from gold to vibrant crimson. Downy serviceberry prefers to grow as a few stems in a clump, but is

The flowers of downy serviceberry usually emerge before the leaves in spring.

often encountered as a single-trunk tree. It reaches about 40 ft. (12 m). The trunks reach a maximum of 12 in. (30 cm) in diameter, and have a smooth light gray bark that persists a long time before becoming fissured into narrow ridges. Branching pattern and bud are typical of the genus.

Having year-round interest and being a small tree, downy serviceberry is widely used in landscaping. The fruit is edible, but is not as palatable to humans as the smooth serviceberry. Birds, however, relish it.

Amelanchier laevis WIEG.

Rosaceae (Rose Family)

Allegheny Serviceberry, Smooth Serviceberry

Sometimes considered a naturally occurring variety of the downy serviceberry, Allegheny serviceberry differs primarily in its soil preference and some characteristics of leaf and fruit. It can be found in moister soils throughout the same range as the downy serviceberry and extending further north in eastern North America. The emerging leaves overlap the later stages of flowering, and are a distinctive coppery red. They also lack the white hairs that are present on the emerging leaves of downy serviceberry. The fruit is very sweet and juicy, and is

The later stages of flowering in Allegheny serviceberry overlap the emergence of the new leaves.

borne in large quantities when the tree grows in the open. Birds relish it, and the ripe fruit can be stripped from a tree within a few days. Autumn color is also a consistent crimson. Like downy serviceberry, which it resembles, Allegheny is widely used in landscaping.

Arbutus arizonica (GRAY) SARG.
Ericaceae (Heather Family)
Arizona Madrone

Arizona madrone is restricted to the canyons, foothills and lower mountain slopes of extreme southeast Arizona, southwest New Mexico and adjacent Mexico. At lower elevations it is associated with riparian habitats, but it is more often found at higher, sunny elevations on well-drained, gravelly soils. It prefers north-, east- or west-facing slopes, and associates with a variety of species in evergreen woodlands, such as New Mexico locust, silverleaf oak, net-leaf oak and Apache pine. Arizona madrone is a slow-growing broadleaf evergreen tree having a maximum height of 50 ft. (15 m), although occasionally shrublike. It forms a compact, round-topped crown of thick, lanced-shaped leathery leaves on stout branches. The bark is initially reddish, peeling in long strips, gradually becoming grayish in color and peeling in papery sheets. From April to September, small, white to fleshy pink urn-shaped flowers are borne in loose clusters at the ends of branches. These are followed by warty, pea-sized

The bark on an older Arizona madrone is grayish and peels in papery sheets.

berries of a brilliant orange-red color, mealy in texture and sweet to the taste.

The berries of Arizona madrone have narcotic properties for humans, but various kinds of wildlife eat them for their food value. The bark has been used as an astringent and the wood to manufacture charcoal and gunpowder.

Arbutus menziesii PURSH
Ericaceae (Heather Family)
Pacific Madrona, Madrone, Arbutus

Pacific madrone is a magnificent tree of the Pacific coastal region. A broadleaved, drought-adapted evergreen tree, reaching heights of about 80 ft.

The peeling red bark of Pacific madrone reveals smooth new bark underneath.

Red multistemmed trunks and evergreen foliage characterize Pacific madrone.

(25 m), it has a broad, spreading crown supported by a single or multiple arching trunk and heavy, crooked branches. The bark exfoliates in large, thin, cinnamon-red scales, mostly from June through September. New, exposed bark is lighter than older bark, and has a polished appearance. Young twigs and stems are chartreuse, deepening to orange before peeling. Eventually, very old bark darkens to brownish-red and fissures. Leaves are oval, smooth-edged or occasionally finely toothed, glossy and leathery, the upper surface dark green, the lower a pale green. They remain on the tree for two years, turning red and orange before falling in June or July when the new leaves are emerging. The sweet-scented flowers are urn-shaped and very small,

borne from April to June in showy terminal clusters ranging from white to pink in color. The pea-sized, brilliant orange-red to red fruit matures from September to October, and is either eaten by wildlife or drops by the end of the year.

Pacific madrone has an extensive distribution from the southern coastal lowlands of Vancouver Island and mainland British Columbia, south to California, and in scattered groves into Mexico; it is also very common west of the Cascades in Washington and Oregon. It prefers sites having mild oceanic winters, hot dry summers, and low summer soil moisture, and consequently, it seldom forms pure stands. It is found in coastal redwood and mixed evergreen forests, oak woodlands and chaparral.

Except in chaparral, Pacific madrone is a moderately long-lived, shade-tolerant species. Barring disturbance, it is eventually replaced by conifers and more shade-tolerant competitors. However, once established it is a very tough tree, surviving a variety of disturbances, especially fire. After a fire, a special organ called a burl, at the juncture of the trunk and root, gives rise to vigorous sprouting to replace the lost above-ground parts. Fire also favors the germination of its seed, so that Pacific madrone is a strong competitor in early succession, until shaded out by conifers. In addition to the burl, the extensive root system forms a symbiotic relationship with ericoid mycorrhizae, which increases its efficiency in absorbing water and nutrients from the soil. Once established, Pacific madrone is very drought-tolerant and wind-firm. In fire-prone chaparral it re-emerges from the burl repeatedly.

Because of its visual characteristics, Pacific madrone is widely used in landscaping, and it has a variety of other uses. Although the wood can check badly, its fine-textured, fluid grain produces a lovely veneer; it has been used for flooring and cabinetry. It also has pulp and fuel-wood potential. In natural settings the berries are eaten by a wide variety of animals, and the trees themselves provide shelter. Native peoples ate the berries and inner bark, which was also used medicinally. The berries are reported to possess some narcotic properties.

KEY FEATURES

Arbutus menziesii PURSH

Form:	Medium-sized tree with broad, spreading crown of irregularly shaped limbs and **broadleaf evergreen leaves**
Trunk:	**One to several** trunks, curving slightly
Bark:	Become **reddish brown, exfoliating** in **papery** sheets
Twig:	Smooth, **chartreuse** green
Leaves:	**Evergreen, leathery, shiny dark green** above, lighter below, oval to 6" (15 cm) long
Flower:	**White, fragrant** in large **drooping clusters**
Fruit:	**Orange-red** berries, 0.5" (1.2 cm) across, with **granular surface**

Arbutus xalapensis KUNTH
Ericaceae (Heather Family)
Texas Madrone

A lovely broadleaved evergreen tree, Texas madrone is extensively distributed from Guatemala northward though Mexico into south-central Texas. Preferring full sun and well-drained soil ranging from slightly acidic to slightly alkaline, it may be found in wooded canyons, on desert mountain slopes, and along dry creekbeds and streams. It is common in canyon forests, particularly in densely wooded stands at the heads of canyons. It also occurs widely scattered in a variety of other habitats.

Commonly reaching a height of 30 ft. (9 m), Texas madrone also occurs infrequently as a large shrub. It has a rounded canopy supported by stout, irregular branches. Leaves are elliptical to oval, smooth-edged, thick and shiny, dark green above

Texas madrone often has a smooth grayish bark.

Asimina triloba (L.) DUNAL
Annonaceae (Custard-apple Family)
Pawpaw

Pawpaw is the northernmost outrider of a group of essentially tropical plants valued for their fruit, such as soursop, custard apple and sugar-apple. Pawpaw is also planted to a minor extent for its edible fruit, although handling it may cause an allergic reaction in some people. The fruit resembles a small white-bloomed yellow-green banana about 5 in. (12 cm) long, and has soft, yellowish, custard-flavored pulp inside; it ripens from July to October. Many animals and birds also relish the fruit. In addition, pawpaw bark was once used medicinally,

Even as a young tree, pawpaw forms a dense canopy, casting heavy shade.

and somewhat hairy and paler below. Older bark is variously black, gray or dark brown, exfoliating annually in papery sheets to reveal new smooth bark in shades of white, apricot, orange, pink, tan or dark red. Tiny urn-shaped white to pale pink flowers are borne terminally in small clusters. These are followed by pea-sized, round, warty berries, ranging in color from bright red through orange to yellow.

Despite being difficult to transplant, Texas madrone makes an attractive landscape tree for its leaves, flowers, and visually interesting bark. The wood has been used for a variety of purposes, from gunpowder to utensils. The leaves provide forage to browsing domestic and wild animals, and many species of birds eat the sweet fruits. Because of grazing, mature trees are becoming increasingly rare.

and a potential anticancer drug is currently being investigated. Other than some use as a small ornamental landscape tree, pawpaw is not highly valued commercially.

Pawpaw is considered a pioneering tree, growing to 35 ft. (10 m), colonizing from root sprouts. It can be found throughout the central and southern Appalachians, northwest to western New York and southern Ontario, west to southeast Nebraska, south to eastern Texas and east to the Florida panhandle. It develops rapidly on disturbed sites in floodplain conditions, but is eventually replaced by shade-tolerant species which grow under it as saplings. The shade it casts is quite heavy since the leaves are individually fairly large, up to 10 in. (25 cm) long and half as wide, and densely borne on wide-spreading branches; they turn yellow in autumn. The purple flowers are about 1.5 (4 cm.) wide, opening with the leaves in mid-spring.

Avicennia germinans (L.) L.
Verbeniaceae (Verbena Family)
Black Mangrove

Black mangrove is one of four species that, in various combinations, dominate mangrove habitats in the coastal areas of Florida, Louisiana, Texas, the Caribbean and South America. Black mangrove is the hardiest of them all, extending the farthest north and the farthest inland. It will grow only where it is exposed at low tide. In southern Florida it attains a height of 60 ft. (18 m), but at the northern limit of its range it is at best a shrub.

Black mangrove is an intriguing plant. In adapting to oxygen-poor soil and water conditions, it has evolved vertical, pencil-thick outgrowths of the

The pneumatophores of black mangrove are clearly visible at low tide.

roots called pneumatophores, which reach to just above the highest water level attained. The pneumatophores extend a considerable distance from the tree, and at low tide take in oxygen to nourish the root. They also provide a rich habitat for a variety of other life forms, including fish, crustaceans and birds. Black mangrove also stabilizes shoreline features that would otherwise be transient. It is an evergreen species with narrowly elliptical, leathery leaves, to 4 in. (10 cm) long. The upper surface is shiny dark green, while the underside is downy and whitish. Salt-secreting glands are also found on the undersides of the leaves. The small, white, fragrant flowers are borne in terminal clusters sporadically throughout the year, followed by the downy, light green, podlike fruit. The flowers are highly prized by beekeepers for the exceptional quality of white honey that is produced. The fruits are unusual in that the seeds they contain germinate while in the fruit. The seeds are dropped to the ground, where they immediately take root, or into the water, which carries them to other potential sites.

THE BIRCHES (*BETULA*)

Birch Family (*Betulaceae*)

Ten species of birch, of which seven are dependably trees, occur in North America. Worldwide, there are about 60 species, confined to the Northern Hemisphere. Birches generally prefer cooler climates and moist soils. They are commonly fast-growing and shade-intolerant both as saplings and as mature trees, although yellow birch is moderately shade-tolerant as a sapling. Not particularly long-lived, birches are usually colonizers of disturbed sites, where mineral soil is exposed. They rarely persist once a full canopy is formed since the seeds require light to germinate and grow. They are usually replaced by more shade-tolerant trees unless disturbance creates opportunities for seeding and sapling development.

Never large trees, birches are generally fine-branched and slender-trunked. They often have exfoliating bark of considerable visual appeal. The leaves are usually oval to elliptical in overall shape, with teeth along the edges, and distinguishing those of one species from another is often a difficult task. They all generally turn a good yellow in the autumn as well. Male and female flowers occur on the same tree; they are individually tiny and have no petals. Male flowers are aggregated into many-flowered catkins at the ends of branches, and expand to become lax and pendulous in mid-spring. Female flowers are gathered into smaller green upright catkins, also at or toward the ends of branches, maturing into brown structures that in some species are conelike and upright, but pendulous and catkin-

Although birches' leaf shapes vary in their details between species, most have an oval shape. Twigs bear male catkins at their ends and female catkins and fruit on short spurs.

like in others. Fruiting structures disintegrate in the late autumn and winter, releasing huge quantities of small winged seed.

Birches are widely utilized in landscaping for their form, bark characteristics and good autumn foliage color, particularly paper birch and river birch. They require good access to water, however, and tend to become stressed during drought and at high temperatures. Under such conditions some species of birch will also be prone to insect pests and diseases. The wood of several species of birch is commercially important. In their natural setting birches are valued by wildlife for shelter, nesting and food. There is high aesthetic value placed on the presence in natural settings of paper and river birches, particularly in association with water and cottages.

Betula alleghaniensis BRITT.
Betulaceae (Birch Family)
Yellow Birch, Swamp Birch

A well-known tree of northern deciduous hardwood and mixed forests of eastern North America, yellow birch has a range extending from southern Newfoundland to northern Minnesota, and south along the Appalachians into Georgia. It prefers moist, well-drained soils in upland areas and mountain ravines. Rarely found in extensive stands, it is more often encountered as individual trees or in small groups mixed with other hardwoods, or with conifers in the north and at higher elevations.

Yellow birch is a slow-growing but large tree of about 70 ft. (23 m). It is usually single-trunked,

The peeling bark of yellow birch becomes heavily marked with horizontal lenticels as it ages.

especially in dense forest. The crown is generally high, and broad when open grown. The leaves, flowers and fruit are typically birchlike. The foliage turns from dark green to brilliant yellow in the autumn. The bark is an intriguing color, yellowish, shining silvery-gray, peeling in thin strips. All parts of the plant, particularly leaves and inner bark, smell and taste sweetly of wintergreen when crushed. The roots are wide-spreading and variably deep depending on the soil type.

An economically important tree, yellow birch is also valuable to wildlife. The heavy, strong, and close-grained wood is valued for a variety of uses, including furniture, cabinetry, trim, and veneer. The sap may be tapped for syrup, much like sugar maple, and an infusion can be brewed from leaves and inner bark. Moose, deer and hare also forage on leaves and tender twigs both in summer and winter.

Betula lenta L.
Betulaceae (Birch Family)
Cherry Birch, Sweet Birch, Black Birch

Closely related to yellow birch, cherry birch shares several of the same characteristics and uses. Foliage, flower and fruit are very similar to those of yellow birch, but with a few distinctions. The leaves are generally smaller, more consistently oval, and less strongly toothed along the margin. The lower leaf surface is not hairy as in yellow birch, but does have gland dots. The conelike fruit points upward when mature, but is thinner than that of yellow birch. Cherry birch has a shiny dark reddish-brown bark with horizontal lenticels. With age the bark darkens and breaks into scaly plates reminiscent of black cherry. When open-grown the crown is quite broad relative to its height, and much denser than yellow birch because of short, leafy spur-branches borne into the crown interior. The inner bark, leaves and wood smell and taste very sweetly of wintergreen.

Cherry birch was once the commercial source of oil of wintergreen. Its wood is used similarly to yellow birch for furniture, plywood, veneer and cabinetry. The sap is distilled to make syrup, and fermented to make birch beer. Because of its dense broad canopy and autumn foliage color, it is used in landscaping as well.

Golden autumn color is characteristic of cherry birch.

Having a strong preference for cool, moist soils, cherry birch has a more restricted range than yellow birch, from southern Maine to Ohio, and south to northern Alabama. There is one population in extreme southwestern Ontario.

Betula nigra L.
Betulaceae (Birch Family)
River Birch

As its common name suggests, river birch is primarily a tree of floodplains, associated with other bottomland hardwoods in wet soils along streams and rivers. It is, however, somewhat drought-tolerant and, being the southernmost birch in

River birch characteristically develops beautiful, peeling, cream to cinnamon-colored bark.

North America has adapted to summer heat. Its range extends south from Connecticut to northern Florida, west to eastern Texas and north to southern Minnesota.

Reaching 80 ft. (24 m), river birch has a spreading, uneven crown on a trunk that is often forked close to the ground. Its bark is an attractive whitish gray tinged with pinkish brown, peeling off in papery strips. With age it becomes very shaggy with thick plates and fissures. The diamond-shaped leaves, twigs, flowers, and fruits are hairy, but otherwise typical of the birches.

The wood of river birch is of limited commercial use because of its tendency to be knotty, but it is used for furniture, and being lightweight, it is also useful for toys and artificial limbs. River birch provides cover for animals, the leaves and twigs provide forage to deer, and various birds eat the seeds. Because of its handsome bark and great tolerance of heat and drought, river birch is widely used in landscaping, especially in the Deep South and Midwest, and is useful in reclaiming strip mines.

Betula occidentalis HOOK.
Betulaceae (Birch Family)
Water Birch, Western Birch, Red Birch, River Birch, Black Birch

Typically found in colonies on a variety of soils overlying coarse stone, water birch is very flood-tolerant. It prefers the edges of streams, springs and rivers, from Alaska south through western Canada and the Great Plains of the United States, and west into California, Oregon and Washington. It is notably absent from the West Coast.

Although a variable species, water birch can reach heights of 25 ft. (8 m). Its crown is narrow and rounded, its branches spreading and tending to droop. It has a strong inclination to sucker prolifically from the base, and forms large and dense thickets as it matures. The leaves, stems, flowers and fruit are typical of the birches. Water birch has smooth, shiny, dark red-brown bark, with thin horizontal lines.

In its natural setting, water birch is prone to sucker prolifically from the base.

Commercially, water birch is used mostly for fence posts. It is an important riparian tree species, however, and provides protective cover for a variety of animals. Many species of birds also feed on the seeds. It is particularly useful for streambank stabilization because its roots are fibrous and mat-forming, and it spreads easily by suckering. It is not much foraged by deer and elk, so has potential for landscape applications in the West.

Betula papyrifera MARSH.
Betulaceae (Birch Family)
Paper Birch, Canoe Birch

An archetypal tree, paper birch has a transcontinental distribution from Newfoundland to Alaska, passing in a wide arc through Canada. It reaches near to the northern limit of tree growth, and extends southward at higher elevations along both the Appalachians, into North Carolina and the Rocky Mountains, into western Wyoming. Sporadic populations may also be found on the northern Great Plains and in Colorado. Paper birch grows best in full sun, on cool, moist, well-drained soils, frequently facing north or east on slopes. However, it is adaptable to different soil textures, except for clay. Availability of soil water seems to be more important than the actual amount or pattern of precipitation. Where its seed is present in the soil, or transported by wind to a recently burnt-over site, it often forms pure pioneer stands, growing rapidly. It lives to about 140 years, although height growth ceases at 60 to 70 years, by which time seed-production also generally tapers off. Being shade-intolerant, it is usually overgrown and shaded out

Paper birch is characteristically found as a multistemmed tree.

In a dense late-winter stand like this one, the white bark of paper birch has a haunting beauty.

by more shade-tolerant species that have become established under its canopy. On the northern Great Plains it forms the climax dominant tree in those areas of north- and east-facing slopes where soil moisture is dependable.

Paper birch is a deciduous broadleaved tree reaching 80 ft. (24 m), although close to the tree line it is usually much shorter. In a forest setting, it most often has a straight single trunk, but will develop multiple stems if browsed. Young trees that are burnt to the ground will sprout multiple stems from the root collar as well; older trees gradually lose this ability. The bark of paper birch is initially reddish brown before it begins to exfoliate in thin, chalky-white, papery sheets. New bark is smooth and thin, randomly and lightly flecked with horizontal gray

lenticels. It is also remarkably water-resistant. With age the bark begins to furrow into dark gray plates. The leaves, flowers and fruit are typically birchlike, the seeds being produced in abundance in alternate years. The autumn foliage color is a rich yellow. Paper birch is shallow-rooted, rarely extending more than a depth of about 2 ft. (0.6 m) into the soil.

Paper birch has a long history of human importance, and plays an invaluable role in the ecology of northern woodlands. The bark was used by Native peoples and later by the *coureurs de bois*, or fur traders, for canoes, containers, and other useful implements, and the wood of paper birch is also used for furniture, veneer, plywood, pulp and fuel. Deer, moose, porcupines and beaver all eat various parts of the tree. Smaller mammals and many birds eat the seeds and catkins. The yellow-bellied sapsucker drills holes into the trunk to feed on the sap, which, once tapped, is also sought out by hummingbirds. The sap has been used by people for medicine, syrup, beer and wine.

KEY FEATURES

Betula papyrifera MARSH.

Form:	Large tree with **open narrow** crown
Trunk:	**One to several**, slender, **penetrating** the crown
Bark:	**Exfoliating** in **chalky-white papery sheets** to reveal pale orange inner bark; **horizontal gray** lenticels
Twig:	Slender, reddish brown
Leaves:	To 4" (10 cm) long by 2" (5 cm) wide; **oval, long-pointed, double-toothed**; dark green above paler below, turning **yellow**
Flower:	**Male flowers** tiny in **pendulous catkins** at ends of twigs; **female flowers** in green, **upright catkins** behind male catkins
Fruit:	**Pendulous**, brown, **conelike**; **disintegrates** to release winged nutlet

Paper birch is also a favorite landscape plant, particularly in its multistemmed form, because of its fine-textured form and white bark, as well as its historical association with the northern forests.

Betula populifolia MARSH.
Betulaceae (Birch Family)
Gray Birch, Wire Birch

Gray birch is a broadleaved deciduous tree extending from southeastern Ontario east to Nova Scotia and south to New Jersey, with isolated populations in northern Ohio, northern Illinois, Virginia and western North Carolina. While having a preference for moist, well-drained soils along water courses, it can also be found growing well on dry, gravelly, and sandy soils. A rapidly growing, short-lived pioneer tree of old fields and clear-cut areas, gray birch is shade-intolerant, and is usually replaced by either

Gray birch has smooth, pale, almost white bark.

balsam fir and white spruce or sugar maple and beech. It reaches 30 ft. (9 m), and has a narrow, open, pyramidal crown with drooping contorted branches. The trunk is usually single, although multi-stemmed individuals are common, due to browsing. The bark is initially thin, smooth and pale gray, almost white, but becomes shallowly fissured into dark, irregular, rough plates. The flowers and fruit are typically birchlike. The leaves have long stems, which allow them to flutter in the slightest breeze, and a very drawn-out, pointed tip. They turn a pale yellow in the autumn.

The wood of gray birch is ideal for turning and is used for many everyday items, such as spools and clothespins. It is also used for firewood. It provides shelter and food for a wide variety of animals and birds, including the yellow-bellied sapsucker which drills the bark for sap. Because of its short lifespan, gray birch is an ideal nurse plant for longer-lived hardwoods that require shade in their early years. Its rapid growth, smooth, light gray bark, slender twigs and small stature make it attractive in land-scaping, despite being short-lived.

Betula uber (ASHE) FERN.
Betulaceae (Birch Family)
Virginia Roundleaf Birch

An exceedingly rare and officially endangered species, Virginia roundleaf birch is endemic to a very small area in Smyth County in southwest Virginia, where it is found in the understory of a mixed hardwood forest along a stream. It shares a few characteristics in common with yellow and cherry birch, but has a few notable differences as well. It is a small tree to 35 ft. (10 m), with a narrow trunk and spreading crown of slender branches. The bark is thin, smooth and gray with horizontal lenticels. Its leaves are very nearly round, unlike other native birches, with a blunt tip and notched base. Both leaves and bark smell of wintergreen when bruised. Its flowers are typical of the birches, but the fruit is small and elliptical in shape.

Virginia roundleaf birch is a very uncommon tree, with rounded leaves unlike those of other birches.

Being an endangered species, Virginia roundleaf birch is not used commercially. Ecologically, it might be expected to fulfill the same sort of wildlife needs that yellow and cherry birch provide; i.e., protective cover and browse.

Bursera simaruba (L.) SARG.
Burseraceae (Frankincense Family)
Gumbo Limbo, West Indian Birch

Gumbo limbo is found in natural coastal hammock communities along the south Florida coast and the Florida Keys. It is also widespread throughout the West Indies. It is a fast-growing softwood tree, reaching heights of about 60 ft. (18 m). Its main limbs are massive and wide-spreading, while secondary branches are quite stout. In the first year of growth they are a greenish color, becoming reddish brown in the second year. The bark, which develops as the limbs and branches age, peels off in coppery strips like paper. It is generally surmised that the flaking bark discourages the attachment of heavy epiphytic bromeliads to the limbs. Leaves are pinnately divided into five or seven leathery, oval to elliptical leaflets; the overall leaf size is up to 8 in. (20 cm) long and wide. Leaves are shed in the autumn. Individually, the greenish flowers are tiny, but they cluster in terminal panicles that emerge just ahead of or with the leaves. Male flowers are found on one tree, female flowers on another. Fruit develops

Gumbo limbo usually has massive, wide-spreading limbs.

only on the female trees, and is small and three-angled with a thick dark red exterior.

Gumbo limbo is often encountered as a land-scape specimen tree, and because it roots easily from pieces of stem it has been used to create living fences. It is widely used for medicinal purposes, and the leaves are occasionally made into a tea.

Calocedrus decurrens (TORR.) FLORIN
Cupressaceae (Cypress Family)
Incense Cedar, California Incense Cedar

Native from Baja California to the southern slopes of Mount Hood in Oregon, incense cedar occurs most frequently in the Sierra Nevada at elevations of 2,000 to 6,900 ft. (610 to 2,100 m). It rarely forms pure stands, being more often encountered as small groups or individuals mixed with a variety of pines, white fir or California oak. It prefers dry, shady sites in climates where summers are dry, and is considered a climax community tree under these conditions. Although it grows best on deep, well-drained sandy loams, it can be found on a wide variety of soil types, from neutral to strongly acid.

Incense cedar is long-lived, some trees attaining an age of 500 years, and usually reaching about 80 ft. (24 m) in height; in the Sierra Nevada 150 ft. (46 m) is common. It has a naturally narrow, dense, pyramidal to columnar habit with flattened branches of overlapping green scales. The mature bark is dark brown with hints of dark magenta and gray, fibrous and fissured vertically into irregular plates. Cones are relatively small, to about 1.5 in. (3.75 cm), and oblong-shaped, hanging at the tips of branchlets under their own weight.

Incense cedar is utilized by wildlife for cover from heat and predators. It is not much foraged, although the seeds are eaten by some birds and small mammals. Oil is extracted commercially from the foliage, and the timber, being decay-resistant, is prized for exterior use, as well as for interior siding and the manufacture of pencils. It also is popular as a land-scape plant, and several named cultivars exist.

Incense cedar usually occurs as a solitary individual tree, with a high narrow crown and reddish bark.

Carpinus caroliniana WALT.
Betulaceae (Birch Family)
Musclewood, Blue Beech, American Hornbeam, Ironwood

Musclewood is an extensive understory tree in bottom-land mixed hardwood forests from the Atlantic coast (central Florida to Maine) to west of the Mississippi (eastern Texas to Minnesota). Its range also extends through southwestern Quebec and southern Ontario, and into Mexico.

As a shade-loving tree on cool, moist, rich soil, musclewood stretches up to 10 or 12 ft. (3 to 4 m) before forming a loose, broad crown, which extends upwards to 40 ft. (12 m). The trunks are usually somewhat crooked and sinuous, like the tendons and bunched muscles of a forearm. The effect is heightened by thin, smooth, mid-gray bark. Twigs are fine-textured and bear doubly serrated, elliptical

Early golden-red autumn color on musclewood will eventually become crimson.

leaves, 4 in. (10 cm) long, drawn out to a point at the tip. Summer color is a dark blue-green turning to vivid orange and scarlet in the autumn. Flowers are borne in catkins, male and female in separate catkins. The fruit is a winged nutlet, paired and associated with a three-lobed bract. These are aggregated into a pendulous, leafy-looking cluster, which ripens and disintegrates in the autumn.

Although the wood is dense and strong, musclewood use is commercially limited to small utensils since it is also slender-trunked and often crooked. Wildlife will only lightly browse it. In forest management it is sometimes considered a weed in that it competes in the understory with saplings of commercially more favored species such as sugar maple. However, it makes an elegant and interesting small-scale tree in landscape applications, and does well in shade or moderate levels of sun.

THE HICKORIES (*CARYA*)
Walnut Family (*Juglandaceae*)

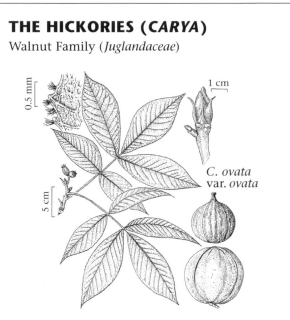

C. ovata
var. ovata

Hickories have pinnately divided leaves and a nut that can split either wholly or partly and shed its husk.

Variously reported as having from 16 to 22 species worldwide, most hickories occur in eastern North America. The remaining two species are located in southeast Asia. They are all larger trees characteristic of many eastern hardwood forest types. Individually each species is characteristically found across a range of topography and soil types, but with a strong preference for one type of soil in particular. They are often found in association with one another wherever their ranges overlap, and naturally occurring hybrids are common. They are all relatively long-lived, and intermediately shade-tolerant, particularly when saplings, although some are more shade-tolerant than others. Hickories range from being slow-growing to moderately quick. They are most often found in late successional and early climax forest communities on sites that are not often disturbed. However, some species are relatively quick to colonize adjacent disturbed areas.

Hickories are medium to large trees, often with a stately, majestic form, especially when open-grown. They have stout branches with a solid pith, unlike the walnuts, to which they are allied, in which the pith is chambered. Their leaves are alternately arranged, and pinnately compound, with five to eleven elliptical leaflets depending on the species, the bottom leaflets smallest and the terminal leaflet largest. The flowers of the hickories are tiny, without petals, and not very noticeable. They emerge with the leaves in spring, male and female flowers on separate branches of the same tree. Male flowers are borne in loose three-branched catkins at the ends of branches, while the female flowers are in smaller clusters at the ends of other branches. The fruit of hickories is a large, smooth-surfaced nut within a relatively thick husk that usually splits halfway to fully open, depending on the species, along several seams when ripe. In a number of species, notably the pecan, the seed inside the nut is edible.

The hickories are an economically important group of trees. The nuts of pecan have been long been harvested commercially, and several other species have nuts that are highly palatable as well. Cultivated varieties and hybrids have been developed for nut production, ease of shelling and hardiness. The wood of several species is also valued, being hard and impact-resistant. Some of the hickories also make superb shade trees on suitable larger sites, and their fall color is usually an excellent warm, antique gold. In their natural settings, hickory nuts are an important food to many birds and mammals.

The leaves of water hickory generally have 11 leaflets, with those at the base being smallest.

In addition, it has a wider tolerance for both wet soils and seasonal variation in soil moisture than other hickories. It can be found as a component of several hardwood forest types.

The tallest of the hickories, water hickory generally reaches a height of 100 ft. (30 m), with a straight tall trunk penetrating a narrow crown of slender branches. The light brown bark is somewhat variable between being tight on plants in drier areas, to shaggy on those growing on wet ground. Flowers are typical of the hickories, and the fruit is characteristically rough, flattened and strongly four-angled, with a dark brown thin-walled nut and bitter seed inside.

As a lumber tree, water hickory is regarded as inferior to other hickories, and generally has no direct commercial value. However, its bitter nuts are eaten by ducks, although it is not an important food source to them. It hybridizes with pecan, and research has been undertaken in evaluating the hybrids.

Carya aquatica (MICHX. f.) NUTT.
Juglandaceae (Walnut Family)
Water Hickory

Aptly named, water hickory can be found in low, wet, wooded sites from southern Illinois to eastern Texas, east to Florida and north to southeast Virginia. It is found on floodplain soils that are generally poorly drained, such as clay, and often submerged.

Carya carolinae-septentrionalis (ASHE) ENGL. & GRAEBN.
Juglandaceae (Walnut Family)
Southern Shagbark Hickory

Although often considered a variety of shagbark hickory, southern shagbark has been shown to have adapted ecologically to soil conditions that are distinctly different from those preferred by shagbark hickory. In addition, even though the two

In later stages of autumn color, southern shagbark foliage turns from antique gold to brown.

Bitternut hickory fruits are oval, generally with four raised seams, as seen here.

Carya cordiformis (WANGENH.) K. KOCH
Juglandaceae (Walnut Family)
Bitternut Hickory, Swamp Hickory

Bitternut hickory is the most widely distributed and common of the hickories, extending from southern Quebec west to Minnesota, and throughout all the eastern states southward to eastern Texas and northwestern Florida. Although found on a variety of soils, bitternut hickory prefers hardwood forests on rich moist bottomlands. It also occurs on dry uplands, particularly in the southwest of its range, and is part of the climax canopy. It is not found at high altitudes, and is completely absent from the forested mountains of northern New England and New York.

Forming a broad crown when open-grown, or a high narrow one in the forest, bitternut hickory is a single-trunked tree, to 80 ft. (24 m). The bark is tight, gray to light brown, shallowly furrowing into ridges. Twigs are slender with yellow buds, which become sulfur-yellow during the winter. The pinnately compound leaves generally have seven or nine stalkless leaflets in the hickory pattern. They turn a rich yellow-gold color in the autumn. Flowers are typical of the hickories. The fruit is round or slightly flattened, about 1.25 in. (3 cm) in diameter. It has a thin green husk, splitting open to release a thin-walled nut containing a very bitter seed. Roots are deep and lateral.

Bitternut hickory has some commercial value for

species occur within the same range, they interbreed infrequently. The range of southern shagbark hickory is much more restricted than that of shagbark. It is found in two large areas on opposite sides of the southern Appalachians, one running from south-central Virginia to northeast Georgia, and the other through Tennessee into northwest Georgia, northern Alabama and northeast Louisiana. Several other smaller populations are found in Alabama and Louisiana. In terms of its height, growth pattern and chief characteristics it is very similar to shagbark hickory. The important differences are that southern shagbark hickory's shoots are much more slender, and it has darker, less rounded outer bud scales.

Southern shagbark hickory has not been exploited commercially the way shagbark hickory has, but a number of cultivars exist.

its wood, which is used in furniture, small utensils, ladders and dowels. It is also used for making charcoal, and as fuel. Smoke from burning bitternut hickory is used to give meats a "hickory" flavor. The nuts are largely as unpalatable to wildlife as to humans, and are rarely eaten.

Carya floridana SARG.
Juglandaceae (Walnut Family)
Scrub Hickory, Florida Hickory

Restricted to 20 counties in central Florida, scrub hickory can be found in association with other scrub vegetation trees, such as evergreen oaks, on hummocks and dry sand ridges. It is generally a small tree with several trunks reaching heights of 20 ft. (6 m), but there are reports of single-trunked trees reaching in excess of 50 ft. (15 m). The bark is initially

Scrub hickory is a small tree that typically grows in dry soils.

smooth gray, but becomes furrowed with age into vertical ridges. The crown is spreading. The pinnately compound leaves reach about 8 in. (20 cm) in length, in the general hickory pattern, with usually five unstalked leaflets. When emerging the leaves are densely pubescent, with rust-colored hairs, which slough off except for some along the veins of the lower leaf surface, which is also dotted with tiny brown glands. Buds are also covered with abundant rusty hairs. The flowers are typical of hickory. The fruit is somewhat pear-shaped, small, to about 1.25 in. (3 cm) long, smooth and brown; the husk splits open to release a hard-shelled nut with an edible seed within. Fruit is often borne while the tree is still young.

Economically unimportant, Florida hickory is mostly a food source to those animals which are capable of cracking or otherwise opening its hard, thick nut-shells.

Carya glabra (MILL.) SWEET
Juglandaceae (Walnut Family)
Pignut Hickory

Although never abundant, pignut hickory is widely encountered from eastern Maine west to southeastern Iowa, then southward through all the eastern states to eastern Texas and central Florida. It is a frequent tree in mixed hardwoods on dry to moist upland soils, rocky hillsides and bottomlands, preferring light, well-drained, loamy soils. It is often found co-dominant with a variety of oaks in climax hardwood forests, where it tends to be shade-tolerant.

A slow-growing, long-lived tree, pignut hickory reaches 100 ft. (30 m) with a high, narrow, oval crown of somewhat pendulous branches. It is usually single-trunked, with the gray bark shallowly ridged and furrowed. The typically hickory-type, pinnately compound leaves consist of generally five (rarely seven), smooth leaflets. Flowers are typically hickorylike. The fruit, which ripens in early autumn, is fig or pear-shaped. The brown husk splits halfway open to reveal a thick-walled nut about 1.5 in. (3.5 cm) in length, containing a small, bitter to sweet seed.

The high narrow crown of pignut hickory becomes rich gold in the autumn.

Pignut hickory provides cover for a variety of animals. The nut is also highly palatable to wildlife. In some areas it is harvested commercially for human use; the wood is heavy, strong and elastic and has been used since colonial times for a variety of implements, tools and wheel-spokes. It is also encountered as a landscape shade tree on larger sites throughout its range.

Carya illinoensis (WANGENH.) K. KOCH
Juglandaceae (Walnut Family)
Pecan

Pecan is arguable the most economically important food crop native to North America. Before the arrival of European settlers, its range was probably much influenced by the dietary and harvesting practices of the Native peoples. In any case, its non-commercial range encompasses the bottomlands of the Mississippi River, from southern Indiana through Illinois south to the Gulf of Mexico, as well as the lower Ohio River and the river systems that empty into the Gulf westward of the Mississippi and reach up through central Texas, into Oklahoma and Kansas. It is also found in the mountains of adjacent Mexico. Pecan has a strong preference for well-drained loamy soils, and is largely limited throughout its range to the alluvial soils of rivers and streams where it is not subjected to too much flooding. It is not found on poorly drained clay soils or low-lying ground prone to extensive flooding. Being intolerant of shade, pecan is regarded as a sub-climax species, which replaces early colonizing species such as willow or poplar, but is in turn replaced by more shade-tolerant species.

Pecan is a long-lived tree, reaching a height of 100 to 150 ft. (30 to 45 m). It is usually a single-trunked tree, with a number of large ascending limbs that develop into a rounded to irregular crown. The bark is light gray to light brown, shallowly furrowed, and ridged. Flowers and leaves follow the typical pattern for hickories. The leaves reach lengths of 20 in. (50 cm), and are composed of up to 17 generally hairless leaflets, which are characteristically slightly curved. The fruits are brown and cylindrical, with four wings running the length. The husk splits along the wings to expose a thin-walled, cylindrically shaped, smooth brown nut with a large,

At maturity, pecans become large trees, as seen here.

The narrow, oval, ridged fruit of pecan encloses the highly valued nut.

sweet, edible seed inside. The root system of the pecan is deep and lateral.

Although the wood of pecan is considered inferior to that of other hickories, it is nonetheless used for veneer, flooring and furniture, and it also

provides charcoal for smoking meats. But the pecan's most important attribute is its sweet, nutritious nutmeat, which is highly valued. It generally starts bearing at about 20 years of age, and in the peak productive years from 75 to 225 years of age, a single tree can produce an average of 100 pounds (40 kg) of nuts each year. Because of the commercial value of its nut, pecans are widely grown in plantations far outside its native range. Many cultivated varieties are available for improved nut production and quality. The nut of wild-growing trees is eaten by a number of birds and small mammals, which also use it as protective cover. Throughout its range pecan is widely grown as a shade tree where soil conditions allow.

Carya lacinosa (MICHX. f.) LOUD.
Juglandaceae (Walnut Family)

Shellbark Hickory, Big Shagbark Hickory, Kingnut

Related to shagbark hickory, but uncommon and with a more restricted range, shellbark hickory has a rambling core range from southwest Pennsylvania and Ohio west to southeast Iowa, south to northeast Oklahoma and east to Tennessee. Scattered populations occur in extreme southwestern Ontario, New York, Mississippi and northern Georgia. Most often found in oak-dominated habitats on moist, fertile, deep bottomlands, it rarely may also occupy drier sandy soils in the northern parts of its range.

Shellbark hickory becomes a large, straight-trunked tree to 100 ft. (30 m), supporting a rounded, narrow crown of stout branches and large leaves. Twigs are also stout, buff to orange in color and hairy, terminating in a large hairy bud. The typical hickory leaf reaches 20 in. (50 cm) long with seven broadly lance-shaped leaflets, shiny above and pale with downy hairs below. The light gray bark exfoliates in loosely attached thick, vertical plates, like the shagbark. Flowers are typically hickorylike. The fruit is the largest of the hickories, about 2.5 in. (6 cm) long, usually light cream-colored, round, somewhat angled, and flattened. It has a very thick husk and a thick shell, with a large, sweet, edible seed.

KEY FEATURES

Carya illinoensis

Form:	Large tree with broad round cown
Trunk:	Single; developing into **several massive spreading branches**
Bark:	Light grayish brown; deep, irregular furrows; zigzag scaly ridges
Twig:	Smooth, medium texture
Leaves:	Pinnately compound to 20" (50 cm) long with 11 to 17 **leaflets, somewhat sickle-shaped**; finely toothed; yellowish green above, paler below, turning yellow
Flower:	Tiny; **males** gathered into catkins, **3 hanging together** on a stalk; **females in groups of 2 to 10** at the end of the twig
Fruit:	Oblong, to 2" (5 cm), thin brown husk **splitting along 4 ridges** to release **thin-shelled** smooth brown nut with **edible seed**

Shellbark hickory develops a rounded crown at maturity, and typically turns antique gold in autumn.

Commercially, shellbark hickory is not as important as other hickories. However, it has given rise to over 40 cultivars and a number of hybrids with pecan and shagbark hickory, all in the attempt to improve the flavor of the nutmeat and reduce the thickness of the shell. In the wild, because of the thick shell, the nut it is not an important food source for animals.

Carya ovalis (WANGENH.) SARG.
Juglandaceae (Walnut Family)
Red Hickory

Red hickory is classified by some authorities as a variety of the pignut hickory, *C. glabra* var. *odorata*.

It has much the same range as pignut hickory, from eastern Vermont west to southeastern Iowa, then southward through all the eastern states to eastern Texas and central Florida. It is more common, however, in the northern and western areas of its range than is pignut hickory, extending into the Niagara Peninsula of Ontario and into northeastern Oklahoma. It tends to prefer well-drained, drier upland soils mixed with other broadleaved hardwoods. It is intolerant of shade and may be replaced by more shade-tolerant species.

A medium tree, reaching 80 ft. (25 m), red hickory is otherwise somewhat similar to pignut hickory in form, differing chiefly in the characteristics of its foliage, fruit and bark. Leaves consist of seven, rarely nine, leaflets, initially smooth but becoming slightly shaggy. The husk of red hickory fruit is somewhat warty, with golden scales and four, slightly winged sutures along which it splits open entirely to release

Red hickory typically has mid-gray bark and golden autumn foliage.

the nut. Pignut hickory, in contrast, is smooth, without scales or winged sutures, and partially splits open. The seed of red hickory is bitter-tasting to sweet. The bark is gray, initially thin, later becoming shallowly fissured, forming intersecting ridges that give an overall scaly effect.

Except for the nut having no value for most wildlife or human consumption, red hickory has the same uses as pignut hickory.

Carya ovata (MILL.) K. KOCH
Juglandaceae (Walnut Family)
Shagbark Hickory, Upland Hickory

Shagbark hickory has an extensive range throughout North America east of a line from southeast Minnesota to eastern Texas, including southern Ontario and the extreme south of Quebec. It is not present in the lower Mississippi Delta or the coastal plains of the Southeast and Gulf of Mexico. Shagbark hickory grows best in humid climates on rich, deep, moist soils of various types. Being in the mid-range of shade-tolerance, it is often a climax species of mixed hardwood forest, especially oak-hickory forests, but may also, especially in the northern part of its range, be replaced by more shade-tolerant climax species such as sugar maple and basswood.

A moderately long-growing tree to 200 years, shagbark hickory reaches 80 ft. (25 m), with a single dominant trunk that penetrates the canopy. When open grown the crown is broadly oblong, but in forested conditions it tends to be narrow and columnar. The dark gray bark is very characteristically shaggy with long vertical straplike plates exfoliating from the ends. The five to seven leaflets create a typical hickory leaf 10 in. (25 cm) in length, which changes to a rich golden color in the autumn. The outer scales of the terminal buds have terminal spines, spread loosely outward and are easily detached. Flowers are of the hickory type. Fruits are generally borne in clusters of two or three at the ends of branches. They are round and smooth, with grooved sutures. The husk splits open to release a light beige, roundish, four-ridged,

Shagbark hickory is aptly named for its peeling shaggy bark.

thick-walled nut that contains a sweet edible seed. The root is a taproot.

Shagbark hickory is an economically important tree for both its timber and its seed. The wood is tough, hard and resilient, and is regarded as the best of the hickories for impact and stress resistance. It is widely used for furniture, flooring, tools, sporting equipment and various other implements. Charcoal made from the wood is used to smoke-flavor foods. The nutmeat is highly palatable not only to people but also to many birds and mammals. They were one of the staple foods of some Native peoples, and the distribution of the shagbark hickory may reflect this importance. Many animals and birds depend heavily on the nuts, especially in years

KEY FEATURES

Carya ovata

Form: **Large** tree with narrow oval crown

Trunk: Single, prominent well into crown

Bark: Light gray, in **long narrow strips curving noticably outward at the ends**, remaining attached in the middle

Twig: Stout, brown, smooth; buds large, light brown, hairy, **scales with long spikes at the tips**, easily detached

Leaves: Generally comprised of **5 leaflets**, terminal leaflet larger than side leaflets

Flower: Without petals: male flowers small, in long drooping catkins, grouped in threes; female flowers in groups of 2 to 5 at the tips of the twig

Fruit: Nearly round to 2.5" (6 cm), splitting completely along 4 grooved sutures; husk thick; nut elliptical to round, flattened and angled, edible

Maryland. It is usually found in oak–hickory forests and in association with species of pine.

Sand hickory reaches heights of 80 ft. (25 m) and is generally characterized by silvery, sometimes yellowish scales on twigs, leaves, and buds. It is single-trunked, with tight, deeply furrowed, rough, blackish bark. It has slender twigs bearing typical hickory-type leaves to 15 in. (13 cm) long, made up of seven to nine leaflets. The mid-rib is characteristically densely tufted with hairs, and the lower surfaces of the leaflets are covered with silvery scales. The bud scales are reddish brown. Flowers are borne in the hickory fashion, and the fruit is about 1.5 in. (4 cm) long, with a thin husk covered in silvery yellow scale. The nut within is roundish, somewhat thick-walled, and contains an edible, sweet, small seed.

In a forest, sand hickory develops a straight, single trunk and high crown.

when bumper crops are produced. Many cultivars and hybrids with other hickories have been developed for nut production. It is also encountered as a shade and specimen tree throughout its range where soil conditions are appropriate.

Carya pallida (ASHE) ENGL. & GRAEBN.
Juglandaceae (Walnut Family)
Sand Hickory, Pale Hickory

Preferring dry rocky or sandy soils in both valleys and uplands, sand hickory extends in an irregular band from the Atlantic coast of Virginia southwest to Louisiana. There are scattered populations in northern Florida, as well as Indiana, Illinois, and

The wood and nut of sand hickory are not commercially important, and wildlife value is restricted to providing cover. The nut is too thick to warrant use, despite the sweetness of the seed. It has some usefulness as a landscape tree where the soil conditions warrant.

Carya texana BUCKL.
Juglandaceae (Walnut Family)
Black Hickory, Buckley Hickory

Found on dry, shallow upland soils of dry rock or sand, black hickory ranges west of the Mississippi River from southern Indiana to south-central Texas. It is most commonly found in association with various oak species.

A small tree, reaching about 30 ft. (9 m), black hickory has a single trunk, developing into a rounded

A small tree, black hickory sometimes develops an irregular crown.

or sometimes mounded and uneven crown. The black-to-dark-gray bark is rough and thick, deeply and tightly fissured in a diamond pattern. Leaves are typically pinnately compound to 12 in. (30 cm) long, in the hickory pattern. They are covered with rust-colored hairs when first developing, but become smooth, shiny and dark green above, paler and lightly covered with rusty hairs along the veins below. The young twigs and buds are similarly covered in rusty hairs. The flowers conform to the typical pattern for the hickories. The fruit is rounded with an often slightly winged brown husk covering a thick-walled nut. The small seed inside ranges from being bitter to edible.

The wood of black hickory is not considered important economically, because of its small size. However, it has some landscape potential, and at least one cultivar exists. It reportedly hybridizes with water and mockernut hickories.

Carya tomentosa (POIR.) NUTT.
Juglandaceae (Walnut Family)
Mockernut Hickory

Mockernut hickory ranges from eastern Texas east to northern Florida, north to Massachusetts and west to southeastern Iowa. A climax species on most sites, mockernut hickory attains its best growth on fertile, deep upland soils. In the south it may be found also on moist bottomlands, but in the north prefers rocky, and especially sandy, slopes and hillsides. It is found associated with a variety of hardwood trees and pines.

Reaching 100 ft. (30 m), mockernut hickory is a single-trunked tree often swollen at the base, with a tap root or deep laterals. In a forest setting it is usually high, open and narrowly crowned, while in the open its crown is lower, wide and more oblong. The bark is gray, tight and furrowed irregularly. Mockernut hickory is densely hairy in twig, leaf and bud, all of which are quite fragrant when rubbed. Twigs are also stout and brown, with a large, silkily pubescent bud at the tip, the outer scales of which, while present in summer, fall before winter.

As shown here, the husk of mockernut hickory fruit often splits only partially open.

The hickory-type leaves are 20 in. (50 cm) long, and composed of seven or nine leaflets. The mid-vein and the lower leaflet surfaces are pale with dense pubescence, while the upper surfaces are shining yellow-green. Flowers are typical of hickories. The fruit is brown, roughly elliptical, with the thick husk splitting partial or totally to release a four-angled, elliptical, thick-shelled nut with a sweet edible seed inside.

Although rarely eaten by people because of the thick shell, mockernut hickory is preferred by a number of animals, including deer, squirrels, foxes, black bears, and beavers. The wood is hard, tough, and strong, making it valuable for tool handles, furniture, gymnasium equipment, and a variety of implements. It is also used for lumber and charcoal.

Castanea dentata (MARSH.) BORKH.
Fagaceae (Beech Family)
American Chestnut

The loss of American chestnut from the hardwood forests of eastern North America due to the introduction of the chestnut blight (*Endothia parasitica*) around 1904 still stands as an example of the potential dangers of the global translocation of plants. Prior to the introduction of the blight, American chestnut could be found from southern Maine west through southwestern Ontario to Indiana, south to Mississippi and east into southwest Georgia. It was most prevalent in the Appalachians, with scattered populations in the Piedmont. Now it is very rare, although trees planted in isolated areas outside its range have remained unaffected. Its preferred habitat is moist, fertile, well-drained soils in upland mixed hardwood forests, in association with oaks, hickories, birches, and sugar maples.

When unaffected by blight, American chestnut has the potential to reach a height of 100 ft. (30 m), with massive spreading branches and a rounded crown. Since the blight remains viable in the environment, any American chestnut growing within its former range is inevitably infected and dies to the ground. Root sprouts will emerge until they are re-infected. It is rare to find a sizeable tree. The bark on sprouts and young trunks is smooth and dark grayish brown. On older trunks it becomes deeply furrowed with flat vertical ridges. Leaves reach 9 in.

Densely spiny green capsules are characteristic of American chestnut.

(23 cm) long and about a third as wide, with many parallel veins ending in curved teeth at the margin, the vein protruding to form a bristle. They are shiny, yellowish green above, paler below, turning a very attractive, rich yellow-gold in the autumn. On young trees the leaves eventually turn brown and persist on the tree into the winter. This tendency becomes less pronounced in older trees. The flowers, borne in early summer, are individually tiny, but the male flowers are grouped into fairly showy, fragrant, creamy white catkins. At the base of some of them there are up to three inconspicuous green female flowers. The fruit that develops from the female flower is a large, 2.5 in. (6 cm) round bur,

---

KEY FEATURES

Castanea dentata

Form:	Massive, often tall trunk; crown dense, broad, round to oval
Trunk:	Single; in forests high-branched; in open branches massive and low
Bark:	Similar to red oak
Twig:	**Green, slender, smooth**
Leaves:	Resembling beech; **elliptical, sharp-pointed, pronounced regular teeth**, 2 to 3 times long as wide
Flower:	In midsummer; males individually small, **gathered in conspicuous, upright, whitish, 8" (20 cm) long catkins**, in the axils of upper leaves; females greenish, in groups of 2 or 3 at the base of male catkins
Fruit:	**Short-stalked bur** to about 2.5 in. (6 cm) in diameter, covered in prominent, branched spines; matures in autumn, splitting along 3 or 4 sutures, revealing up to three **ovoid, somewhat flattened shiny, mahogany-colored nuts, very sweet and palatable**

---

covered in very prickly branched spines. It ripens in autumn, splits open along three or four sutures to release up to three egg-shaped, shiny, brown chestnuts about 0.75 in. (2 cm) long. They are sweet and highly palatable.

American chestnut no longer has commercial value. Before the blight eliminated it from the forest, its wood was highly valued for many purposes, from log cabins, to furniture, to barrels. Because it is resistant to decay, it found particular use in railway ties, posts and split-rail fences. The nuts were also an important cash crop. It was considered by many that the nut of American chestnut was more flavorful than the European species. In addition, the nuts were a major food source to many animals. In the last century, American chestnut was a popular landscape shade tree, and was widely planted in cities and towns in parks and as street trees. Current attempts to breed resistance to the blight into American chestnut by cross-breeding with Asiatic species has not proven very successful, although there is still hope that the effects of the blight may be overcome through this strategy.

Catalpa bignonioides WALT.
Bignoniaceae (Bignonia Family)

Southern Catalpa, Indian Bean, Common Catalpa

The range of southern catalpa prior to European settlement is a matter of conjecture, but it seems likely that the center of distribution was Alabama, extending west into Mississippi and east into southwest Georgia and northwest Florida. It has since become naturalized throughout all of eastern North America, as far north as southern New England. Southern catalpa prefers moist, fertile soils in more open areas.

At 50 ft. (15 m), southern catalpa forms a short-trunked tree with a broad, rounded crown of spreading, coarse branches and large, coarse leaves. The bark is scaly grayish brown. Twigs are smooth, thick, crooked and initially green, turning brown over winter. Leaves are large, to 10 in. (25 cm) long by

Southern catalpa bears showy flowers even when quite young.

of crooked branches and hanging fruits. It is occasionally pollarded to accentuate the large leaf size.

Catalpa speciosa (WARDER) WARDER ex ENGELM.
Bignoniaceae (Bignonia Family)
Northern Catalpa, Western Catalpa, Hardy Catalpa, Catawba

Northern catalpa has many general features in common with southern catalpa, and only the chief differences will be highlighted here. Like southern catalpa, its original range, prior to European settlement, is a matter of conjecture. Probably it was restricted to open sites, in moist fertile soils along streams and rivers feeding into the lower Ohio

As a large mature tree, northern catalpa in flower is bold and attractive.

7 in. (18 cm) wide, heart-shaped, smooth-edged, dull mid-green above, and paler, and softly hairy beneath, blackening in the autumn with the first hard frosts. They are borne three to a node, and when bruised emit an unpleasant odor. They are prone to bacterial leaf spot, which often disfigures them by midsummer. The flowers are slightly fragrant, irregularly bell-shaped, and white with yellow and purple markings inside. They are grouped into very showy, upright clusters emerging in late spring. They are followed by cylindrical capsules, 12 in. (30 cm) long and 0.33 in. (1 cm) wide, which turn brown in the autumn. They remain into winter, gradually splitting open to release numerous fringed, winged seeds.

Southern catalpa is widely grown for its showy flowers, large leaves, and interesting winter aspect

River, and downstream along the Mississippi into northeast Arkansas. It is now widely naturalized throughout eastern North America as far north as southern Ontario.

Northern catalpa tops out at about 80 ft. (24 m). The crown is higher and more cylindrical in profile than southern catalpa. The bark, branches, and leaves are virtually identical to those of the southern catalpa, and share the same problems. The flowers are similar also, but larger in northern catalpa, to 2.25 in. (6 cm) long, with a pair of orange lines and purple dots inside. The fruit is similar as well, but thicker, about 0.75 in. (15 cm).

Northern catalpa is used in landscaping in the same ways that southern catalpa is. Both kinds of catalpa need attention when grown as specimens. The bacterial leaf-spot can ruin the visual effect of the leaves. Insect infestations are common as well.

THE HACKBERRIES (*CELTIS*)

Elm Family (*Ulmaceae*)

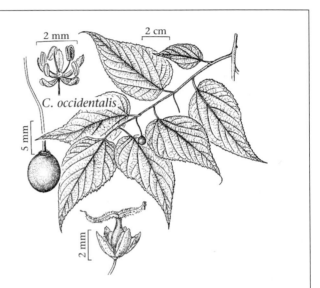

C. occidentalis

The hackberries are closely allied to the elms but differ from them in having a round fleshy drupe as a fruit rather than a samara. There are about 600 species of hackberries in temperate and tropical regions of the world. However, only five species occur in North America, and one of these, the netleaf hackberry (*Celtis reticulata*), which is not covered in this book, is variable between shrub and tree depending on environment and genetics. The remaining four species are characteristically trees of moist to wet ground, commonly found along rivers, streambanks and the edges of wetlands. They are fairly fast-growing, moderately long-lived, and shade-intolerant. They typically colonize disturbed sites, particularly flood-disturbed ones, but are shaded out by longer-lived, more shade-tolerant deciduous trees.

The hackberries form elegant, medium-sized trees with fine-branched crowns and characteristically warty bark. There leaves are alternate along the somewhat zigzagging twigs. They have leaf blades that are unevenly shaped at the base, where the blade joins the leafstalk. The leaves of all species are very similar, sharing the same general shape, texture, milky blue-green summer color, and pale yellow autumn hues. The flowers appear in spring just ahead of the emerging leaves, and are inconspicuous, tiny, and unisexual, male and female flowers being grouped

The leaves of hackberries are elmlike, but the fruit is a small, dry and mealy berry.

togther in same-sex clusters on the same tree. The fruit is an orange to red to purple, mealy-fleshed drupe ripening in the autumn.

Hackberries make fine, generally durable shade trees, and are used widely as such, and as street trees. When well-grown, and sited to exploit form and leaf color, they provide quietly elegant foils to other vegetation. They are much unsung in landscape applications and deserve better treatment. They are prone to leaf gall which can badly disfigure the foliage, but this is a very treatable condition. They are not commercially important for their wood. In their natural setting they are exploited by birds for their fruit and for shelter.

Celtis laevigata WILLD.

Ulmaceae (Elm Family)

Sugar Hackberry, Sugarberry, Southern Hackberry

Occurring in scattered areas through the southeast United States, sugar hackberry covers a range from Florida north to southeast Virginia, west to central Illinois and south to southwest Texas. It also occurs in local populations in Maryland and northeast Mexico. It strongly prefers humid climates at low elevation, although it is not particular as to soil type so long as it is moist, fairly well drained and not prone to flooding. Sugar hackberry is fairly shade-tolerant as a young tree and, along with a number of other species, such as American elm and sweet gum, will replace early colonizing trees, only to be ultimately replaced itself by climax-forest trees.

Sugar hackberry is a generally trouble-free, fine-textured tree with a rounded crown.

At 100 ft. (30 m), sugar hackberry is a tall, single-trunked tree, with a generally high spreading or rounded crown. It grows slowly and is relatively short-lived, to about 150 years. The gray bark is initially smooth before developing the warty bark characteristic of hackberries. The twigs, flowers, fruit, and leaves are all typical of hackberries. The roots of sugar hackberry are shallow, and wind-throw is sometimes observed when the tree is open-grown.

The berries of sugar hackberry are a favored fruit of many birds, including grouse, pheasant, quail and turkey. Apparently the fruit is also quite palatable to humans as well. The wood is used mostly for furniture but is used for flooring, crates and posts as well. It is widely planted as a relatively problem-free and attractive ornamental shade tree. However, the leaves produce several chemicals that will suppress the growth of lawn grass.

Celtis occidentalis L.

Ulmaceae (Elm Family)

Common Hackberry, Northern Hackberry

Common hackberry has a distribution that can only be described as simultaneously extensive and erratic. It has a core range that extends from southern Ontario south to Tennessee, west to Oklahoma and north to North Dakota. It has a subsidiary distribution, from Connecticut to Virginia, which is connected to the core range through West Virginia and southern Pennsylvania, along rivers. Scattered localized populations are found higher on the southern Piedmont, extreme southern Quebec and extreme southern Manitoba. In general, common hackberry grows best on fertile, moist, limestone soils that do not have a high water table. It will tolerate some flooding, and is notably tolerant of drought. However, repeated drought tends to stunt it. On the Great Plains it tends to follow stream and river courses. It is also fairly shade-tolerant, particularly when young. In the west of its range, particularly where fires are suppressed, it tends to

Common hackberry is a mid-sized tree with a high, broadly oval canopy.

depending on genetics and location. It generally has a straight single trunk penetrating a high oval crown of spreading fine-textured branches. Its light gray to brown bark is typically smooth in youth, gradually developing the corky warts and ridges common to hackberries. Its leaves, flowers and fruits are typical of the hackberries. The leaves are a pleasant mid-green turning pale yellow to yellow-green in the autumn. Because of the genetic variability in common hackberry, there are some individuals in which both the summer and autumn leaf-color is quite beautiful. The sweet fruit is variable in color, from orange-red to crimson to brown to black, borne in equal amounts every year. After ripening in the autumn the fruit gradually drops off during the winter.

become the dominant tree of climax forest. There are several varieties of common hackberry, each adapted to regional climate and soil conditions and variable in a number of features, including overall form and height.

A deeply rooted tree, common hackberry is widely variable in height, from 50 ft. (15 m) to 90 ft. (27 m),

KEY FEATURES

Celtis occidentalis L.

Form: Large tree with rounded crown

Trunk: Single, **ascending high into canopy**

Bark: Light grayish brown; smooth developing **corky warts and layered ridges**

Twig: Light brown, slightly hairy, zig-zagging, **last bud on twig hooked** over the tip

Leaves: To 5" (13 cm) long by 2.5" 6 cm) wide, long-pointed oval with **unequal-sided base**, sharply toothed

Flower: Tiny, green male and female at base of twigs

Fruit: Dry to sweet **orange-red to purple drupe**; single-seeded

Common hackberry produces an abundance of round red berries that ripen in the autumn.

The fruit of common hackberry is eaten by over 25 species of birds, including larger game birds, such as turkeys and pheasants, as well as songbirds. Numerous small mammals also consume the fruit. It is a favored food source of numerous insects, none of which kill the tree, and only a few of which are nuisances. It makes a superlative shade tree, especially on the Great Plains, where its relative drought-tolerance is an asset. However, not all individual trees are equally tolerant of drought, and where drought is more than an occasional event, the common hackberry will tend to become stunted. It should be remembered that tolerance is not preference. Some individual trees of common hackberry are beautiful, having excellent form with milky green summer foliage turning soft yellow in the autumn. They make an excellent replacement for the American elm, which has been devastated by Dutch elm disease. Common hackberry is also used extensively as a wind break on the Great Plains, where its intermediate wind resistance, deep-rootedness, drought and shade tolerance, and self-seeding habit favor its use in self-regenerating mixed shelterbelts.

Celtis tenuifolia NUTT.
Ulmaceae (Elm Family)
Dwarf Hackberry, Georgia Hackberry

Dwarf hackberry has a scattered distribution throughout the southeast United States from northern Florida to Maryland, west to southeast Kansas and south to eastern Texas. It is also found locally in southwestern Ontario, where it is designated a vulnerable species. Dwarf hackberry is found with other hardwoods favoring well-drained sandy loams in open, exposed conditions on rocky limestone outcroppings, ridges, bluffs and sand dunes. It is somewhat shade-tolerant when young, but in maturity is intolerant.

On difficult sites, dwarf hackberry is a large shrub. Under good conditions, however, it reaches 25 ft. (7.5 m), with a finely branched, narrow, high-domed

Dwarf hackberry is a small tree with a high-domed crown.

crown, deeply penetrated by a single trunk. The gray bark develops with the typical corky ridges of hackberries. The slender twigs tend to be hairy. The leaves have the general hackberry pattern, but are smaller, to 3 in. (7.5 cm) long, with the irregular base of the blade less obviously uneven. Leaves on the fruiting branches also tend not to be toothed. The leaves are gray-green above and may be rough or smooth; the lower surface may be hairy. The fruit conforms to the hackberry type, ranging from brown though orange to red, and may be sweet or dry.

Songbirds relish the fruit, which is also consumed by other wildlife. Dwarf hackberry makes a fine, small-scale shade tree for landscaping on appropriate soils, and deserves wider use for this purpose, although its deep lateral roots can make transplanting difficult. Because of its scattered distribution and small size, the wood is not commercially important.

Cercis canadensis L.
Fabaceae (Bean Family)
Eastern Redbud, Redbud, Mexican Redbud

Ranging from extreme southwestern Ontario to Texas and adjacent Mexico, eastern redbud has no strong soil preferences, except that it does not like either soggy or dry soils. If air circulation is poor, especially in damp situations, it is subject to a variety of diseases. And occasionally, when stressed, it may be bothered by insects. Despite such intermittent problems, it is justifiably one of the more appreciated native trees.

Eastern redbud is a small, elegant tree, rarely exceeding 40 ft. (12 m) in its preferred understory haunts of moist deciduous forests. In cultivation, particularly when open-grown, it usually reaches heights of only about 25 ft. (7.5 m), with a quite short trunk, and a more wide-spreading habit. In the middle spring months, small pink, pealike flowers emerge, before the leaves, in tight clusters all along the twigs, branches and main limbs of the tree, sometimes right down along the main trunk. On some trees this profusion of bloom can be so dense that the actual bark is not visible. In cool weather the display can last for up to three weeks, before the broadly heart-shaped leaves finally conceal the last blooms.

The clear, mid-green leaves are about 5 in. (13 cm) wide, with the leaf stem swollen just below the

The bright pink flowers of eastern redbud emerge early in spring, before its own leaves or those of other trees.

point of attachment to the blade. They turn a dependable warm yellow in the autumn. The flattened pods, reminiscent of peapods, and resembling the shuttlecock of weaving looms (hence the botanical name, *Cercis*, pronounced 'kerkis', which is Greek for shuttlecock) hang onto the tree well into the winter.

Chamaecyparis lawsoniana (A. MURR.) PARL.
Cupressaceae (Cypress Family)
Port Orford Cedar, Lawson False Cypress

Port Orford cedar has a very restricted range along a 220-mile (365-km) stretch of the Pacific coast from Coos Bay, Oregon, south into extreme northwestern California. Beyond 40 miles (65 km) inland it is found only in scattered populations. Port Orford cedar is a shade-tolerant climax tree, occasionally forming small pure stands, but more often co-dominating with other coniferous trees. It is dependant on abundant soil moisture and humid air, but grows well on a wide variety of soils. Typically it is found in the west-coast fog belt along drainage channels of various kinds within areas that have cool, wet winters and warm, dry summers.

Port Orford cedar typically lives to 600 years, and reaches 200 ft. (60 m) in height. It develops a tapering bole free of branches for about 60 ft. (18 m), supporting a narrow spirelike crown of horizontal and pendulous branches. The leaves are small, green, and scalelike, pressed tightly to the branches, creating flattened sprays. The seed-cone is typically 0.5 in. (1.2 cm) in diameter and globular, ripening in early autumn to release small winged seeds. The root is shallow and wide-spreading.

Port Orford cedar is an economically important tree. In the past it has been widely used for a huge variety of goods ranging from airplanes to yardsticks, furniture, telephone poles, boats and arrow shafts. Currently most Port Orford cedar timber is exported to Japan, where it is very highly regarded as a substitute for Hinoki false cypress wood. As a landscape tree, it is also important, especially in

Golden cultivated varieties of Port Orford cedar make superb specimens.

Europe, with many cultivars in commerce. Wildlife value is low, with few animals either browsing the foliage or eating the seed.

Chamaecyparis nootkatensis (D. DON) SPACH
Cupressaceae (Cypress Family)
Nootka False Cypress, Nootka Cypress, Yellow Cypress, Alaska Cedar

Native to the Pacific Northwest, Nootka false cypress occurs in the coastal mountain ranges from south-central Alaska to southern Oregon. It is found in a variety of climatic conditions from shoreline to tree-line, although in the southern part of its range it is found at higher elevations. It has a very strong preference for deep well-drained soils rich in calcium and magnesium, but can also be found in poor alpine soils where other conifers will not grow. It is one of the few trees that can grow and recolonize land subject to avalanches. Nootka false cypress is very shade-tolerant and depending on local conditions it may either be a successional or climax canopy tree associated with other conifers.

Nootka false cypress is a long-lived tree, usually 1,000 to 1,500 years, with some reported as old as 3,500 years. It is most often a shallow-rooted large tree, reaching 125 ft. (38 m), although at the tree-line it is reduced to a layering shrub. Its habit is narrowly conical, with primary branches horizontal and sweeping, while secondary branches hang

The weeping variety of Nootka false cypress develops into a commanding and attractive tree.

vertically from them, like curtains. The blue-green leaves are small, scalelike and pressed against the twigs to produce flattened sprays. Seed cones are small and round, about the size of a pea, with each scale bearing a coarse spike in the center. Small winged seeds are released in the autumn. The trunk often becomes buttressed and fluted at the base. The bark is initially thin and scaly brown, becoming grayish brown and shedding in shaggy narrow vertical strips. When bruised, all parts of the plant have a disagreeable odor, variously described as similar to cat urine or potato.

The yellow wood of Nootka false cypress is commercially valuable for a variety of products ranging from boats and doors, to greenhouse construction and marine pilings. It is exported to Japan as a substitute for Hinoki false cypress wood. Native peoples have also used the wood extensively for masks, bowls, bows, paddles, and other everyday utensils. The roots were split and used for basketry. The leaves were used to make medicinal teas, and the cones and bark had a variety of medicinal uses as well. Nootka false cypress is also valued as a landscape specimen plant because of its appealing form and pendulous branching pattern. A number of

Normally, Nootka false cypress is columnar to conical in shape, and only slightly pendulous.

cultivars are currently available. In a natural setting living trees provide thermal and protective cover for deer and small mammals, although the foliage and seed are a minor food source. Bears are reported to scrape the bark off the up-slope sides of trees in the spring to get at the rising sap, which is sweet with sucrose. Being virtually rot-free, the snags persist for a long time and provide nesting and perching sites for raptors.

KEY FEATURES

Chamaecyparis nootkatensis

Form:	Very tall tree with high relatively narrow conical to oval evergreen crown
Trunk:	Single, straight, **buttressed at the base** penetrating the crown
Bark:	Grayish brown **fissuring into narrow vertical** strips
Twig:	Fine, slender, long, **pendulous**
Leaves:	Small, **scalelike**, pressed against the twigs
Flower:	Male cones tiny yellow, female cones small greenish in clusters
Fruit:	Seed cones **round**, cone scales with **prickle** in the center

Chamaecyparis thyoides L. (B.S.P.)
Cupressaceae (Cypress Family)
Atlantic White Cedar, White Cedar False Cypress

The range of Atlantic white cedar is discontinuous along the Atlantic and Gulf coasts in a narrow band

Atlantic white cedar is characteristically found in groups in swampy areas.

from Maine to Florida and west to Mississippi. It is found extensively in the Great Dismal Swamp of Virginia, but elsewhere occurs in isolated groups, never more than 130 miles (215 km) inland. It prefers the highly acid, peaty soils of bogs and swamps and sandy soils underlain with sand, but not clay. It commonly occurs in either pure stands or mixed with other dominant tree species such as eastern hemlock, but is usually replaced by hardwoods. Even though it is moderately shade-tolerant, seedlings cannot survive in the understory to replace them.

Atlantic white cedar reaches average heights of 60 ft. (18 m). While they can live as long as 1,000 years, they are generally supplanted after about 200 years. They form a narrowly spirelike crown of slender horizontal branches bearing small, scalelike leaves pressed to the twigs in sprays. The bark is reddish brown and fibrous, shredding into narrow, long, flat ridges that become scaly and loose. The seed-cone is dark reddish brown, small and round with tiny winged seeds. The root is very shallow on peat soils, rarely more than 2 ft. (0.6 m) deep.

The wood of Atlantic white cedar is fragrant, decay-resistant and insect-repellent, and valued for a wide variety of products that come in contact with water or soil. Deer browse the foliage heavily, and find cover within dense stands. Living plants are used in wetland restoration. Atlantic white cedar is an attractive and hardy landscape tree for appropriate soil conditions. Over 20 cultivars are commercially available.

Chionanthus virginicus L.

Oleaceae (Olive Family)

American Fringetree, Grancy Greybeard, Old Man's Beard

American fringetree is a slow-growing, smaller understory tree. From southern New Jersey to Florida and west to Texas, it is found growing to heights of 30 ft. (9 m), and equal widths, on well-drained moist acidic soils along bluffs and ridges in small windfall gaps. In cultivation, however, it tops out at about 20 ft. (6 m), tending to be shrubby, often wider than it is high. It is never common in the wild, because its seed has a complicated set of dormancies that keeps numbers relatively low.

Fringetree in flower is a treat for the eye and the nose. From mid-May to early June, the soft-textured,

Fringetree in flower has a fresh and delicate appeal.

fragrant white flowers are borne in profusion above the leaves, which are just finishing their expansion. It tends to bear male and female flowers on separate trees, although trees with both types do occur. Male flowers are larger-petaled, so all-male trees are showier. It flowers most heavily in full sun. The small, fleshy blue fruits are produced only by female flowers, however, and mature in August and September, attracting songbirds. Fringetree has fairly large oblong leaves, mid- to dark green, and usually quite shiny on the top. The leaves can turn a warm golden yellow in autumn when soil conditions are moist.

Fringetree is an excellent small-stature tree for landscape purposes when sited to mimic its natural setting. Unfortunately, it is also one of the more difficult trees to propagate from seed and cuttings, so is not widely available commercially.

Chrysolepis chrysophylla (HOOK.) HJELMQVIST
Fagaceae (Beech Family)
Giant Chinquapin, Golden Chestnut

A broadleaved evergreen native to the Pacific Coast region, giant chinquapin is found from central California to extreme southwestern Washington. It has an ecologically complex relationship to climate, topography, soil, and the plant communities in which it is found. Generally, it can be found in two forms. North of the San Francisco Bay area the tree

Giant chinquapin is often found with conifers; as a tree it tends to be conical in habit.

form is prevalent. The shrub form is found in the southern part of its range and sporadically throughout the northern part. Giant chinquapin is drought-hardy and, once established, very fire-resistant, enabling it to survive in chaparral habitats where brushfires are common. It is also moderately shade-tolerant, which allows it to persist as an understory tree or shrub in mixed coniferous forests, where soil water and humidity favor the tree form once gaps open up in the canopy and allow the plant to grow in response to higher light levels.

Given its preferred environmental conditions of moist soil, full sun, and a Mediterranean type climate, giant chinquapin readily assumes the tree form, reaching heights of 50 to 100 ft. (15 to 30 m). The largest trees are usually single-trunked. The bark is gray and smooth when young, becoming thick and fissured into reddish-brown plates as it ages. The crown is conical in shape, supported by stout spreading branches. Leaves are smooth-edged, leathery, narrow, and evergreen. They are dark green above, and fold up along the mid-rib thus showing the golden

---

KEY FEATURES

Chrysolepis chrysophylla

Form:	Large tree with conical **evergreen broadleaved crown**
Trunk:	Usually single, penetrating the crown
Bark:	Gray and smooth becoming **reddish brown**, **thick and fissuring** into plates
Twig:	Moderately coarse
Leaves:	**Evergreen, leathery, narrow, dark green above, golden below; curved upward along mid-rib**
Flower:	Tiny; male flowers gathered in **catkins** at the end of twigs; female flowers tiny, green at the base of male catkins
Fruit:	**Spiny bur** splitting open, with one to three **edible nuts** inside

Giant chinquapin bears clusters of golden spiny fruit at the ends of branches.

American yellowwood typically develops a broad, dense crown when open-grown.

lower surface. The flowers and fruits are very similar to the American chestnut, to which it is related. The spiny bur fruit is only sporadically produced, and has up to three sweet nuts inside. Giant chinquapin can live up to 500 years. This longevity is made possible by a woody regenerative organ, called a burl, found at ground level. In the event of fire or any other catastrophic disturbance destroying the crown, buds on the burl re-establish the above ground parts, usually as multiple, rapidly growing stems. The burl also imparts wind-firmness to the tree.

Giant chinquapin does not grow in quantities and sizes that would economically justify harvesting its wood, which is hard, strong and attractively pink-colored. The wood was used during the settlement period for making utensils of various kinds. Being notoriously difficult to transplant out in the open, giant chinquapin is also not widely available commercially for landscaping, although it has a graceful beauty as a tree. Its nuts have some value to wildlife but, being erratically produced, are not of commercial importance. Native peoples used to collect, roast and eat them. A number of small mammals eat the nuts also.

Cladrastis lutea K. KOCH
Fabaceae (Bean Family)

American Yellowwood, Virgilia

Even in its native habitat on limestone cliffs and ridges from North Carolina to Kentucky, Tennessee, Alabama and Arkansas, American yellowwood is not common. Being fairly shade-tolerant, it grows as a sub-climax tree in hardwood forests on moist sandy loams that are well drained and not prone to flooding.

It reaches heights of 50 ft. (15 m), with a crown of similar width. The foliage of American yellowwood is a fresh, clean, somewhat blue-green color. Individual leaves are large but usually fine-textured, being pinnately compound. In the autumn they turn a rich golden yellow. In addition the bark remains thin, gray, and generally smooth, even when mature. Although it tends to flower heavily in alternate years (or in every third), the flower display in late May to early June is quite stunning, with even young trees entirely covered in what appears to be dripping, fragrant, white rain. On close inspection the individual flowers are pealike, and are followed by fairly inconspicuous papery pods. The roots are deep, coarse and lateral.

Although the flower is pollinated by bees American yellowwood is not an important commercial bee-plant. It is becoming more familiar in cultivated settings, particularly in cities, not just because it is adaptable but also because it is handsome in all seasons, as either a single specimen or in groups. Aside from a tendency to develop crotches that can split and crack in wind-storms, American yellowwood is not prone to many environmental problems, nor is it susceptible to many diseases or insects.

Cornus alternifolia L.

Cornaceae (Dogwood Family)

Pagoda Dogwood, Alternate-leaved Dogwood

Pagoda dogwood is distributed from Newfoundland to west of Lake Superior, south to northern Arkansas and east to northern Florida. It is a dominant understory tree in young hardwood and coniferous forests, and at the shaded edges of woods next to meadows, old fields, marshes, streams and swamps. It prefers moist, somewhat acid, deep and well-drained soil.

Pagoda dogwood develops a slender vertical main trunk, or occasionally two or three closely set together, to a height of 40 feet (12 m), with branches arranged in well-spaced horizontal disks. The leaves are elliptical, minutely toothed, to 2.5 in. (6 cm) long, clustered toward the ends of branches. Twigs are green, becoming red. Bark is reddish brown, turning rough and broken in very small plates. In June, the creamy-white flowers appear in fluffy clusters over the top surface of each tier of branches and leaves. Later in the summer, clusters of blue berries on bright red stems cover the tiers, weighing them down so that they look like the sloping roofs of a pagoda. Later in the fall, the leaves turn a smoky maroon or plum.

The berries of pagoda dogwood are eaten by over ten species of birds, as well as black bears. Deer, rabbits and beavers eat the leaves and stems, and small animals use it for protective cover. It is often used in landscaping as a shrub or small tree, since it is quite adaptable to a range of light intensities. However, it is far more attractive in its tree form, and high light intensities will only tend to encourage a more shrubby habit.

Cornus florida L.

Cornaceae (Dogwood Family)

Flowering Dogwood

An understory tree of hardwood and coniferous forest, flowering dogwood ranges from southern-

Pagoda dogwood develops a pronounced tiering of branches as it grows.

The flowers of flowering dogwoods, such as these of Pacific dogwood, are tightly clustered at the center of showy white bracts.

The ever-popular flowering dogwood is one of the first native trees in the east to flower in the spring.

most Maine south to northern Florida, west to eastern Texas, and north to southern Ontario. A variety is also found in the mountains of eastern Mexico in Nuevo Leon and Veracruz. It is found as a scattered dominant or co-dominant forest understory in moist deciduous woods, in ravines and on slopes, bluffs and floodplains. It also is found at the edges of swamps and old fields, and along old fencerows. It prefers slightly acidic, medium- to coarse-textured soils, but can be found growing well on a range of soils from moist, deep soils to light-textured, well-drained ones. It is not found on heavy soils that are poorly drained. Flowering dogwood is very shade-tolerant and will persist beneath a forest canopy in a suppressed state, growing slowly. It is capable, however, of adapting to a range of microclimatic conditions, so that it can be found in a variety of plant communities, from old fields in all stages of succession to open gaps in the forest canopy.

Interestingly, since birds are the principal means of seed dispersal, seedlings are occasionally found concentrated under power lines.

Flowering dogwood generally becomes a small tree to 50 ft. (15 m) having one to several trunks supporting a broad, rounded crown, tending to have a horizontal layered aspect to its branching pattern. The bark is reddish brown, broken into squarish plates, resembling alligator skin. The leaves are elliptical to 6 in. (15 cm) long, with very minute teeth along the edges. They are smooth and green above, paler and variably hairy beneath. The upper surface turns vivid red in the autumn. The flowers are actually quite tiny and yellow, densely clustered at the center of four large, showy, white bracts (occasionally pink) to about 4 in. (10 cm) in length, which resemble thick petals. Each bract has a notch at its apex. The flowers are borne facing upward on the layered branches before the

KEY FEATURES

Cornus florida L.

Form:	Small, **flowering** tree with broad crown of **almost horizontal branches**
Trunk:	Short, penetrating into the crown
Bark:	Deep reddish-brown fissuring into **small irregular squarish scales**, like alligator skin
Twig:	Slender, greenish or reddish, sometimes bloomy, ending in **onionlike bud**
Leaves:	Simple, ellipical, pointed with **parallel veins, very minutely toothed**, green above, paler with fine hairs below, turning red
Flower:	Small, several clustered tightly together and surrounded by **4 white bracts**, rounded at the ends and **notched**
Fruit:	A cluster of small **bright red drupes**

Crataegus crus-galli L.
Rosaceae (Rose Family)
Cockspur Hawthorn, Hog-apple, Newcastle-thorn, French Mulberry

Cockspur hawthorn is distributed from southern Quebec through southern Ontario, southwest to Iowa, south to eastern Texas, and east to eastern Florida. It is generally found on moist soils in stream and river valleys as well as on upland slopes. It is common in rural hedgerows and in abandoned old fields. It often forms extensive thicket at forest edges of fields, eventually being shaded out by larger canopy trees.

Reaching heights of about 30 ft. (9 m), cockspur hawthorn has a short, stout trunk, or several stems tightly pressed together, supporting a broad, dense crown of wide-spreading, horizontal branches. The bark is a silvery grayish brown and scaly. The branches and twigs are densely covered by slender, slightly curved red-brown thorns up to 3 in. (7.5 cm) long. The leaves are leathery, shiny, dark green above, paler below, and turning orange and scarlet in the autumn. They are narrowly obovate, to about 2 in. (5 cm) long, wider toward the rounded tip, with gland-tipped teeth along the outer half of the leaf-edge. The flowers and fruit are generally typical of hawthorns, the fruit ripening to a dull dark red and

Cockspur hawthorn typically develops a very wide-spreading domed crown.

persisting into the spring. Cockspur hawthorn is typically tap-rooted.

Easily distinguished, cockspur hawthorn has long been planted to create impenetrable hedging, and for ornament, its broad, dense crown being quintessentially characteristic of rural landscapes throughout the east. Its thorns have been used for needles and hooks. Many species of birds feed on its fruit. It is prone to several bacterial and fungal diseases, although it is one of the most fire blight–resistant hawthorns.

Crataegus douglasii LINDL.
Rosaceae (Rose Family)
Douglas Hawthorn, Black Hawthorn, River Hawthorn, Western Thornapple

Douglas hawthorn ranges along the Pacific coast from southern Alaska to northern California, and inland in a broad arc that reaches its most easterly point in western Wyoming. There are also isolated populations in Saskatchewan, Minnesota, Michigan and northwestern Ontario. It prefers moist, deep and fine-textured soils in a variety of exposures on undisturbed sites, and reaches its best growth in riparian habitats as an understory tree, but may also form pure stands.

The tree form of Douglas hawthorn reaches 40 ft. (12 m), although it becomes smaller and more shrubby when exposed. Usually several stems arise in a tight cluster from the ground and support a broad, dense canopy of interlacing, very flexible branches supporting leaves and straight thorns up to an inch (2.5 cm) long. Lower branches are shade-killed by higher ones, but are persistent, forming a dense thicketlike mass. The bark is gray, scaly, and rough. The leaves are broadly oval, coarsely toothed to almost lobed, three to five times, and about 2.5 in. (6 cm) long. They are leathery, dark green above but paler below. The small, white, clustered flowers have a sickly sweet odor and are followed by blackish, smooth fruits about 0.5 in. (1 cm) long. Douglas hawthorn is tap-rooted.

and west to Arkansas. It has been introduced and become naturalized throughout eastern North America as far north as southern Ontario. It is typically shade-intolerant, and when found at the forest edges of old fields is generally shade-killed by canopy trees as they invade the field.

Infrequently a large shrub, Washington thorn is typically a tap-rooted small tree reaching 30 ft. (9 m) in height, with a short trunk supporting a rounded, dense crown. The bark is thin, smooth, and light brown initially, becoming scaly with age. Thorns are about 1.5 in. (3.5 cm) long, and more numerous when the tree is young. Leaves are most typically three-lobed, with a flat base and pointed tip, coarsely toothed. They are a lustrous dark green above, paler below, turning a beautiful crimson to orange in mid-autumn. The flowers and fruit are generally typical of hawthorns. However, the hard, dry and very small fruits are numerous, brilliant, shiny red to scarlet, borne in flat clusters in mid-autumn.

Washington thorn is probably the showiest of the hawthorns, and the one most often used in landscape applications, having strong visual appeal though all seasons. It is one of the most resistant hawthorns to leaf rusts, so its beautiful foliage is seldom blemished. It makes a fine specimen, and works well as both formal and informal hedging. Many birds relish the fruit, which is persistent on the tree through the winter.

Thornapple usually begins as a suckering shrub, as shown here, later becoming a multistemmed small tree.

Largely valued for the refuge and food it provides to wildlife and its potential for streambank stabilization, Douglas hawthorn has few other direct uses. Native peoples have variously eaten the fruit, made medicines from the bark, and used the thorns for various implements such as needles and fish hooks.

Crataegus phaenopyrum L. f.
Rosaceae (Rose Family)
Washington Thorn

Washington thorn is typically found on moist, well-drained soils of stream and river valleys from southern Missouri to Virginia, south to northern Florida

Washington thorn makes an excellent small landscape tree, with glossy rich green foliage.

THE CYPRESSES (*CUPRESSUS*)

Cypress Family (*Cupressaceae*)

The cypresses consist of between 20 and 25 species of trees with mostly local distribution in North America, the Mediterranean, and Asia. They are closely allied to both the junipers and the false cypresses, and there arc a few species that are considered by some to belong to the cypresses, and by others to the false cypresses. North America is home to ten species of cypress, nine in the west, and one species in the southeast. They are characteristically trees of hot, dry locations, fast-growing and shade-intolerant. Although relatively long-lived, they tend to be replaced by more shade-tolerant and longer-lived trees, except where fire clears mineral soil and provides light for seedling re-establishment.

The cypresses tend to have a columnar to slender pyramidal habit, except when exposed to wind and harsh conditions in which they become stunted and wind-swept. Their trunks are usually single with shredding bark, while in most species their fine branches radiate in all directions. The foliage consists of evergreen, small, scalelike leaves pressed against the twigs and persistent after they die. The female and male cones are borne on the same plant, with pollination occurring in the spring. The female cones generally become quite large and woody, with shieldlike scales having a prickle centred on the back of each. They are borne in clusters towards the ends of twigs, mature in two years, but often remain closed for years on the tree, waiting for fire to open them and release their seeds on mineral soil. The cypresses generally have deep root systems,

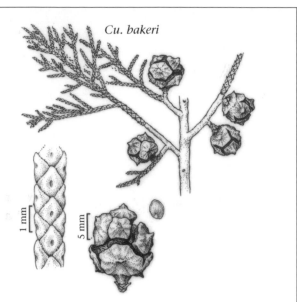

Cu. bakeri

The mature female cones of cypresses are round. Each cone scale has a prickle in the center. Needles are generally scale-like.

except in one or two species, and are either tap-rooted or have several strong lateral roots.

Several of the cypresses are highly valued as evergreen specimen plants, because of their narrowly conical habit and ability to withstand drought. They are sometimes used as windbreaks and in shelterbelts as well. The wood of the more abundant species is used in a variety of products, and because of their deep-rooted habit cypresses are also useful in restoration work for retaining erodible soils. High aesthetic value is frequently placed on some in their natural habitat, such as the coastal Monterey cypress. Several species are endemic to California, with very restricted natural ranges, although most are cultivated as well. In their native habitat cypresses are fairly valuable to wildlife for shelter.

Cupressus abramsiana C.B. WOLF

Cupressaceae (Cypress Family)

Santa Cruz Cypress

Existing in only five populations, comprising some 5,100 individuals, Santa Cruz cypress is found along a 15-mile (24-km) range of the Santa Cruz Mountains in Santa Cruz and San Mateo Counties in California. It is considered at both state and federal levels to be an endangered plant species. Santa Cruz cypress is found on dry ridges within coastal chaparral and evergreen forests above the altitude where fog is present.

An endangered plant, Santa Cruz cypress has vivid green foliage and conical to columnar form.

Cupressus arizonica GREENE not HORT.

Cupressaceae (Cypress Family)

Arizona Cypress

Arizona cypress has a restricted distribution in the United States from southeastern Arizona to the Chisos Mountains in Texas. It is more prevalent in the adjacent areas of Mexico. It is found locally within mountain canyons as a common component of riparian plant associations, and at higher elevations mixed with other conifers, where it occasionally forms small pure stands with a closed canopy. Another species similar to Arizona cypress, *Cupressus stephensonii*, or Cuyamaca cypress, has an extremely restricted distribution to a few sites in San Diego

It prefers well-drained sandy or gravelly soils.

Reaching a potential height of 82 ft. (25 m), Santa Cruz cypress has a columnar crown of bright green foliage in sprays of shoots covered in scalelike leaves. The gray bark is thin and fibrous, breaking into vertical strips or plates. The seed-cones are round to elliptical, shiny brown, about an inch (2.5 cm) in diameter. The eight to ten cone-scales have a distinct prickle in the center of each. The cones generally do not release their seeds except though fire.

Given its endangered status, Santa Cruz cypress is not commercially used. Part of the recovery plan formulated by the U.S. Fish and Wildlife Service requires the establishment of a seed bank under controlled conditions in order to maintain a genetic backup in the event the wild populations decline further or are lost.

Arizona cypress sometimes forms small pure stands of blue-green trees.

County, California and adjacent Baja California. It is regarded as endangered throughout its range in California, threatened by fire and changing land use. Arizona cypress has a preference for well-drained, dry soils on cool gravelly slopes with north exposure, although at higher elevations it can be found facing south. Being intolerant of shade and a colonizer of soil-disturbed sites, it is eventually either removed by fire or replaced by climax species that are more shade-tolerant as saplings.

Arizona cypress reaches a potential age of about 700 years and an average height of 50 ft. (15 m), with a single trunk penetrating a dense, pyramidal crown, which may branch out close to the ground but is often higher. The bark is gray to dark reddish brown, breaking first into large, irregular, thin scales, later becoming fibrous, fissured and shredding. The blue-green to gray-green leaves are small, scalelike and pressed close to the branch, forming fine textured sprays of foliage. The dark brown cones are roundish and typical of cypresses, the scales opening from the heat of fire or with age. Arizona cypress forms a strong tap root with deep laterals.

Although the wood of Arizona cypress is workable, it is nowhere prevalent or accessible enough to be commercially important. It is occasionally used to control erosion, and is planted for windbreaks and Christmas trees. It is also valued as an landscape specimen tree.

Cupressus forbesii JEPS.
Cupressaceae (Cypress Family)
Tecate Cypress

Tecate cypress has a restricted and highly localized distribution. Isolated groves occur in the northern portion of Baja California and the off-shore island of Guadalupe, but only four groves occur in southern California, where it is considered very threatened, and in at least a portion of its range endangered. Three groves are found on Tecate Peak, Otay Mountain and Guatay Mountain in San Diego County; the fourth is located in Orange County on Sierra Peak. Tecate cypress is found in closed-cone coniferous

In cultivation, Tecate cypress develops a columnar crown.

forest, and also occurs as even-aged stands in dense, fire-maintained forest surrounded by chaparral. Shade-intolerant in all life stages, Tecate cypress reproduces only from seed in contact with mineral soil following its release from the cones after fire. It prefers well-drained, coarse soils on dry, exposed slopes and ridges, usually facing north, but also occurs along moister drainage channels.

Usually a multistemmed tree to about 23 ft. (7 m), Tecate cypress forms a small, bushy evergreen tree with thin exfoliating bark. Leaves are small, scalelike and pressed against the fine shoots that radiate in sprays from the branches. Seed cones are solitary, about 1.2 in. (3 cm) in diameter and remain closed on the tree for many years until opened by the heat of fire. Tecate cypress forms a tap root supported by deep lateral roots.

As a threatened species, Tecate cypress is not commercially exploited, although land-use pressures affect its viability in the wild. It has been planted to control erosion and as an agricultural windbreak. Given its slow growth rate and small size, it can also be used as a bonsai subject.

Cupressus glabra SUDW.
Cupressaceae (Cypress Family)
Smooth Arizona Cypress

Smooth cypress is often considered a variety of Arizona cypress, but varies in bark and foliage characteristics and has a distinctly localized distribution in central Arizona. It is restricted to mountain canyons

Smooth Arizona cypress typically grows in small groups on dry gravelly slopes.

as a common component of riparian plant associations, and at higher elevations mixed with other conifers. Smooth Arizona cypress has a preference for well-drained, dry soils on cool gravelly slopes with north exposure, although at higher elevations it can be found facing south. Being intolerant of shade and a colonizer of soil-disturbed sites, it is eventually either removed by fire or replaced by climax species whose saplings are more shade-tolerant.

Reaching to 50 ft. (15 m), smooth Arizona cypress forms a dense, broad and regular conical crown supported by a single trunk. The bark is reddish to deep purple, blistering after several years and shedding in small roundish scales to reveal paler patches beneath. Foliage is silvery blue-green composed of small scales flattened against brownish-orange twigs. The seed cones and root system are similar to those of Arizona cypress.

Highly prized as a landscape tree for its form, foliage color, bark characteristics and drought tolerance, smooth Arizona cypress is widely planted as a specimen tree, and as a Christmas tree, not only in the Southwest but also in the Southeast and on the East Coast. It is also grown in New Zealand and Australia, where many cultivars have been developed. There are several named American selections as well, which are commercially available.

Cupressus goveniana GORD.
Cupressaceae (Cypress Family)
Gowen Cypress, California Cypress

Gowen cypress is restricted to two areas in Monterey County: a discontinuous strip along the Pacific coast in Mendocino County, and one grove in Sonoma County of California. It is considered to consist of two subspecies, one of which largely occupies the Monterey sites, while the other is found in the remainder of the range. Gowen cypress is found on exposed sites of poorly drained, acidic soils, often in dense thickets following fire disturbance. The Mendocino subspecies is a component of the Mendocino pygmy cypress forest, while the other is a component in some places of closed-cone

On rich soils, Gowen cypress develops an open, conical to columnar crown.

coniferous forests. Shade-intolerant in all life stages, Gowen cypress relies on periodic burning to create conditions suitable for regeneration from seed.

Gowen cypress varies considerably in form, depending on the nature of the soil. In the poor soils of the pygmy cypress forest it rarely exceeds 6 ft. (2 m). However, on richer soils it averages about 65 ft. (20 m). on a single trunk supporting a sparse crown. The bark is grayish brown, rough, and exfoliating in fibrous strips The leaves are dark green, blunt-pointed, about 0.4 in. (1 cm) long, angled away from the shoot but in-curving at the tip. When bruised, the foliage has an odor of citronella. Seed cones are solitary, oblong, about 0.8 in. (2 cm) long, and dark grayish brown. The root structure of Gowen cypress is reportedly variable between tap-rooted and shallow.

Gowen cypress is not extensively used for wood products. It has some applicability in landscaping, especially on acidic, nutrient-poor soils.

Cupressus macnabiana MURR.
Cupressaceae (Cypress Family)
MacNab Cypress

Endemic to California, MacNab cypress is found as scattered groves throughout the North Coastal Ranges, the Cascade Range and the foothills of the Sierra Nevada. It is a component of several distinct plant habitats, depending on soil conditions. It prefers the dry slopes of ridges and hills, often facing north or northeast, and is commonly found on serpentine soils. However, it is also found on other fine-textured mineral soils as well. Shade-intolerant in all life stages, MacNab cypress relies on periodic burning to create conditions suitable for regeneration from seed.

MacNab cypress grows to about 33 ft. (10 m), usually with several main trunks supporting a broad, rounded crown of dense foliage arranged in flattened sprays. The bark is grayish brown, fibrous and furrowed, and becomes quite thick. Leaves are dark green, small, scalelike, and have a citrus odor when bruised. The seed cone is round, brown, about an inch (2.5 cm) in diameter, and borne solitary.

MacNab cypress is characteristically found on dry rocky soils.

MacNab cypress has a tap root supported by deep lateral roots.

Because of its close association with serpentine soils, MacNab cypress was heavily used as a fuel in the extraction of mercury in the underlying serpentine rock. Because of its broad dense crown and tendency to be multistemmed, it also has some potential for windbreaks and hedges. Otherwise it is not much used in landscape application.

Cupressus macrocarpa HARTW. exGORD.
Cupressaceae (Cypress Family)
Monterey Cypress

Monterey cypress is restricted to two stands in Monterey County in California. However, it is widely planted along the California coast and many other places in the world. It prefers acidic sandy soil derived from granite on rocky coastal headlands and bluffs, and is usually windswept from constant onshore winds. It is a component of several plant habitats depending on soil and exposure.

Away from the constant winds of the coast, which distort and sculpt its form, Monterey cypress may grow to 80 ft. (24 m), initially narrowly columnar, but becoming flat-topped with tiered levels of branches, or otherwise broadly oval. The bark is brownish gray, furrowed, fibrous and thick. The leaves are dark green,

Monterey cypress is typically found on rocky headlands along the California coast.

small, scalelike and pressed to the shoots, which are arranged densely all around the branches in plume-like sprays. The seed cone is about 1.5 in. (3.5 cm) in diameter and round, each cone-scale having a shallow ridge across the centre. Monterey cypress forms a tap root supported by deep lateral roots.

By far the most planted of the native cypresses, Monterey cypress is valued in landscape applications for its form, wind resistance and salt tolerance, particularly in coastal settings. Despite this, encroaching changes in land use threaten its natural habitat. Inland plants are susceptible to cypress canker and infestation from a bark beetle and two species of moth. In Britain a hybrid of the Monterey cypress with Nootka false cypress is used for hedging.

Cupressus sargentii JEPS.
Cupressaceae (Cypress Family)
Sargent Cypress

Regarded as closely related to Gowan cypress, Sargent cypress is restricted to California along the Coastal Ranges in numerous scattered stands from Mendocino to Santa Barbara Counties. It is usually found on dry slopes of ridges and hills and rocky outcroppings in well-drained, serpentine soils. However, it also occupies riparian sites. It is a component of several forest-type plant habitats forming either dense thickets or open groves. It is also a component of several kinds of chaparral plant communities. Shade-intolerant in all life stages, Sargent cypress relies on periodic burning to create conditions suitable for regeneration from seed.

Normally growing to 50 ft. (15 m), Sargent cypress has a slender trunk supporting a generally narrow conical crown of grayish-green foliage. On exposed sites it becomes more shrublike. The bark is vertically furrowed, fibrous, grayish brown, and 1.2 in. (3 cm) thick. The leaves are glaucous-bloomed, small, blunt-pointed scales. Seed cones are borne solitary, ripening grayish brown, and are about an inch (2.5 cm) long. Sargent cypress forms a tap root supported by deep lateral roots.

Sargent cypress is typically found in open groves on dry rocky outcroppings.

Because of its close association with serpentine soils, Sargent cypress, along with MacNab cypress, was heavily used as a fuel in the extraction of mercury in the underlying serpentine rock. It is rarely cultivated.

Diospyros virginiana L.
Ebonaceae (Ebony Family)
Common Persimmon

Common persimmon ranges from eastern Texas to southeastern Iowa, east to Connecticut, and south to southern Florida. It is found in many plant communities on a variety of soils, but prefers moist clays and heavy loams in valleys, in mixed forests, old fields, clearings and roadsides. Common persimmon is very shade-tolerant. It will also regenerate from the root after fire or cutting.

Occasionally either a large shrub or a large tree, common persimmon usually reaches 40 ft. (12 m), with a single trunk supporting a cylindrical, dense crown of branches borne at right angles to the trunk. The thick bark is brownish black, furrowed into small, squarish plates resembling alligator skin. Leaves are elliptical, somewhat thick, with a smooth edge, shiny green above, and pale green, often densely hairy beneath. Common persimmon has male flowers in twos and threes on one tree, females solitary on another. They are small, bell-shaped, white and fragrant. The fruit is a persistent orange-to-purplish brown berry, about 1.5 in. (4 cm) in diameter, having a sweet, juicy, orange pulp inside, tasting datelike. Each berry contains up to eight large flat seeds. Common persimmon is strongly tap-rooted.

Native peoples dried the fruit of common persimmon, which is edible when ripe, like prunes for winter use. Both bark and unripe fruit are astringent with tannic acid, and have been used medicinally. The fruit is relished by many animals as well. Being tap-rooted, common persimmon has some application in erosion control. It is also planted as an ornamental tree, although it is difficult to transplant because of its tap root. The flowers provide nectar for bees to produce honey.

Female trees of common persimmon bear edible fruit in the autumn.

Fagus grandifolia EHRH.
Fagaceae (Beech Family)
American Beech

American beech has a wide distribution throughout eastern North America, from northern Michigan through southern Ontario to Cape Breton Island, Nova Scotia, south to northern Florida, and west to eastern Texas. The variety *F. grandifolia 'mexicana'* is found isolated in the mountains of northeastern Mexico. American beech prefers moist to somewhat dry, well-drained, course textured soils that are not limestone in origin. In the northern part of its range it is found at low altitude, seldom above 3,000 ft. (915 m), while in the south it can be found to 6,000 ft. (1,830 m), where it is also more abundant on moist, cool northern slopes. It sometimes occurs in pure stands, but is more often co-dominant with other hardwoods. American beech is a climax forest tree. As a sapling it is shade-tolerant and grows slowly under the canopy of conifers or other hardwoods until a gap appears. It then develops quickly until it has filled the gap and becomes part of the canopy. In addition, American beech will sucker from the root or stump, or from below a wound on the trunk. In this way an individual tree may maintain itself after losing its crown.

American beech is a relatively slow-growing, long-lived tree that reaches ages of about 300 years. It usually attains a height of 80 ft. (25 m), but under

American beech may occur in pure stands as a climax forest tree.

good conditions can reach 130 ft. (40 m). In a forest setting it forms a high crown of ascending limbs. In the open it retains limbs right to the ground, forming a wide, domed crown of dense foliage. Its bark is characteristically a smooth silvery-gray throughout its life. The leaves of American beech reach about 3 in. (7.5 cm) long, and are elliptical with regular pronounced teeth along the margin; in color they are dark blue-green in summer, changing to rich yellows and golds before turning brown in the autumn. On young trees, the brown leaves are retained well into winter. Older trees mostly lose their leaves soon after turning brown. Flowers are male or female on the same tree, very small and very inconspicuous. The fruit develops from female flowers, and is a coarsely spiny bur that splits open four ways to release two three-angled chestnut-brown beechnuts, about 0.75 in. (1.8 cm) long. American

KEY FEATURES

Fagus grandifolia

Form:	Large tree with high rounded crown
Trunk:	Single, straight, penetrating deep into the crown
Bark:	**Smooth, thin, silvery gray**
Twig:	Slender, reddish brown, **zig-zagging**, with widely angled, **long, narrow, sharp-pointed buds**
Leaves:	Elliptical, sharp-pointed to 5" (13 cm) long by 3" (7.5 cm) wide; **veins parallel** to leaf edge into **sharp, curved teeth**; dark green above, lighter below becoming **golden, persisting** on young trees
Flower:	Tiny; male flowers clustered in 1" (2.5 cm) **ball hanging** on slender stalk; female flowers **reddish** with stiff hairs
Fruit:	Light brown, **prickly bur** opening to release 2 **three-angled, edible nuts**

The fruits of American beech split open to release two nuts in late summer to early autumn.

beech has a very shallow, fibrous root system, which suckers when it is exposed to air.

Because of its dense, full form in all seasons when open grown, and its foliage colors in summer and autumn, American beech makes a choice landscape specimen tree where soil conditions and space allow. It is not as tolerant of urban conditions as its European counterpart, and is prone to a number of diseases and insect pests. The beechnuts are consumed by a large variety of birds and mammals, and its foliage provides cover to small birds. The leaves and bark have been used to manufacture dyes, and the nuts when roasted can be eaten or made into a substitute for coffee. A tar is made from the wood of American beech for use in treating medical disorders. The wood is used for flooring, veneer, furniture, and railway ties.

Franklinia alatamaha MARSH.
Theaceae (Tea Family)
Franklin Tree, Franklinia

Originally found in a single grove along the Alatamaha River near Fort Barrington close to the Georgia coast, Franklin tree has been extinct in the wild since about 1804. Previously, it had been found growing in sandy soil by William Bartram in 1765. Several years later he collected seeds for propagation in his garden in Philadelphia. It is from these plants that all current ones derive. It has been suggested that

Franklin tree makes a small multistemmed specimen tree, valued for its autumn flower.

Franklin tree was already on the road to full extinction prior to settlement. It was only fate that put Bartram in the right place at the right time to salvage it for cultivation.

Under ideal conditions of full sun and moist, well-drained acid soil, Franklin tree forms a small tree to 30 ft. (9 m) high and 20 ft. (6 m) wide, although it is generally smaller, and in less ideal conditions a large shrub. The bark is smooth, thin, and dark brown, becoming furrowed and gray. Leaves are elliptical, with a short point and fine teeth along the margin, shiny green above, paler below. They turn brilliant red or orange in the autumn, especially in full sun. Creamy-white flowers are borne singly in autumn, and are 3 in. (7.5 cm) across. They consist of five rounded petals, slightly wavy along the edges, forming a shallow cup around a cluster of rich yellow stamens. The fruit is a round, hard, brown capsule, about 0.75 in. (1.8 cm) in diameter, splitting open to release several flat seeds.

Franklin tree is justifiably prized as a small specimen tree for its autumn flowers and foliage color.

THE ASHES (*FRAXINUS*)
Olive Family (*Oleaceae*)

Of the 60 to 65 species of ash found in the temperate regions of the Northern Hemisphere, 16 are native to North America. Of these, 10 are dependably trees in their natural setting. The ashes are generally characteristic of moist to wet soils along waterways and the edges of wetlands, or in floodplains. A few species are fairly tolerant of drought or drier soils. The ashes tend to be shade-tolerant as seedlings and young saplings, but require light as they mature. They are usually fast-growing and moderately long-lived, but give way to other dominant climax forest trees in the absence of disturbance.

The ashes characteristically have a single, relatively slender trunk, reaching high into the crown with tight, fissured bark. The leaves are borne oppositely on stout twigs and are pinnately compound, the oval leaflets generally five to eleven, depending on the species, and all leaflets in a leaf of the same size. Usually, the autumn color of ashes is attractive, ranging from yellow to maroon, but this is variable depending on the species, as well as site conditions. The flowers of ashes are in some species fairly showy, but not in the majority of native species. Those of trees described in this book are tiny, without petals, primarily unisexual with male and female flowers borne on separate trees. They appear in spring

F. pensylvanica

5 cm

1 cm

Ashes have pinnately compound leaves and a dry-winged fruit borne in clusters behind the tip of the twig.

before the leaves from side buds close to the tips of branches, with many flowers gathered in a large cluster. Female flowers develop the slender, elongated, dry, winged fruit characteristic of ashes. They are borne in loose clusters and ripen in late summer and early autumn and are shed through the autumn and winter.

Several ashes are highly valued landscape amenity trees, and are widely used for shading and as street trees. Those with good autumn color are particularly and dependably attractive. As well, the wood of several ash species is commercially important, and a few have had other economic values as well.

Fraxinus americana L.
Oleaceae (Olive Family)
White Ash

White ash occurs from Nova Scotia to northern Florida, west to eastern Texas, north to eastern Minnesota, and east into southern Ontario and southwestern Quebec. It prefers deep, moist, well-drained, loamy soils high in calcium and nitrogen. It occurs along valley slopes of streams and rivers

with other deciduous hardwood species, as well as eastern hemlock and eastern white pine. Seedlings are shade-tolerant for several years, allowing them to exploit gaps that appear in the canopy. However, they are shade-intolerant after several years and are generally replaced by more shade-tolerant trees.

A long-lived tree, white ash reaches 100 ft. (30 m). In a forest it has a single long trunk bearing a high, narrow pyramidal crown. In the open its trunk is shorter with an oval crown. Bark is thick, dark gray,

White ash typically develops plum-colored autumn foliage, as shown here.

furrowed into a diamond pattern of tight ridges. Leaves are typical of ashes, with five, seven or nine leaflets, dark green above and paler, often whitened, or hairy below, turning purple and pale yellow in autumn. White ash is dioecious with tiny inconspicuous flowers borne in loose clusters in the spring. The fruit is a typical ash samara (key), persisting on the tree into winter.

The wood of white ash is valued for its shock resistance and is used for baseball bats, tool handles, furniture, canoe paddles, snowshoes and cabinetry. The fruit is widely consumed by many birds and mammals. White ash snags are favored nesting sites of many cavity birds and small mammals. The juice of the leaves relieves the swelling and itch of mosquito bites, and crushed leaves carried in the pocket are said to produce an odor repellent to rattlesnakes.

White ash is a valued shade and ornamental tree for landscaping. However, it is sensitive to atmospheric pollution.

Fraxinus berlandieriana DC.
Oleaceae (Olive Family)
Mexican Ash, Berlandier Ash

Mexican ash has a relatively restricted distribution, in south-central Texas and adjacent northeastern Mexico. Largely found on moist, rich soils along streams and rivers in warm, dry climatic conditions, it associates with other trees characteristic of riparian habitats. It tends to colonize sites disturbed by flood scouring, but being shade-intolerant, it is ultimately displaced by larger, dominant shade-tolerant trees that grow as saplings beneath its canopy.

Mexican ash is a small tree to about 30 ft. (9 m), with a rounded crown of spreading branches supported by a short trunk. Its bark is thick and gray, furrowed and narrowly ridged. Leaves are typically ashlike, with three or five leaflets, shiny and green above, paler below. A dioecious species, Mexican ash

Mexican ash is typically found on flood-scoured ravine bottoms.

has typical, small, inconspicuous, ashlike flowers borne in clusters in the late winter or spring before the leaves. Female trees carry clusters of light brown samaras (keys) in the summer.

Being a small tree, and never numerous, Mexican ash is not exploited commercially for its wood. It makes a good small shade tree for landscaping on moist soils, and has potential for slope stabilization and control of soil erosion. Small mammals and birds eat the fruit, and shelter under it from sun and predators.

Fraxinus caroliniana MILL.
Oleaceae (Olive Family)
Carolina Ash, Pop Ash, Florida Ash, Water Ash, Swamp Ash

Carolina ash bears broad, flat-winged fruit on female trees in autumn.

Carolina ash extends along the Atlantic coastal floodplains from northeastern Virginia through to southern Florida and west to southeast Texas. It occurs on wet soils subject to flooding along rivers, and in swamps, mixed with other species of wetland trees and shrubs. It is shade-intolerant and on undisturbed sites it usually replaced by longer-lived, more shade-tolerant species that emerge from under its canopy.

The average height attained by Carolina ash is about 40 ft. (12 m). It usually has one trunk, but several are not uncommon. The crown may be narrow to rounded, depending on how crowded it is. The trunks often lean and develop a swollen base. Carolina ash develops a furrowed, rough, light gray bark. Leaves are smaller than is common among ashes and somewhat thicker, but otherwise similar, with three or five leaflets. The color is green above, paler below. Flowers are typically ashlike, male on one plant and female on another. The fruit is also typically ashlike, but the wing of the samara (key) is quite broad and elliptical, with the cylindrical body of the samara winged along the sides. It ripens late summer into the autumn and persists on the tree into winter.

The wood of Carolina ash is not commercially harvested, being soft and weak. The fruit is eaten by a variety of birds and mammals, and the tree is useful in wetland restoration projects.

Fraxinus latifolia BENTH.
Oleaceae (Olive Family)
Oregon Ash

Oregon ash is the only ash native to the Pacific Northwest, being found in western Washington, Oregon and south along the Sierra Nevada and Coastal Range into central California. It occurs in riparian habitats on moist or wet soils that are seasonally flooded. It is shade-tolerant as a sapling, and occasionally forms pure stands, but is more often associated with other riparian tree species. It tends to be shade-intolerant as a canopy tree, and is usually shaded out by larger, more shade-tolerant trees which emerge from under its canopy.

Oregon ash may occasionally be shrubby in youth, as shown here, but at maturity is usually single-trunked.

Reaching to 80 ft. (24 m), Oregon ash usually has a single straight trunk supporting a dense narrow crown. The dark, grayish-brown bark is thick and furrowed into a reticulated net of scaly ridges. Leaves are typically ashlike with five or seven leaflets, green above, paler below, turning yellow or brown in the autumn. Flowers are typical of ashes, male on one plant and female on another, small, inconspicuous and gathered in clusters. The fruit is a samara (key) characteristically ashlike, borne in clusters on female trees.

Oregon ash is valued as an ornamental landscape tree for moist soils. Its foliage is prone to late season fungal blight which can detract from autumn color. However, it is not a serious disease. Being a riparian plant, it also has usefulness in restoration work and

prevention of erosion. It provides cover to a variety of birds, mammals, and when adjacent to streams and wetland, to fish as well. Its seeds provide forage to a variety of birds and small mammals, and its vegetation is also browsed by larger mammals.

Fraxinus nigra MARSH.
Oleaceae (Olive Family)
Black Ash, Swamp Ash, Hoop Ash, Basket Ash

With a distribution centred on the Great Lakes–St. Lawrence River drainage basin, black ash extends from the extreme northeast corner of north Dakota and adjacent Manitoba east to western Newfoundland, south to northern Virginia, then west to central Iowa. It is a major hardwood of lowland forests, found in

Black ash develops a narrow, rounded crown of coarse, ascending branches.

several plant communities associated with bogs, swamps, poorly drained areas and slow-moving streams. It prefers moist or wet peat, or shallow organic soils, as well as sands and loams over poorly drained clay with high water tables. Black ash is regarded as a pioneer species with low shade-tolerance; however, it is occasionally present in mature forest, where canopy gaps have occurred.

Black ash grows slowly to a potential height of 60 ft. (18 m), with a single narrow trunk, occasionally leaning, supporting a narrow, rounded crown of coarse, ascending branches and twigs with stalked buds. Its bark is corky and gray, fissuring into irregular soft scaly plates which rub off easily. The leaves follow the ash pattern with seven, nine or eleven leaflets, dark green above, paler below, turning brown in the autumn. Flowers are typically ashlike, dioecious, inconspicuous, borne in clusters. The fruit is an ashlike samara (key), with a broad elliptical wing running down the sides of a flatten body. The root of black ash is fibrous and shallow, rendering the tree prone to wind-throw.

The wood of black ash is not extensively used, although it has been split to make barrel hoops, baskets and woven chair bottoms. The twigs and leaves are consumed by deer and moose in spring and summer, while the fruits are consumed by song birds, game birds, and small mammals.

Fraxinus pennsylvanica MARSH.
Oleaceae (Olive Family)
Green Ash, Red Ash, Swamp Ash, Water Ash

With the most extensive distribution of any ash in North America, green ash may be found from Cape Breton Island, Nova Scotia west to southeastern Alberta, south to eastern Texas and eastward to northern Florida. It is absent north of Lake Superior and from the Florida peninsula, as well as higher elevations in the Appalachians from Maine through Pennsylvania. Green ash is found in many plant communities throughout its range. In the east it is generally a successional tree, often in small pure, even-aged stands

Green ash is undemanding, resilient, and popular as a shade and park tree.

until replaced by more shade-tolerant species such as elm and red maple. On the Great Plains it is more characteristically a dominant climax canopy tree. It is at best moderately tolerant of shade when young but intolerant at maturity. It is mostly confined to floodplains, where it is subjected to seasonal flooding, along rivers and streams, or at the edges of swamps. However, under cultivation it will grow wherever there is adequate soil moisture. It prefers deep, well-drained loams but occurs on a variety of soils.

Green ash tops out at about 60 ft. (20 m). In forested circumstances in the understory it grows slowly, and often has several stems. However, when it responds to an opening gap in the canopy one stem generally asserts dominance and becomes a straight trunk supporting a narrowly oval canopy.

In the open the trunk is straight, but shorter, supporting a dense rounded canopy. The bark is a dark grayish brown, shallowly furrowed with scaly ridges, often supporting lichen. The leaves are shining bright green above, paler below, turning yellow in the autumn. They are typically ashlike with five, seven or nine leaflets. Flowers are borne in typical ash fashion with males on one tree, females on another. Fruit is an ashlike samara (key) with a narrow body and narrow wing. Green ash has a wide-spreading, moderately shallow root system.

Green ash wood is used mainly for rough lumber, boxes, tool handles and pulp. On the Great Plains it provides valuable cover to both livestock and wildlife. It is extensively browsed by a variety of insects. In general, green ash woods provide a critical habitat in terms of cover and insect food sources for a variety of birds and mammals. It is also exten-

Female trees of green ash typically produce large quantities of winged fruit.

sively used in land rehabilitation, restoration and as windbreaks. A tough, tenacious and adaptable tree, green ash is extensively used in residential and park landscaping as a shade tree. It is also widely used as a street tree in urban environments because of its high tolerance for air pollution.

KEY FEATURES

Fraxinus pennsylvanica

Form:	Medium-sized tree with dense rounded crown
Trunk:	Single, slightly tapered, penetrating into the crown befor developing several large spreading limbs
Bark:	Gray, furrowing into a **diamond or zigzag pattern** of tight, narrow ridges
Twig:	Slender, gray, **flattened at nodes**, sometimes hairy
Leaves:	**Pinnately compound** to 10" (25 cm) with 5, **7** or 9 lance-shaped leaflets, slightly toothed; shiny green above, lighter beneath, sometimes hairy, **turning yellow**
Flower:	Tiny; in loose clusters at the ends of twigs, **dioecious**
Fruit:	**Samara**; slender **cylindrical body** with **narrow wing** attaching to the end, brown; in clusters

---

Fraxinus profunda (BUSH) BUSH
Oleaceae (Olive Family)
Pumpkin Ash, Red Ash

Pumpkin ash has an erratic distribution along the Atlantic coast from southern Maryland to northern Florida, west to Louisiana, and sporadically up the Mississippi and Ohio river valleys. It is confined to wet soils in swamps and river valleys that are inundated part of the year. It is poorly shade-tolerant and is usually replaced by dominant climax trees.

Growing to about 80 ft. (24 m) pumpkin ash is a single-trunked tree with a usually buttressed base, supporting a narrow oval crown. Its gray bark is furrowed into a diamond pattern of narrow ridges. Leaves are typically ashlike, with seven or nine leaflets, dark green above, yellowish green and softly hairy below. Flowers are tiny and inconspicuous, borne in characteristic ash fashion with males on one tree and females on another. The fruit is a typical ash samara (key), yellow, with a thick cylindrical body and a wide wing extending along the sides to near the base. The root system is extensive, shallow, and fibrous.

Pumpkin ash is typically a single-trunked tree, supporting a narrow oval crown.

Pumpkin ash has no commercial value. Its seed is a source of food to a variety of small birds and mammals. Snags provide nesting to hollow dwelling birds and small mammals.

Fraxinus quadrangulata MICHX.
Oleaceae (Olive Family)
Blue Ash

Blue ash has a sporadic distribution from western Ohio south to northwest Georgia, westward to northeast Oklahoma and north to southern Wisconsin. It is also found locally in extreme southwestern Ontario, where it is considered threatened. Blue ash is found as a scattered tree, mixed with other hard-woods on moist floodplain soils, as well as on dry, rocky, limestone outcroppings and alvars. It is the most drought-tolerant of the ashes.

A slow-growing tree to 70 ft. (21 m), blue ash forms a single tapered trunk penetrating a high narrow and irregular to rounded crown of stout s-curved branches. The bark is light gray, fissuring into irregular shaggy scales and plates. The inner bark turns a blue color when exposed to air. The twigs when young are characteristically stout, four-angled and somewhat winged or ridged. Leaves are typically ash-like with seven, nine or eleven leaflets. They are yellowish green above, paler below, turning yellow in the autumn. Flowers are a purplish color, with both male and female parts in the same flower, small, and clustered in the usual ash pattern. While more noticeable than other ashes, they are not particularly showy. The fruit is a typical ash samara (key) with a broad flattened body with a wide, slightly

When open-grown, blue ash typically forms a rounded dense crown on a short trunk.

twisting wing extending down the sides of the body to the base.

Blue ash is nowhere now common enough to exploit for its lumber, although until recently it was used locally for that purpose. The inner bark was also used by both Native peoples and settlers to make a blue dye by soaking it in water.

Fraxinus texensis (GRAY) SARG.
Oleaceae (Olive Family)
Texas Ash

Sometimes considered a variety of white ash, Texas ash is generally smaller in all features and adapted to a drier environment. It is found sporadically in southern Oklahoma and Texas. It prefers open

Texas ash makes a very useful, drought-tolerant landscape tree; its foliage is darker green than that of other ashes.

woodland on dry rocky soils of limestone origin. It is shade-intolerant.

Texas ash grows to about 40 ft. (12 m), with a short trunk supporting a wide-spreading crown of stout, crooked branches. The grayish-brown bark furrows into wide scaly ridges. The leaves are dark green above, whitish, sometimes hairy beneath, turning golden in the autumn. They are borne in typical ashlike fashion with usually three or five, or occasionally seven, leaflets. The flowers are purplish, borne in the characteristic ash pattern, males on one tree and females on another. The fruit is a typical ashlike samara (key), with a narrow cylindrical body and narrow wing, maturing, unlike other ashes, in the spring.

Nowhere common, Texas ash is not commercially exploited for its timber. It is grown commercially as a drought-tolerant shade tree for landscape purposes. The fruit is eaten by a variety of small birds and mammals.

Fraxinus velutina TORR.
Oleaceae (Olive Family)
Arizona Ash, Velvet Ash

Distributed throughout the Southwest, Arizona ash is found in a patchy distribution from western Texas through New Mexico, Arizona, Colorado, Nevada and into Utah and California. It is restricted to riparian habitats along the bottoms of canyons on various, well-drained soils, solitary or mixed with other trees. It is partially shade-tolerant and adapted to reflected heat.

Fraxinus velutina is a fast-growing, small, single-trunked tree to 40 ft. (12 m). The trunk is generally straight, supporting a spreading, open crown of stout branches, pubescent when young. Its grayish-brown bark becomes furrowed with age into a diamond pattern of narrow ridges. Leaves are characteristically ashlike with five, seven or nine leaflets, but are velvety with downy white hairs when they emerge. The upper leaf surface loses this characteristic as it expands, and becomes a bright

Arizona ash is a typical tree of riparian habitats along canyon bottoms.

shiny green, while the lower surface remains downy white. In autumn they turn yellow. The leaves are also leathery and smaller than those of other ashes. These adaptations enable the tree to survive in dry, hot climates and desiccating winds. The inconspicuous flowers are borne crowded into a cluster in typical ash fashion, males and females on different trees. The fruit is a typical ash samara (key).

Principally used as a street and shade tree throughout the southwest because of its tolerance for arid environments, Arizona ash has given rise to several cultivars. In its natural setting, it provides shade and protective cover to many kinds of small birds and mammals, which also eat the seed. Its wood has been used as fuel, but is otherwise not commercially exploited.

Gleditsia aquatica MARSH.
Caesalpinaceae (Caesalpine Family)
Water Locust

Water locust is found from South Carolina to central Florida along the Atlantic coast, along the Gulf coast from Florida to eastern Texas, and inland along the Mississippi to southern Illinois and Indiana. It is restricted to wet loamy to clay loam soils along rivers, stream, floodplains and swamps, where it is subjected to prolonged flooding. Under these conditions it produce enlarged lenticels on the stem probably to increase oxygen uptake through the stem. It is found singly in association with other wetland tree species, and is partially shade-tolerant.

A tree to about 50 ft. (15 m), water locust has a single, short trunk and a broad crown of spreading, often crooked branches. The bark is grayish brown fissuring into small scaly plates. Multibranched thorns dot the trunk and limbs. Leaves are about 8 in. (20 cm) long, pinnately to bipinnately compound, composed of small leaflets. They are dark green above, yellowish green below, turning yellow in the autumn and disintegrating. The flowers are tiny in small inconspicuous clusters, male and female flowers in separate clusters either on the same tree or different ones. The fruit is a 2-in. (5-cm) long, flat, shiny brown, elliptical pod. It is tough with papery divisions inside and no pulp, shedding one to three flat, round seeds in late autumn.

Multibranched thorns and pinnately compound leaves are typical of water locust.

Water locust is not commercially exploited for its wood. It is used in a limited way as a landscape tree on moist soils and in wetland restoration.

Gleditsia triacanthos L.
Caesalpinaceae (Caesalpine Family)
Honey Locust, Thorny Locust

Honey locust is naturally distributed from central Pennsylvania west through extreme southwestern Ontario to southeastern South Dakota, south to eastern Texas and east to the western slopes of the Appalachians in Alabama. It occurs as isolated populations in northwestern Florida. It has been introduced and become naturalized east of the Appalachians as far north as Nova Scotia. Honey locust is a widely adapted tree found in a range of different plant communities throughout its range, although it is never numerically numerous in any. It is found on rich moist bottomlands near streams and rivers and on rocky dry hillsides and uplands. It grows in the open or in open woods. It is tolerant of both flooding and drought, acid and alkaline soil as well as salinity. It is shade-intolerant and is eventually shaded out by larger more shade-tolerant species that develop under its canopy and then emerge above it.

Potentially a very large tree, honey locust generally reaches only about 80 ft. (24 m) in height. It is fast-growing and lives to about 125 years. It has a single trunk, often short, and heavily armed with

Most honey locusts in the wild are heavily armed with branching thorns.

The thornless varieties of honey locust, like this sunburst locust, are very popular landscape amenity trees.

multibranched thorns which extend onto the main limbs. The crown is open, airy, and wide spreading. Its grayish brown bark is fairly thick, fissuring into vertical narrow ridges. The leaves are pinnately to bipinnately compound, made up of many small oval leaflets, green above, yellowish green below, becoming rich gold in the autumn. The flowers are tiny, yellowish green, and crowded into inconspicuous clusters. Male and female flowers are in separate clusters either on the same tree or separate ones. The fruit is a twisting curved pod to about 16 in. (41 cm) long and 1.25 in. (3 cm) wide, dark maroon-brown, with numerous flat seeds, and an edible pulp inside. The fruits are dropped late in the autumn without opening. Flowering and fruiting are usually heavier in alternate years. Honey locust has deep thick, wide-spreading lateral roots.

KEY FEATURES

Gleditsia triacanthos

Form: Large tree with **open, wide-spreading crown**

Trunk: Single, straight, developing into several large irregular branches

Bark: Grayish brown fissuring verically into long scales lifting on the edges; **multibranched spines** abundant

Twig: Coarse, zigzagging, shiny brown, **with large spines**

Leaves: **Pinnate to bipinnately compound** to 8" (20 cm) long; leaflets small, oval, shiny green above, paler below, turning **golden**

Flower: **Tiny, clustered, greenish**; males and females in separate clusters on separate limbs of the same tree or on different trees

Fruit: **Flat pod** to 16" (41 cm) long by 1.25" wide; **leathery, maroon-brown, twisting** with many flat seeds and **edible pulp**

Honey locust wood is too scattered to be considered a commercial wood, although it has been used for furniture, rough lumber, interior finishing and firewood. It is deliberately planted to provide high-protein forage for cattle and sheep. Wildlife of many kinds eat the pods and seeds, and deer and rabbits eat the bark of young growth in the winter. Its adaptability has led to its use in landscape rehabilitation and erosion control. The thornless variety of honey locust has been developed into several cultivars for use in landscaping. It is a tough, resilient tree for use as a street tree, and is rarely bothered by diseases and pests. It casts a light dappled shade, and is regarded as self-cleaning in the autumn since its leaves disintegrate into tiny leaflets which decompose quickly.

Gordonia lasianthus (L.) ELLIS
Theaceae (Tea Family)
Loblolly Bay

Loblolly bay is found along the Atlantic and Gulf coastal plains, from North Carolina to halfway along the Florida peninsula, and westward to Mississippi. It is found on acid, wet soils with a high watertable for most of the year. It prefers flat or shallow depressions having slow runoff, poor drainage and rapid soil permeability. It is generally associated with a variety of acid-loving hardwoods. It is shade-tolerant.

An evergreen broad-leaved tree, loblolly bay grows to about 65 ft. (20 m), with a single trunk supporting a narrow, dense, columnar crown. The bark is thick reddish brown, deeply furrowed into narrow

Loblolly bay is prized for its fragrant showy summer flowers and shiny evergreen foliage.

Mountain silverbell develops an open oval crown on a short trunk, but is otherwise similar to Carolina silverbell.

Although in its native setting mountain silverbell is a large tree, in cultivation it is generally closer to 40 ft. (12 m). It makes a striking single-trunked spring-flowering tree on appropriate soils. Its wood is very occasionally used for lumber as well.

Hamamelis virginiana (L.)
Hamamelidaceae (Witch Hazel Family)
Common Witch Hazel

Common witch hazel is found from Nova Scotia to northern Florida, and inland through southern Ontario west to central Wisconsin and south to eastern Texas. It is a very common understory tree or large shrub, in near to full climax forests of many types. It may form relatively pure stands in the understory or, more commonly, be mixed with a variety of other understory trees and shrubs such as flowering dogwood, eastern redbud, rhododendron and ironwood. It is also a common tree of forest edges abutting on fields, meadows and road-cuts. It is very

shade-tolerant, preferring moist, fertile, well-drained soils. In the northern part of its range it prefers drier and warmer slopes, while in the south it is found in cooler, moist valleys facing north and east.

Reaching a height of 35 ft. (10 m), common witch hazel is a short-trunked small tree or large shrub supporting a broad crown of crooked limbs and crowded twigs. The light brown bark is smooth to slightly scaly, and the twigs are velvety yellow-brown. Leaves are borne alternately, and are broadly elliptical, widest toward the end, with large wavy coarse teeth or small lobes, and a short leafstem. They emerge hairy, becoming dull, and smooth, dark green above, paler below, turning lemon yellow in the autumn. As the leaves turn, or shortly after, small flowers emerge in short-stemmed clusters along the twigs. Each flower has four yellow,

Common witch hazel is usually a small multistemmed understory tree, turning golden in the autumn.

The yellow threadlike petals of common witch hazel appear in autumn and curl up in inclement weather.

threadlike petals which curl up in cold weather and unfurl when it is warm. Depending on location, they will flower from late September to late December. The overall effect is like a yellow hazy glow over the limbs. The fruit takes a year to ripen, and is a pea-sized, knobby, explosive, woody capsule. The explosive force will expel two to four hard, black, shiny, narrowly elliptical seeds up to 30 ft. (9 m) away. The seed has double dormancy and generally requires two winter cycles before it germinates. The roots are deep, coarse laterals.

KEY FEATURES

Hamamelis virginiana

Form: Usually multistemmed with broad, open crown

Trunk: Slender

Bark: Smooth to scaly; light brown

Twig: Slender; **zigzag**; **pubescent** with rust-gray hair

Leaves: Broad, elliptical; rounded or pointed tip; **wavy-toothed** beyond middle toward tip; **parallel veins**

Flower: Small, **bright yellow**, with **4 narrow, straplike petals**; opening in **autumn**

Fruit: An **explosive** brown elliptical **capsule with 4 blunt points**

The seeds of common witch hazel are of minor importance as food for birds, particularly northern bobwhite, ring-necked pheasant, and ruffed grouse, as well as mammals such as rabbits, beaver and deer. Astringent extracts, salves and lotions are made from the leaves, twigs and bark, and are used to stop bleeding, inflammation and excessive secretion of mucous membranes. Twig extracts were used by shamans to confer occult power. In geomantic practice, a forked branch of witch hazel is used to douse for underground water. Common witch hazel is also planted as an ornamental small tree or large shrub, primarily for its late-season flower. Because of its shade tolerance it will also flower in shaded positions. There are several cultivars available in which the flowers are somewhat larger or open after the leaves have fallen. It has also been crossed with Asiatic witch hazels to produce various hardy hybrids that flower in the early spring.

Ilex opaca AIT.
Aquifoliaceae (Holly Family)
American Holly, White Holly, Holly

American holly is found from central Florida north to eastern Massachusetts, southwest to southeastern Missouri and south to central Texas. It prefers moist, slightly acidic, well-drained soils, but is widely adaptable, growing in places along the Atlantic in nearly sterile sandy soils, and on inland

The bright red berries of American holly are typically borne on female trees.

Juglans californica S. WATS.

Juglandaceae (Walnut Family)

California Black Walnut

California walnut is endemic to California in scattered locations between Ventura and San Diego Counties. A northern California subspecies, *J. californica 'hindsii,'* is sometimes treated as a separate species. Due to urbanization and livestock grazing, its natural range is declining, with the extensive stands on north-facing slopes in the Puente and San Jose Hills of eastern Los Angeles County. It is found in relatively pure stands, or mixed with coast live oak, occasionally in chaparral communities or coastal sage scrub, where climates are Mediterranean. California black walnut prefers moist, deep, alluvial soils, especially clays, on north-facing slopes, creek beds, and canyon bottoms. It is frequently subjected to fire, and has adapted to sucker from the root crown and trunk.

A relatively short-lived tree, California black walnut is variable in form depending on age, site conditions and fire damage. In dense stands it is usually single-trunked to 50 ft. (15 m), but in more open settings prone to fire it usually attains only half that, and is multitrunked supporting a broad, open crown. The black-brown bark becomes furrowed with age and is strongly scented. Leaves are typically walnutlike but small, to 3 in. (7.5 cm) long, mid-

California walnut produces copious catkins of male flowers; female flowers are less visible at the tips of branches.

green and aromatic when bruised. Flowers are also borne in the walnut fashion, and the walnut fruit is globose and not usually produced in dry years. California black walnut tends toward having a deep tap root.

California black walnut is widely planted in urban forestry projects, and makes a handsome small to medium-sized ornamental tree. It has also been used to control erosion on steep road embankments where the soil is deep. The nuts are edible, but not grown commercially. Many rodents eat the nuts, and dense stands provide shelter for an abundance of bird species and small mammals. California black walnut is prone to both crown rot and heart rot; the latter renders the tree susceptible to termites and wood-boring beetles.

Juglans cinerea L.

Juglandaceae (Walnut Family)

Butternut, White Walnut

Butternut ranges from southwest New Brunswick, south to extreme northern Georgia, west to Arkansas, north to eastern Minnesota and northwest to southern Quebec. Throughout its range it is uncommon and is in decline in many areas due to butternut canker, a fungal disease. It is found as a canopy tree with other hardwoods and conifers, and is only partially shade-tolerant as a seedling. Butternut prefers deep, moist soils over limestone with good drainage, and is usually found in valleys above the floodplain, and on slopes.

Butternut reaches 70 ft. (21 m) on a short single trunk, bearing a high, broad, open crown of stout branches. It grows rapidly but lives to only about 75 years. The light gray bark ages from smooth to rough and furrowed. Leaves are typically walnutlike, aromatic when bruised, to 24 in. (60 cm) long, with up to 17 leaflets, yellow-green above, paler and softly hairy beneath, turning yellow-brown in autumn. Flowers are borne in typical walnut fashion, the females in clusters of up to eight. The walnutlike fruits are clustered, and individually large, egg-shaped, and thick-husked, with sticky rust-colored

A dense, broad, domed crown is characteristic of butternut.

hairs; they are borne heavily in alternate years. The nut inside contains an aromatic, oily seed. Occasionally tap-rooted on deep soils, butternut usually forms deeply penetrating lateral roots.

Butternut wood is soft and not much used commercially, except for small utensils and interior finishes. The seed is highly palatable, and a number of varieties are cultivated for the nutmeat and its oil. The nut is an essential ingredient in maple-butternut candy in New England, and the oil was used by Native peoples for consumption and ritual anointing. The husk yields an orange or yellow dye. Butternut is occasionally found as a shade tree in parks, but it is not commonly planted as an ornamental. The nut is consumed by squirrels and other rodents, and deer will eat the foliage.

Juglans elaeopyren DODE
Juglandaceae (Walnut Family)
Arizona Walnut

Found from central Arizona eastward to central Texas, Arizona walnut is also found in adjacent Mexico. A Texas subspecies, *J. elaeopyren 'microcarpa,'* is sometimes treated as a separate species, and commonly called "little walnut." It is found in a variety of riparian plant habitats in pure or mixed stands or as isolated individuals. Arizona walnut commonly occurs on coarse, rocky to sandy loams, often deep, usually low in organic content, common to moist, occasionally flooded sites along ephemeral and perennial streams. It is also found along river floodplains, canyons, and dry terraces and hillsides. It is relatively shade-tolerant, but seedlings are prone to drought-kill, and may be found in early successional habitats all the way through to climax ones.

Living to 400 years, Arizona walnut may reach 65 ft. (20 m), with a thick, short trunk supporting a wide, rounded crown of stout branches. The bark is gray and furrowed into rough ridges. The leaves are typically walnutlike, to 14 in. (35.5 cm) long. Flowers and fruit are walnutlike as well. The female flowers tend not to be produced in dry years, and the nut is small, about 1.5 in. (3.8 cm) in diameter, and hard-shelled. The root is typically tap-rooted.

The wood of Arizona walnut has been used for small items and fence posts, but is not commercially harvested. The nut, like all walnuts, is edible and gathered for consumption. It is also eaten by a variety of small mammals and birds. Arizona walnut provides valuable habitat for a wide variety of breeding bird species as well. It is valued and planted as a shade tree, although it is susceptible to walnut anthracnose, a fungal disease easily transmitted to commercial walnuts. As a sapling it is also prone to root and crown rots.

Juglans nigra L.
Juglandaceae (Walnut Family)
Black Walnut, American Walnut

Black walnut is found from southern Ontario west to southern Minnesota, south to east-central Texas, east to northwest Florida and north to Long Island. Isolated populations are found scattered along its northern boundary from Connecticut and western Massachusetts through to southern Vermont and southern New York. Others are found in Texas, western Oklahoma, central Kansas and southern South Dakota. It is conspicuously absent from the southern Piedmont, southern Mississippi valley and Mississippi delta. Black walnut can be found on a variety of soils but grows best on deep, fertile, well-drained moist soils, especially loams of neutral

A low, wide-spreading crown of stout branches on a short trunk is typical for open-grown black walnut.

character (i.e,. neither acidic nor alkaline). It prefers river valleys, but may also occupy slopes and dry ridges. It is found as scattered individuals mixed with other hardwoods and conifers in a large number of forest types, but because it is shade-intolerant it is not considered a climax forest canopy tree. However, it maintains itself in climax forests by occupying any gaps that occur in the canopy.

KEY FEATURES

Juglans nigra L.

Form:	Large tree, open, rounded crown
Trunk:	Single, straight
Bark:	Dark to light brown, deeply fissured into forking, narrow, vertical ridges
Twig:	Stout, brown, **chambered pith**, ashy gray pubescent buds
Leaves:	Pinnately compound; **9 to 21** lance-shaped, fine-toothed, **long-pointed leaflets, terminal one usually aborting**; hairy below; aromatic
Flower:	Male and female separate; male in catkins, females in clusters of 1 to 4 at ends of branches; not showy
Fruit:	Large, green-brown, thick-husked, **rounded, smooth**, hard-shelled; **edible walnut seed within**

The large, nearly spherical fruit of black walnut is borne in small clusters at the ends of branches.

Black walnut grows to be a large tree, between 80 and 125 ft. (25 to 38 m) in height. In forest settings its trunk supports a small, high rounded crown, while in the open it is short-trunked, developing a low wide-spreading crown of stout branches. Its bark is dark brown, matte black when wet, furrowed into narrow tight diagonal ridges. The typically walnut leaves are aromatic when crushed, up to 24 in. (60 cm) long with as many as 21 leaflets, and dark green turning yellowish in the autumn. The flowers are typically walnutlike as well, the female flowers in clusters of two to five at the ends of branches. The walnut fruits are borne single or in pairs, or occasionally in threes. They are round, to 2.5 in. (6 cm) in diameter, with a smooth thick green or brown husk over a thick-walled grooved shell. The seed within is edible, but fruit-set tends to be heavier in alternate or third years. Black walnut has a deep tap root supported by deeply penetrating laterals.

The wood of black walnut is probably the most prized of North American hardwoods. It is strong, heavy, durable and highly shock resistant, with a generally straight grain. It takes a smooth finish and is used for furniture, cabinetry, gun-stocks, interior detailing, hand tools, and the highest-grade veneer and plywood panelling. It is particularly valued for sporting rifles and expensive shotguns. The nuts are also commercially harvested for human consumption. Plantations are sometimes interplanted with black alder or Russian olive, because these trees increase the availability of nitrogen in the soil, which in turn increases the yields of black walnut. A brown-black dye is extracted from the husk and root. The ground-up shells find a variety of uses: to clean jet engines, as a filter in smokestack scrubbers, and as a nonslip additive in automobile tires. Black walnut is also grown as an ornamental, but is prone to European canker, which will slowly kill a tree. It has a strong suppressing action on other plants growing within its root system, particularly apples, conifers, rhododendrons, many vegetables, and herbaceous plants. It has also been used to rehabilitate strip mines.

THE JUNIPERS (*JUNIPERUS*)
Cypress Family (*Cupressaceae*)

The junipers consist of about 60 species of evergreen shrubs and trees throughout the Northern Hemisphere. They are closely allied to the cypresses, from which they most clearly differ in the nature of the ripened female cone. There are 15 species native to North America, of which eight are dependably trees throughout their respective ranges. A number of species are immensely variable in habit, from low spreading shrubs to more upright shrubs to trees. In some cases the harshness of their environment greatly influences the form of individual plants. For the most part, junipers are trees of dry locations and hot conditions during the growing season. They often occur in pure stands, at times extensively so; however, they may also be found in small groves or singly. Although some species are shade-dependent when very small, junipers are otherwise very intolerant of shade. They are also generally slow-growing and very long-lived, and in extremely hot and dry environments constitute a component of the climax plant community.

The native junipers are mostly small trees, occasionally reaching 70 ft. (20 m) in some species. Their overall form has no typical pattern. However, conical upright and rounded to irregular and open are some of the more commonly encountered

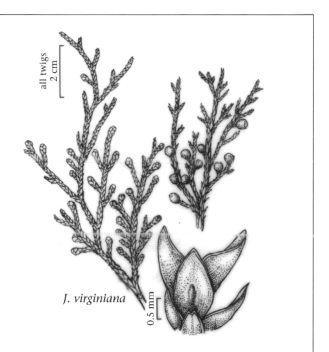

J. virginiana

all twigs 2 cm

0.5 mm

The needles of junipers can be scale-like or sharp-pointed. Female cones are fleshy.

forms. The bark is often scaly and shredding. The leaves of junipers are of two general kinds. Juvenile leaves are small, sharp-pointed, awl-like scales, usually borne in whorls of three, pointing outward at their tips from the twig. Mature leaves are minute, rounded at the tips, borne in pairs, or very rarely in whorls of three, and tightly pressed against the twig. A few species bear only juvenile foliage, while others have nearly all mature foliage. Most have a mix of the two types over the whole plant in all life stages. The foliage is generally a dark green, although in some species waxes create a more silvered appearance. In the winter the foliage tends to bronze from the cold. The male and female cones of junipers may occur on the same plant in some species, and on different trees in other species. Pollen is shed in the spring from the tiny male cones. The female cones, after pollination, develop into small, rounded "berries," composed of somewhat succulent, fleshy cone-scales that do not dry out, become woody, or split apart at maturity. They are usually black to red with a glaucous surface and they mature in the first, second, or third year after pollination, depending on the species. They have evolved to be eaten and pass through the gut of an animal. Stomach acids corrode both the fleshy scales and the hard woody coating over the seed, enabling it to germinate once excreted. Junipers generally have deeply penetrating root systems, most often tap roots or deeply penetrating lateral roots.

The junipers constitute an important group of trees, highly valued by both people and wildlife. The wood of some species is commercially important, and the berries of others are used locally in a variety of foods. A number of the native species are cultivated and widely used in landscape applications as specimens, in informal groupings of shrubs and trees, in hedges, windscreens and foundation plantings. Because of their deep root systems, junipers have high potential for use in soil stabilization on erodible slopes. Juniper berries provide an important source of food to many animals, and the plants themselves are excellent shelter from heat and winter storms as well.

Juniperus californica CARR.
Cupressaceae (Cypress Family)
California Juniper, Desert White Cedar

California juniper is found primarily in California from Shasta County south to Baja California, through the inner coastal range, and in the interior portion of southern California to the western slope of the southern Sierra Nevada. It is also found in isolated populations in western Arizona and western Nevada. California juniper is found in several plant habitats, principally pinyon–juniper woodlands, but also in chaparral that borders desert, Joshua tree woodlands and coastal sage shrub. It usually either co-dominates with single-leaf pinyon, or in chaparral is itself dominant. The seedlings are shade-tolerant, and in the absence of disturbance replace those trees that die. California juniper prefers shallow, poor, rocky, sandy or silty soils, low in nutrients, and clay. It can be found on both outwashes and steep slopes. Climatically it is found where winters are moist, sunny and mild, and summers dry and hot.

Under the best of conditions, California juniper reaches 40 ft. (12 m), but is usually less. It is most often multistemmed and stiffly upright, with a crooked branching habit and irregular, open branching. Seedlings under a foot (30 cm) are shade-dependent. Its bark is reddish brown, fissuring vertically and somewhat shedding. The leaved are tiny, mid-green scales borne in threes usually, and pressed tightly to the twigs. Cones are blue "berries," which ripen red-brown.

California juniper is most often multistemmed and stiffly upright, with irregular, open branching.

The principal human uses of California juniper are as fence posts and Christmas trees. Wildlife, principally birds, depend heavily on the fleshy cones as a food source, and larger mammals browse the foliage. It also provides thermal and protective cover when large. Native peoples used the ground-up cones to make a molded cake.

Juniperus erythrocarpa CORY
Cupressaceae (Cypress Family)
Redberry Juniper

Redberry juniper occurs in isolated populations from the Trans-Pecos in western Texas through to southwestern New Mexico, southern Arizona and into adja-

Minute scale leaves and dark orange-red "berries" are characteristic of redberry juniper.

cent Mexico. It associates with oaks and pinyon in a number of plant habitats. Redberry juniper prefers rocky, dry poor soils in full sun at elevations between 4,000 ft (1,200 m) and 6,500 ft. (2,000 m). Except as seedlings, when light shade helps to maintain soil moisture and thus survival, redberry juniper is shade-intolerant. It is often replaced by pinyon where the two types of tree are found together.

Redberry juniper usually has a straight central trunk branching low to the ground, forming an open, irregular crown of ascending and spreading branches to a height of 15 ft. (4.5 m). It may at times assume a large shrubby habit. The bark is red-brown, fissuring tightly, but somewhat scaly. Leaves are minute scales borne in pairs. On rapidly growing stems the scale-leaves are somewhat larger, with a white band on the inner surface. The cones are 0.3 in. (0.8 cm) in diameter, fleshy, orange to dark red, overlaid with a whitish bloom that makes them appear pinkish or rose-colored. Redberry juniper is able to recover from fire by sprouting from buds at the base of the trunk.

The wood of redberry juniper is used locally for fence posts and fuel. The cones were used by Native peoples for beads, or ground into a flour. Many bird species and mammals rely on the berries as a food source.

Juniperus flaccida SCHLECT.
Cupressaceae (Cypress Family)
Drooping Juniper, Mexican Juniper, Mexican Weeping Juniper

Although the most common juniper in Mexico, drooping juniper is found only in Big Bend National Park in Texas. It is found as scattered individuals in grassland, scrub and woodland plant communities, generally on dry, rocky or sandy soils of igneous derivation, in canyons, and along hillsides and ridges.

Drooping juniper is a slow-growing, long-lived tree to about 42 ft. (12 m) with a single trunk supporting a broad conical crown of pendant branches. It may also be found growing as a large shrub. The

Pendant sprays of fine branches on an open crown are the hallmark of drooping juniper.

Juniperus occidentalis HOOK.
Cupressaceae (Cypress Family)
Western Juniper

Western juniper ranges from southeastern Washington through Oregon east of the Cascades, and on through California to the upper slopes of the Sierra Nevada and San Bernardino Mountains. It also occurs in adjacent Idaho and Nevada. Western juniper is a co-dominant tree with many other trees and shrubs in a variety of habitats. It occurs in open stands or as isolated individuals on mountain slopes, high plateaus and rock outcroppings in all exposures. At lower elevations and along streams it is found more densely. It prefers shallow, stony,

bark is red-brown and shredding into long strips, and deeply fissured in an interlacing pattern. The adult leaves are small rounded scales pressed in pairs against the slender twigs. Immature leaves are about four times the size of adult leaves and borne in pairs or in threes, and are a lighter green. The cones are round, about 0.8 in. (2 cm) in diameter, ranging from tan to reddish brown to dull black, leathery or fibrous, with up to 13 seeds.

Drooping juniper makes a very attractive landscape tree reminiscent of a false cypress, and is widely planted for its pendant habit. Its wood is used locally for fence posts. A wide variety of birds and animals eat the cones.

Living to a thousand years, western juniper develops a massive buttressed trunk with age.

coarse sands or sandy loams that are slightly acidic and deeply and rapidly drained. It favors very dry conditions, hot summers and cold winters.

Western juniper is a slow-growing, very long-lived tree, reaching ages of between 800 and 1,000 years. Generally, it grows to about 40 ft. (12 m) as a tree, with one or several trunks supporting a broad-spreading crown of heavy limbs. The bark fissures into long red-brown strips. The gray-green leaves are small, blunt scales borne in threes and pressed against the slender twigs. The cones are round, blue-black with a light bloom, about 0.3 in. (0.8 cm) in diameter, ripening in the second year. Plants are occasionally single-sexed, but can change sexual condition from year to year as prompted by climatic conditions.

The wood of western juniper is used for a wide variety of products, but not extensively. The cones and foliage are palatable to a wide range of birds and animals, and provide thermal cover to wildlife as well. The cones are edible, especially when dried. In one of its oddest uses, the berry is fed to chickens to produce gin-flavored eggs.

Juniperus osteosperma (TORR.) LITTLE
Cupressaceae (Cypress Family)
Utah Juniper

Utah juniper is found throughout the Great Basin of western North America, from southern California north to Wyoming and southern Montana, and east to Colorado, Arizona, and New Mexico. It is found in a number of different plant habitats, often co-dominating with single-leaf pinyon, or pinyon at higher elevations, but forming pure stands at lower elevations where the pinyons cannot survive the drought. Utah juniper grows on shallow, coarse, rocky, slightly alkaline soils, clay loams, or sandy loams, where summers are hot, with low precipitation, low humidity, high evaporation, intense sun, and strong wind.

A small but long-lived tree, Utah juniper can reach 40 ft. (12 m), but is generally smaller. It is short-trunked with a spreading crown of stout

Utah juniper is typically found growing on shallow, hot, rocky soils.

branches. Its bark is reddish-brown to ashy gray, furrowed and shedding in long strips. Leaves are pale yellow-green, small and scale-like, borne in pairs, or on vigorous shoots in threes. The abundantly produced cones are round, 0.75 in. (1.8 cm) in diameter, reddish brown and bloomy when ripe, generally remaining on the tree for two years.

The wood of Utah juniper has been used for railway ties, fence posts, firewood and charcoal, as well as for novelty items, panelling, furniture, pulp and particleboard. A large number of birds and animals consume the fruit, although individual trees vary in the palatability of their fruit. Many small mammals and birds nest in Utah juniper and larger mammals use it for protection from heat and cold. It is used as an ornamental in landscaping. The essential oils of Utah juniper are used as flavorings or scents for a variety of products.

Juniperus scopulorum SARG.
Cupressaceae (Cypress Family)
Rocky Mountain Juniper

Rocky Mountain juniper extends from central British Columbia and Alberta south to Arizona, and from eastern Nevada to western Texas and the Dakotas. It is found in a wide variety of habitats, but occurs most commonly in open woodland with other conifers, and occasional broad-leaved trees,

Often found on cliff edges, few Rocky Mountain junipers attain the tenacious old age of this specimen.

growth forms. These are used as specimens, in small groups with other conifers, as ground cover and as both formal and informal hedging. The wood has been used for fence posts, firewood, and novelty items. The cones are eaten by a large variety of birds and mammals. Essential oils of Rocky Mountain juniper are used as flavorings and scents in a variety of products.

Juniperus silicicola (SMALL) BAILEY
Cupressaceae (Cypress Family)
Southern Red Cedar

Southern red cedar has a fairly restricted range, mostly near the coast from southeastern Texas to

but sometimes forms pure stands. Rocky Mountain juniper occupies a wide range of sites varying in elevation, climate and soil type, but performs best on dry alkaline soils on limestone cliffs, bluffs, and slopes, or on shallow, stony soils.

A highly variable, slow-growing and long-lived tree, Rocky Mountain juniper reaches 50 ft. (15 m). It is usually single-trunked, supporting an eventually irregular, rounded, open crown. The bark is red-brown to gray, furrowed, and shedding. Adult leaves are blue-green tiny scales borne in pairs and pressed to the slender twigs. Juvenile leaves are larger, sharp-pointed and angled away from the twig in threes. The cones are round, to 0.3 in. (0.8 cm) in diameter, maturing blue-black with a heavy bloom, borne more heavily on a two- to five-year cycle, and taking two years to mature. Trees are occasionally unisexual.

Horticulturally, Rocky Mountain juniper has given rise to a large number of varieties of various

Southern red cedar forms a conical open crown of somewhat drooping slender branches.

northern Florida and north to North Carolina, skirting the range of its close relative, the eastern red cedar. It is found in a variety of habitats, from dry, limestone uplands to swamps, but prefers the wet sandy soils of riverbanks.

Southern red cedar grows to 50 ft. (15 m) with a conical to open crown of somewhat drooping slender branches and twigs. Otherwise, it is very similar in appearance to eastern red cedar (q.v.) in most respects. Its cones are smaller, about 0.2 in. (0.5 cm) in diameter, and it is overall less hardy.

The wood of southern red cedar is aromatic and has been used in a wide range of items from fence posts to cabinetry to household utensils to firewood. Because of its rot resistance, it was used by early colonists for log cabins. It is also grown ornamentally. The berries are sweet and relished by many birds and small mammals.

Juniperus virginiana L.

Cupressaceae (Cypress Family)

Eastern Red Cedar, Pencil Cedar, Red Juniper

Eastern red cedar has the most extensive range of any conifer in eastern North America, from southern Ontario east to Maine, south to northern Florida, west to central Texas and north to North Dakota. It is characteristic in early successional plant commu-

Eastern red cedar is occasionally found growing in pastures.

The glaucous blue "berries" of eastern red cedar are borne only on female trees.

nities of various kinds. On harsh rocky sites, it is the dominant canopy tree, forming pure, scattered stands. Eastern red cedar grows on a wide variety of soils but performs best on deep, well-drained, slightly alkaline soils derived from limestone. It can be found, however, from poor, rocky sites with shallow soils on dry ridgetops and uplands to moist sites along rivers, streams, lakes, and swamps. Eastern red cedar is shade-intolerant, and is usually overtopped by trees growing beneath that are shade-tolerant when young. It is an alternate host to the fungal disease cedar apple rust, which infects apples and crabapples.

Although quite variable in form, with one variety a matted shrub, eastern red cedar tends to become a tree to about 60 ft. (18 m), with a single trunk supporting a dense, narrowly pyramidal to columnar crown that becomes open and irregular with age. It has a potential life-span of 300 years. The bark is thin, fibrous, red-brown to gray, exfoliating in long, vertical, narrow strips. The leaves are quite variable, but adult leaves tend to be small, round-tipped, borne in pairs and pressed tightly to the fine twigs. Juvenile leaves are larger, sharp-pointed, borne in threes and angled out from the twig. The color of the foliage varies from yellow-green to dark green to blue-green. Cones are about 0.4 in. (1.0 cm) in diameter, blue-black and very bloomy, borne only on female trees, maturing in a single season. Occasional trees have both male and female cones. The roots are fibrous and moderately deep.

Alpine larch typically grows on gravelly slopes with other high-altitude conifers.

A potentially long-lived tree, alpine larch reaches 40 ft. (12 m), forming a slender tapering trunk that penetrates a narrow, conical, but raggedly open crown. Main limbs are sporadic along the trunk, often gnarled and twisted from the severity of the growing conditions, spreading widely and drooping at the tips. The smooth gray bark becomes thicker, fissuring into irregularly shaped red-gray plates. Its pale blue-green needle-leaves are stiff, four-sided and tend to be borne only toward the tips of the stout, densely hairy twigs. On young trees the needles will remain green for two seasons before falling. On older trees the needles are deciduous annually. The female cones are about 2 in. (5 cm) long, purple-brown with hairy scales and long, exserted, fringed bracts, standing out from the twigs in all directions.

Seed crops are infrequent. The root of alpine larch is deep and wind-firm.

Although alpine larch can have a pleasing appearance under favorable conditions, it is very susceptible to spring frosts when cultivated. It is valuable in its habitat for providing shelter for small birds and mammals, as well as providing watershed protection and some degree of control over avalanches.

Larix occidentalis NUTT.
Pinaceae (Pine Family)
Western Larch, Western Tamarack

Western larch is found in the mountains from southeastern British Columbia to northeastern Oregon, east to central Idaho and north to western Montana and the extreme southwest corner of Alberta. It occurs between elevations of 1,300 and 7,000 ft. (400 and 2,100 m) in association with a variety of other conifers, although it often forms small, pure stands. It prefers deep, moist but well-drained, coarse gravelly to sandy soils that are slightly acidic.

Living to 400 years, western larch is the largest larch worldwide, growing to 230 ft. (70 m). Its trunk can reach 6.5 ft. (2 m) in diameter, and is often free of branches for much of its length. The crown is short and narrow, with main limbs horizontal to slightly drooping toward the bottom of the crown. The bark is red-brown, scaly when young and becomes quite thick and very deeply furrowed into wide flaky ridges. Its needle-leaves are pale green, somewhat shiny, keeled below but flat above, and borne in the characteristic larch pattern: singly on rapidly growing shoots but tufted on spur-twigs. The female cones are red-brown, about 2 in. (5 cm) long, with the narrow bract tips extending beyond the scales, which are hairy on the lower side. Seed is produced annually, but is most abundant every four or five years. Western larch has a deep, wide-spreading root system.

Western larch is an important timber tree, its wood being hard, heavy, strong and somewhat resistant to decay. The wood is used for construction, finishing, pulp and flooring. In its habitat it is useful

Western larch, with its enormous height, wide straight trunk, and fine, delicate needles, is a study in contrasts.

for controlling avalanches and erosion, and for watershed protection. It also provides protective habitat and seed for birds and small mammals. It is cultivated, but uncommon, due to its large size.

Liquidambar styraciflua L.
Hamamelidaceae (Witchhazel Family)
American Sweetgum, Redgum, Star-leaf Gum

American sweetgum ranges along the eastern seaboard from extreme southwestern Connecticut to central Florida, west to eastern Texas, north to southern Illinois. It is absent from the upper slopes of the Appalachians north of Georgia. American sweetgum is found mixed with other hardwoods such as pin oak, bald cypress, sycamore, American elm, river birch and tulip tree on the floodplains of river and stream valleys and on lower valley slopes. It prefers deep, moist, well-drained, slightly acid clay to silty loam soils. It is tolerant of flooding and wet ground, but is not shade-tolerant. It often colonizes logged areas, old fields, and urban wastelands where it is eventually replaced by more shade-tolerant species of canopy trees.

Potentially living up to 400 years, American sweetgum is a moderately fast-growing large tree, reaching 120 ft. (36 m). The trunk is straight and long, generally penetrating the conical to broadly rounded crown of ascending stout branches and

A broad conical crown and orange-red autumn foliage are typical of American sweetgum.

Scarlet foliage is often found on American sweetgum in autumn.

coarse, corky, winged twigs. The silvery-gray bark becomes deeply furrowed into slender scaly ridges. The leaves are borne alternately on long leaf-stems, and are shaped like five-pointed stars, or somewhat like maple leaves, with fine, regular teeth along the margin. They are up to 6 in. (15 cm) long and wide, bright shining green, turning scarlet in the autumn, although this is variable according to the individual and site conditions. They may sometimes be

KEY FEATURES

Liquidambar styraciflua L.

Form:	Large tree with rounded, spreading crown
Trunk:	Single straight
Bark:	Gray-brown,, deeply fissured into vertical, scaly, narrow ridges
Twig:	Stout, often with **corky projections**, green, turning red-brown
Leaves:	**Maple-shaped**; generally with 5 pointed lobes, **finely toothed**, lustrous green above, turning red
Flower:	Inconspicuous, in small **green, pendant, ball-like clusters**, male and female separate on same tree
Fruit:	**Spiky**, light brown **ball on pendulous stalk**

yellowish or purple. When crushed the leaves are aromatic. The flowers are greenish, borne in spring, and are not conspicuous. Male flowers are tiny, clustered into small balls each attached to a central stalk. Female flowers are in drooping clusters. The fruiting structure is a hard, pendulous, brown, spherical cluster about 1.25 in. (3 cm) in diameter. It is made up of individual fruits, each with a pair of long curved points. The fruiting cluster in aggregate resembles a miniature medieval mace. Each individual fruit opens to release one or two small winged seeds. The fruit clusters tend to remain on the tree, gradually dropping off through late winter and early spring. American sweetgum forms a deep tap root.

As an important hardwood American sweetgum is commercially logged for timber. It is used extensively in the manufacture of furniture, flooring, cabinetry, plywood, veneer, barrels and pulp. Early settlers extracted a resin from the inner bark, which was used as a gum, as well as medicinally. American sweetgum is also used in landscape applications where soil is appropriate. It performs poorly on alkaline or otherwise inappropriate soils. Being taprooted it can be slow to re-establish itself after planting, and is suitable only for large sites. It is not overly prone to pathological disease, and is resistant to most insects. It is decidedly windfirm, and strong-wooded. It makes a superb shade tree and cultivars are available that color dependably in the autumn.

Liriodendron tulipifera L.
Magnolicaceae (Magnolia Family)
Tuliptree, Tulip Magnolia, Yellow Poplar, Whitewood

Tuliptree ranges from Michigan east through extreme southern Ontario to Vermont, south to northern Florida, and west to Louisiana to altitudes ranging from 1,000 ft. (300 m) in the north to 4,500 ft. (1370 m) in the south. It is found in various hardwood forest types as an isolated tree, and occasionally in pure even-aged stands. It prefers rich, moist,

Vibrant yellow autumn foliage is just one attractive feature of tuliptree.

The leaf blade has four, or occasionally six, pointed lobes, arranged so that two lobes form a broad, shallow V-shaped notch at the tip. The base of the blade is flat where the leaf-stalk joins it, but then curves up the sides to the first pair of lobes. The leaves are a shiny dark green above, paler beneath, turning a rich yellow in the autumn. The flowers of tuliptree are borne terminally on branches, and are large and showy, reminiscent of lilies or tulips. They are about 2 in. (5 cm) wide, cup-shaped and consist of six round-tipped, light green-yellow petals with an orange blotch at the base, surrounding clustered golden stamens and a greenish spike of pistils. The fruiting structure of the tuliptree is 3 in. (7.5 cm) in length, a light-brown, cone-like collection of overlapping, stiff-winged nutlets, each containing one or two seeds. As the leaves yellow and fall in autumn, the winged nutlets detach and gradually fall off the "cone." The root system of tuliptree is fibrous, fleshy, and poorly branched but tending to be deep.

KEY FEATURES

Liriodendron tulipifera L.

Form:	Very large tree with high narrow crown, wide-spreading with age
Trunk:	Single, straight, high
Bark:	Dark gray-brown; furrowing into forking, narrow, tight ridges **with white lines in the valleys between**
Twig:	Stout, brown, lustrous; **buds flattened with 2 scales**, like a duck's bill
Leaves:	Large, 4 (6) **paired lobed; V-shaped notch at tip**; dark green turning bright yellow in autumn
Flower:	Showy, large, **cup-shaped, whitish yellow-green**; solitary at ends of branches in spring
Fruit:	Large, narrow, **conelike**, tan-brown, **fragile and disintegrating**

slightly acidic, well-drained, sandy to loam soils along rivers, streams and swamps, and on valley slopes. It is tolerant of flooding and moderately shade-tolerant, particularly when young.

A fast-growing, moderately long-lived tree, tuliptree reaches heights of 120 ft. (37 m), and has a long, straight trunk, often free of branches for half to two-thirds the height of the tree. The crown is narrow and small on forest-growing trees, but long, spreading and irregular in the open. Branches and twigs are smooth, brown, and stout. The dark gray-brown bark becomes thick and furrowed deeply into flat intersecting ridges. The 6-in. (15-cm) long and wide leaves are borne alternately on long slender leaf-stalks, having paired rounded, leafy stipules at the base, which dry up and fall off as the leaf expands.

Tuliptree is one of the more spectacular forest trees of eastern North America and is widely planted for its showy flowers. It makes a large tree, and because it generally does not flower until it is 20 or more feet high, it is best used on large sites. A number of varieties have been developed with different branching patterns and leaf characteristics. Its soft, fine-grained, easily worked wood is used for furniture, toys, crates and a variety of implements. It is also used for pulp. The flowers are visited by bees, which find it a rich source of pollen.

Lyonothamnus floribundus A.GRAY
Rosaceae (Rose Family)
Catalina Ironwood, Lyontree

Catalina ironwood has a highly restricted natural distribution, being found on only four of the eight Channel Islands off the coast of southern California: Santa Cruz, Santa Rosa, San Clemente and Santa Catalina. Two subspecies have been defined based primarily on differences in leaf morphology: subspecies *floribundus*, exclusively on Santa Catalina Island, and subspecies *aspleniifolius*, on the other three islands. Fossil and pollen evidence suggests that it was far more common on the mainland in the recent geological past. It usually grows in canyons and on dry slopes in more moderate environments than those that prevail in surrounding areas. Catalina ironwood prefers well-drained soils in full sun or partial shade, is adapted to summer drought, and associates with other hardwoods and conifers.

A fast-growing, evergreen broadleaved tree, Catalina ironwood reaches a maximum height of 60 ft. (18 m), forming a narrow cylindrical crown in youth, becoming rounded in maturity. Its bark is red-brown to gray and exfoliates in thin narrow strips, hanging from the trunk, giving it shaggy appearance. The evergreen, glossy, dark green leaves are palmately compound, and very fernlike in the subspecies *aspleniifolius*, while in the subspecies *floribundus* they are simple and lanceolate. Its cream-white flowers are borne in summer in slender panicles, tending to hang on the tree after their best display, making it appear somewhat shabby.

The feathery foliage of this Catalina ironwood indicates it belongs to the subspecies 'aspleniifolius'.

Catalina ironwood is threatened in its natural habitat by grazing. However, it is commercially available and has been used as a street tree and in residential landscaping, where it forms an attractive evergreen summer-flowering tree. It needs protection from hot, dry winds, however, and tends to perform better near the coast than inland.

Lysiloma latisiliquum (L.) BENTH.
Fabaceae (Bean Family)
Wild Tamarind, False Tamarind

Wild tamarind is found along the coast of southern Florida and over the Keys. It is also a native of the Bahama Islands and West Indies. It is a characteristic dominant tree of tropical hardwood hammock habitats, preferring full sun.

Wild tamarind makes a fine-textured landscape tree, whose flowers are attractive to butterflies.

Wild tamarind is a tree up to 60 ft. (18 m) in height with a trunk to 3 ft. (90 cm) in diameter, and stout branches forming a wide-spreading and flat-topped crown. New branches are bright red-brown, becoming slightly paler as they age. Its leaves are bipinnately compound, to 7 in. (18 cm) long. The leaflets are very small, light green above and paler below. Its flowers are clustered in a round ball, about 0.5 in. (1.2 cm) in diameter, borne on a slender stalk about 1 in. (2.5 cm) long. The balls occur singly or in small groups in the axils of the outer leaves. The individual flowers are tiny, usually green-white. The dark red to brown fruit is a pod, pointed at both ends, to 7 in. (18 cm) long by 1 in. (2.5 cm) wide, usually several borne together. They split open gradually, shedding several flattened seeds, 0.25 in. (0.6 cm) in diameter.

Wild tamarind is attractive to butterflies, and is sometimes planted for that purpose. Its wood is heavy, hard, and tough, but is used only occasionally, in the construction of boats.

Maclura pomifera (RAF.) SCHNEID.
Moraceae (Mulberry Family)
Osage Orange, Hedge Apple, Bodark, Bowwood

The native range of the osage orange is, conservatively, from extreme southwest Arkansas west into southern Oklahoma, and south into central Texas. Its distribution is obscured because of its being widely planted and naturalized throughout the eastern United States and southern Ontario. It prefers the moist silty to loamy sands of floodplains, but will also grow on drier, coarser sandy soils of hillsides and open pastures. It is heat-, drought- and salt-resistant, and shade-intolerant.

Osage orange will reach 50 ft. (15 m) with a broad rounded crown of spreading branches supported by a short, often irregular trunk. The stout branches arc upward and outward in a characteristic repeating pattern. Its bark is gray to dark orange-brown, thick and deeply furrowed into fibrous, narrowly forking ridges. The orange inner bark of the roots parts into thin papery scales. The leaves are long-pointed, narrow, oval, shining dark green above, paler below, turning yellow in autumn. They exude a milky sap when cut, and are frequently accompanied at the node by stout persistent spines. Flowers are individually very tiny, green and densely crowded into round clusters an inch (2.5 cm) across, with male and female flowers on separate trees. The fruit on female trees is a hard, heavy, fleshy ball to 5 in. (13 cm) in diameter, green-yellow with fibrous hairs covering it. It ripens and soon falls in autumn. Osage orange has a shallow, fibrous root system.

Before the appearance of barbed wire, thorny osage orange was planted as natural "fencing" on the Plains. A yellow cloth dye can be extracted from the inner root bark. Native peoples used its wood for bows, and fence posts have also been made from the wood. Livestock eat the fruit.

Osage orange has a large, hard, heavy fruit, greenish in color and spherical, with a rough hairy surface.

THE MAGNOLIAS (*MAGNOLIA*)

Magnolia Family (*Magnoliaceae*)

Of the about 80 species of magnolia found in tropical and temperate regions of the world, seven are native to North America. A subspecies of bigleaf magnolia is sometimes recognized as a distinct species, Ashe's magnolia. Other species are distributed in east and southeast Asia, the West Indies, and Central and South America. The native species of magnolia are found in the east, especially the southeast. In general, these species are found scattered throughout forested habitats or in small groves; all prefer moist, rich soils. Some will tolerate occasional seasonal flooding. They are all fairly shade-tolerant as young saplings, but most species require full sun at maturity. The native magnolias are moderately fast-growing, and range from fairly short-lived to moderately long-lived, depending on the species.

Ranging from small trees with shrubby tendencies to fairly tall trees, the native magnolias generally have short trunks and well-developed broad crowns. Leaves are evergreen in a few species, but are otherwise deciduous. They are alternately arranged on the twig, and are simple, oval to elliptical in shape, with smooth edges and short leaf-stalks. Some species have hairy undersides to the leaves. The flowers of magnolias are large and very showy, sometimes fragrant, and borne at the ends of branches in the spring. The fruit that follows the flowers is a spiralling set of fleshy follicles, in some species richly colored pink or red, that split open in the autumn to release one or two red-coated seeds.

The native magnolias, as well as numerous

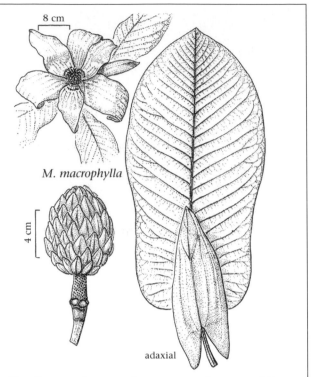

M. macrophylla

adaxial

The flowers of magnolias are very showy and the fruit is composed of clustered follicles. The leaves are generally smooth-edged and simple.

introduced species and innumerable hybrids, are highly prized as ornamental landscape trees. Their flowers are large and visually highly attractively. Those that are scented are especially esteemed. They are not tolerant of drought, and are prone to some fairly troublesome insect pests. They also require some protection from winds, especially the evergreen species, but are otherwise adaptable and very rewarding ornamental trees. With the exception of southern magnolia, the wood of the native magnolias is not commercial of much importance. Wildlife uses, primarily as shelter, are minimal.

Magnolia acuminata L.

Magnoliaceae (Magnolia Family)

Cucumber Tree

The most northerly distributed of the Magnolia family, cucumber tree occurs in scattered populations in southern Ontario north of Lake Erie. It ranges primarily from western New York south to northern Florida, west to Louisiana and north to Missouri. Cucumber tree occurs singly or in small groups, mixed with other hardwoods, along the lower slopes of valleys and mountains in sheltered locations.

golden stamens. The fruit cluster is 3 in. (7.5 cm) long, a pink-red, conelike structure of numerous somewhat pointed fruits, which split open to release two seeds that hang by a thread before falling. The root system of the cucumber tree consists of deep, coarse, fleshy laterals.

Sometimes planted as an ornamental shade tree on large, favorable sites, cucumber tree has a reputation for being difficult to transplant due to its fleshy roots. Its wood is soft and easily worked, but is not commercially harvested.

Magnolia fraseri WALT.

Magnoliaceae (Magnolia Family)

Fraser Magnolia, Umbrella tree, Mountain Magnolia

Scattered through southern West Virginia and western Virginia, south to northern Georgia, Fraser magnolia can be found scattered among other hardwoods along valley slopes in the Appalachians between 800 and 5,000 ft. (245 to 1525 m). It prefers moist, well-drained loamy soils, and full sun.

Fraser magnolia grows to about 70 ft. (21 m) under ideal conditions, but is generally smaller. It forms an open, spreading, round-headed crown of coarse branches supported by a straight, single trunk. The leaves reach about 18 in. (46 cm). Generally magnolia-like, they are widest beyond the middle, with two large, rounded lobes at the base, bright green above, very pale beneath. The buds are smooth, purple-green. The fragrant, creamy flowers are also very large, to 10 in. (25 cm) across, consisting of six to nine "petals" (correctly referred to as "tepals" in the magnolias) borne in the magnolia fashion in the spring. The fruit is a rosy-red, elongated, egg-shaped, conelike structure to about 5 in. (13 cm) long, made up of numerous, long-pointed fruits which split open in autumn to release two seeds each. The root system of Fraser magnolia consists of deeply penetrating laterals.

The principal use of Fraser magnolia is as a shade and flowering tree for large sites. It is too visually coarse to be suitable in most residential applications.

Cucumber tree forms a narrow oval crown, with the lower limbs bending to the ground with age.

It prefers moist, well-drained, coarse to fine, loamy soil. As a young sapling it is moderately shade-tolerant, but is intolerant at maturity.

Moderately long-lived, cucumber tree reaches 80 ft. (24 m), with a straight trunk penetrating into an oval, narrow to broad crown of spreading branches, the lower ones bending toward the ground. Young twigs and buds are densely hairy. The dark, gray-brown bark is shallowly furrowed, forming scaly, long, vertical, flat and narrow ridges. The leaves are typically magnolia-shaped with a pointed tip, to 10 in. (25 cm) long and 6 in. (15 cm) wide, somewhat softly hairy beneath, green above, becoming yellow-brown in the autumn. The bell-shaped flowers are borne in the spring and reach 3.5 in. (9 cm) across. The six petals are yellow to yellow-green and surround a tight cluster of

The first few large and fragrant blooms of a Fraser magnolia opening on a wooded slope.

The rich mahogany foliage in autumn is appealing, if brief.

Magnolia grandiflora L.

Magnoliaceae (Magnolia Family)

Southern Magnolia, Evergreen Magnolia, Bull Bay

Southern magnolia extends from southeastern North Carolina along the coastal plain to central Florida and west into eastern Texas. It can be found singly or in small groups associating with a variety of hardwoods on moist, well-drained, slightly acidic loams in valleys and lower uplands. However, it will tolerate periodically wet soils. It is tolerant of shade, and may be found as an understory tree as well as in the canopy of late successional and climax hardwood forests.

A majestic evergreen tree, southern magnolia reaches a height of 80 ft. (24 m) on a straight, generally short trunk supporting a dense, conical to pyramidal crown. Lower limbs and branches are wide-spreading. Twigs and buds are covered in rust-colored hairs. The dark gray bark is initially smooth, but furrows and becomes quite scaly. Leaves are typically magnolia-shaped, with a pointed tip, to 10 in. (25 cm) long and half as wide, firm, almost leathery, lustrous dark green above and often with a rust-colored pubescence below. The wonderfully fragrant, cup-shaped flowers are white, about 8 in. (20 cm) across and composed of three sepals and six thick petals. They are borne in the typical magnolia fashion in late spring and sporadically into summer. The fruit is a pink-brown conelike structure to about 4 in. (10 cm) long, consisting of many individual

Dense columnar form, evergreen foliage, and lovely fragrant white flowers all account for the popularity of southern magnolia as a landscape tree.

The flower of southern magnolia is creamy-white and fragrant.

short-pointed fruits that split open in the autumn to release two seeds each. The root structure of southern magnolia is deep and wide-spreading.

An undeniably beautiful tree, southern magnolia is planted as an ornamental shade tree throughout the world in agreeable climates for its evergreen foliage, form and flower. There are numerous excellent cultivars with larger or smaller flowers, larger, smaller or narrower leaves, and faster or slower

KEY FEATURES

Magnolia grandiflora L.

Form:	Large, broadleaved evergreen with dense, conical crown
Trunk:	Single, generally short, straight
Bark:	Smooth, dark gray, becoming fissured and scaly
Twig:	Fairly stout **rusty-haired when young; buds have rusty hairs**
Leaves:	Large, elliptical, thick, **edges rolled under,** lustrous green above, **pale or rusty-hairy below**
Flower:	Large, **cup-shaped, white, fragrant,** borne at ends of branches in late spring and early summer
Fruit:	**Pink-brown,** small, **conelike;** in autumn

growth. "Gloriosa" is considered one of the best. The fragrance of the flower is refined. Since it generally begins flowering about 15 to 20 years from seed, it is more often commercially grown from cuttings. It makes a superb specimen tree for larger sites where it has the room to develop well. The leafy branches of those trees with densely rusty pubescence on the buds, twigs and leaf undersides are widely used in the florist industry. The wood of southern magnolia has also been used for cabinetry, furniture, doors and boxes.

Magnolia macrophylla MICHX.
Magnoliaceae (Magnolia Family)
Bigleaf Magnolia

With a distribution centered in Louisiana and Mississippi, local populations of bigleaf magnolia may be found in southeastern South Carolina, Tennessee, Alabama, Kentucky, northeastern Arkansas, and southern Ohio. It is usually an understory tree of deciduous hardwood forests, preferring the moist, well-drained loamy soils of valleys. It is tolerant of shade and periodically wet soil.

A small tree, with a maximum height of just 40 ft (12 m), bigleaf magnolia forms a single trunk supporting a broad, round crown of spreading, stout limbs, and branches. The twigs and buds are covered in white hairs. The magnolia-like leaves are huge, to 30 in. (76 cm), about a third as wide, and generally widest beyond the middle of the leaf, with two rounded, short-pointed lobes at the base of the blade. The upper surface is bright green, while the lower is paler and silvery. The fragrant, cup-shaped flowers are likewise very large, to 12 in. (30 cm) across, composed of six creamy-white petals with a red spot at the base of each. They open in late spring and sporadically into summer. The fruit is a rosy red, egg-shaped, cone-like structure to about 3 in. (7.5 cm) long, composed of numerous fruits, which split open in autumn to release two seeds each. The root system of bigleaf magnolia consists of deeply penetrating laterals.

Although grown as an ornamental as far north as southern Ontario, bigleaf magnolia requires a

Large leaves and large fragrant white flowers characterize bigleaf magnolia.

large site protected from winds, which will otherwise lacerate the large leaves. It is visually too coarse for most residential applications, being better suited to golf courses, parks, and large public spaces.

Magnolia pyramidata BARTR.
Magnoliaceae (Magnolia Family)
Pyramid Magnolia, Mountain Magnolia

A rare and sporadically distributed tree found along the coastal plain from South Carolina to eastern Texas, pyramid magnolia is usually a solitary tree, occasionally growing in small groups in the understory of deciduous hardwood forests. It prefers the rich, moist, well-drained, loamy soils of river, and stream valleys. It is tolerant of shade, as well as seasonally wet ground.

Pyramid magnolia is a small tree, to 40 ft. (12 m), with a short straight trunk supporting a pyramidal crown of upright, stout branches. The dark brown-gray bark is smooth when young, but becomes scaly with age, and is always thin. The leaves resemble those of Fraser magnolia and are bright green above, paler and silvery below, to 9 in. (23 cm) long and half as wide, widest above the middle, and very narrow above the two large lobes at the base of the blade. The flowers are creamy white, to 4 in. (10 cm) in diameter, composed of six to nine petals, and borne in the usual magnolia fashion in the spring. The rosy-red, cone-like fruiting structure ripens in the autumn.

It is about 2.5 in. (6 cm) long, and composed of many small fruits with short, arching points, which split open to release two seeds each. The roots of pyramid magnolia are deep and spreading.

An uncommon tree in its native habitat, pyramid magnolia is sometimes planted as a specimen tree on moist soils in the south.

Magnolia tripetala L.
Magnoliaceae (Magnolia Family)
Umbrella Magnolia

Umbrella magnolia has a patchy distribution from southern Pennsylvania to northwestern Florida, west to southeastern Mississippi, and north to southern Indiana, with local populations scattered through

The attractive white cup-shaped flowers of the umbrella magnolia are rank-smelling.

Arkansas into southeastern Oklahoma. It can be found individually or in small groups as an understory tree in deciduous hardwood forests, along river and stream valleys at lower elevations. It prefers moist, well-drained loams and is shade-tolerant.

A small tree to 40 ft. (12 m), umbrella magnolia generally forms a single trunk supporting an open, broad crown of stout branches, occasionally suckering at the base. The bark is smooth, thin and pale gray. The leaves of umbrella magnolia are fairly large, to 20 in. (50 cm) long and half as wide, broadest beyond the middle, green above, and somewhat white with hair below when young. They are crowded toward the ends of twigs and arranged so as to appear umbrella-like. The cup-shaped flowers are large also, to 10 in. (25 cm) in diameter, with three pale green sepals and six to nine shorter white petals. They are borne in the spring and are rank-smelling. The rose-red fruit is a cone-like structure about 4 in. (10 cm) long, comprising numerous short-pointed individual fruits, which split open in autumn to release two seeds each. The root system of umbrella magnolia is deep and wide-spreading.

Umbrella magnolia is not widely used horticulturally due to the unpleasant odor of its flowers. The arrangement of its foliage gives it some architectural interest, which can be exploited on larger sites, such as golf courses and parks.

Magnolia virginiana L.
Magnoliaceae (Magnolia Family)
Sweet Bay, Laurel Magnolia, Swamp Magnolia, Swamp Bay

Sweet bay is a near-evergreen tree found along the eastern seaboard from Massachusetts to southern Florida and west to southeastern Texas. It grows inland up to elevations of 500 ft. (150 m). Sweet bay prefers the wet acidic soils of the banks of ponds, streams, and rivers, as well as coastal swamps and bogs, where it grows in association with other wet-soil trees and shrubs in a wide range of plant habitats. It is somewhat shade-tolerant, although more so as a young tree than at maturity. It is drought-intolerant.

Sweet bay has lovely, sweet-smelling, creamy white flowers.

In the northern parts of its range sweet bay reaches heights of only 20 ft. (6 m); in the south it can attain 60 ft. (18 m). It is either single stemmed or multistemmed, especially in the north. It generally has a rounded to narrowly pyramidal crown, but more open, loose, and upright in the north. The gray bark is thin, smooth and aromatic when bruised. The leaves are deciduous in the north to near-evergreen in the south, typically magnolia-shaped, to 6 in. (15 cm) long and half as wide, bright green above, and

KEY FEATURES

Magnolia virginiana L.

Form:	**Nearly evergreen**, deciduous small to medium tree with narrow, rounded crown
Trunk:	One to several, slender trunks
Bark:	Thin, smooth, gray, aromatic
Twig:	Medium texture, buds with white hairs
Leaves:	Oval, blunt tipped, short-stalked, lustrous green above, **densely white-hairy below**, somewhat thick
Flower:	Fairly large, **cup-shaped**, **white**, **fragrant**, late spring and early summer
Fruit:	Deep red, **conelike**, small, ripening in autumn

the bud but opening white, tinged pink, with a fragrance resembling that of violets, and about 1.5 in. (4 cm) in diameter. The fruit is a yellow-green crabapple about 1.25 in. (3 cm) in diameter, maturing in late summer. Wild sweet crabapple has a fibrous, shallow root system.

The fruit of the wild sweet crabapple when over-ripened is relished by many birds and small mammals. Native peoples dried the fruit for winter use. It is also made into preserves and cider. Its hard, dense wood has been used for utensils and tool handles. Because of its attractive and fragrant flower it is planted as an ornamental specimen or in small groups. However, it is susceptible to rust, which disfigures both leaf and fruit.

Malus fusca (RAF.) SCHNEID.
Rosaceae (Rose Family)
Oregon Crabapple, Pacific Crabapple

A native of the Pacific Northwest, Oregon crabapple extends along the coast from the Alaska panhandle to California, and inland along rivers and streams. It prefers moist to wet ground along the edges of forests, swamps, streams and rivers, as well as at the backs of beaches and around estuaries. It is somewhat shade-tolerant and is normally shaded out by larger canopy trees with time.

Oregon crabapple bears its flowers, which may also be tinged pink, along with the new leaves.

Oregon crabapple reaches 40 ft. (12 m), and has a short trunk supporting an open, irregular to rounded crown of several stout limbs and numerous branches, armed with sharp-pointed spur-twigs. Its bark is red-brown and deeply fissured into flat scaly vertical ridges. The leaves are 3 in. (7.5 cm) long, oval, finely toothed, rounded at the tip, with a pair of glands at the base of the blade. They are yellow-green above, paler below, turning yellow-orange-red in the autumn. The typically crabapple flowers are white to pink-white, and about 0.75 in. (2 cm) across. The fruit is an oblong, somewhat pear-shaped crabapple, about 0.75 in. (2 cm) long, yellow with a reddish blush, tart-tasting and ripening in late summer. Oregon crabapple has a shallow, fibrous root system.

Many birds and mammals consume the fruit. Native peoples gather the fruits and preserve in oil, or a mixture of oil and water, what cannot be eaten immediately. The bark has been used medicinally. Although attractive in flower, Oregon crabapple is not extensively planted as an ornamental.

Malus ioensis BRITT.
Rosaceae (Rose Family)
Prairie Crabapple

Mainly distributed from Missouri north to southeastern South Dakota, eastward to northern Indiana and south through Illinois, prairie crabapple is also found in scattered local populations southwestward into central Texas. It is found in a variety of prairie and open forest habitats, usually in full sun along streams and rivers, at the edges of open woods, and on rocky hills and open pastures. Prairie crabapple grows on a variety of soils, from coarse, well-drained gravelly loams to poorly drained clays, but is most common in soils on limestone.

Prairie crabapple is a small tree, to 30 ft. (9 m), its short trunk supporting several crooked main limbs and an open, wide-spreading, twiggy crown with numerous thornlike spur-twigs. It may also be a large spiny shrub, in less favorable situations. The bark is

An upright form of the prairie crabapple with light pink double flowers.

silver-gray, flaking off in paper-thin scales. Leaves are slightly thickened, dark shiny green above, paler below, hairy when young, turning yellow in the autumn. They are 4 in. (10 cm) long, about half as wide and are coarsely toothed and somewhat three-lobed, with prominent veins. The typically crabapple flowers are sweetly scented, pink in the bud, opening white to pale pink on long stalks, each flower about 2 in. (5 cm) across, and open in spring. The fruit is a long-stalked, yellow-green crabapple, about 1.25 in. (3 cm) across, maturing in late summer. Prairie crabapple has a shallow, fibrous root system.

Often planted in windbreaks and shelter belts, prairie crabapple is a lovely small tree in flower. There is a double-flowered form that is particularly appealing. It is very susceptible to cedar-apple rust, however. Birds and small mammals relish the fruit when over-ripe.

Mastichodendron foetidissimum (JACQ.) H.J. LAM
Sapotaceae (Sapodilla Family)

Mastic

Mastic is found in Florida along the coast, from Brevard through to Lee Counties, and in the Florida Keys.

It is a large, evergreen, broad-leaved tree, growing to a height of 80 ft. (24 m) with a large straight trunk, to 4 ft. (1.2 m) in diameter, topped with coarse branches and smooth, red-brown branchlets forming an uneven crown. All parts of the tree exude a milky sap when wounded, and leaves and bark have an unpleasant odor when bruised. The leaves are clustered at the ends of shoots, and are oval, smooth, bright green and lustrous above, and yellow-green below. They are up to 6 in. (15 cm) long by about a third as wide, thin but firm, remaining green for more than a year, and are formed sporadically during the

Mastic, with its glossy evergreen leaves, makes an excellent landscape shade tree.

(q.v.), but differs in its leaf and habitat requirements. It prefers deep, permanently wet, slightly acid, soils along the edges of swamps, and will not tolerate drought. Soil that is not acidic enough will often result in chlorotic foliage.

Swamp tupelo reaches 50 ft. (15 m). It forms a single, generally short and narrow trunk, buttressed at the base and penetrating midway into the canopy. It is usually conical in youth but becomes flat-topped with age as a result of the many slender, strongly horizontal branches having numerous short spur branches. In most respects, it resembles black tupelo, except that its leaves are thicker and leathery, narrower and oblong, its fruits are paired, and the trunk-base is buttressed.

Swamp tupelo is not suitable for landscape applications due to its requirement for permanently wet soils. It is useful for wetland protection and restoration, however, and in preventing erosion. As with black tupelo, birds and small mammals relish the fruit, and a good honey can be made from the flower.

Nyssa ogeche BARTR. ex MARSH.
Cornaceae (Dogwood Family)
Ogeechee Tupelo, Ogeechee Lime, White Tupelo, Sour Tupelo

A small tree of restricted distribution, Ogeechee tupelo is found from northern Florida through southern Georgia, and just into southern South Carolina. It is found in wet, acidic soils bordering swamps, lakes, streams and rivers where it is seasonally inundated, and water tables are within 2 ft. (60 cm) of the surface. It is shade-intolerant and is often replaced by larger canopied trees.

Ogeechee tupelo reaches a height of 40 ft. (12 m) on one to several crooked trunks supporting an open narrow crown of slender, hairy, red-brown twigs. It is occasionally a large shrub. Its thin dark brown bark is irregularly furrowed into scaly plates and ridges. Leaves are elliptical to 5.5 in. (14 cm) long and half as wide, somewhat leathery, smooth-

Ogeechee tupelo, a small tree, often grows with more than one trunk, and is usually found very close to water.

edged, glossy green above with a few hairs, paler beneath and velvety along the veins. The flowers are tiny, hairy, and greenish, male and female on separate trees, opening in the spring. Male flowers are gathered into small heads on a long stalk; female flowers are borne solitarily. The oblong fruit is a shining red, succulent but sour-tasting drupe, to 1.5 in. (4.0 cm) long, ripening in late summer; the pit inside is a 10-to-12-ribbed stone.

The fruit of Ogeechee tupelo is used like limes, and a preserve can be made of the pulp. A superb honey is also produced from its flowers. Propagation is easily achieved through seed, or suckers from the base of the trunk or from the roots. Its fruit is also relished by a variety of birds and small mammals. It is a useful tree in maintaining riparian and wetland habitats and in the management of watersheds.

Nyssa sylvatica MARSH.
Cornaceae (Dogwood Family)
Black Tupelo, Black Gum, Sour Gum, Pepperidge

Black tupelo ranges from southwestern Maine through southwestern Ontario to central Michigan,

Black tupelo typically has brilliant crimson autumn foliage and noticeably horizontal branching.

of the canopy. It is usually conical in youth but becomes flat-topped with age, the many slender, strongly horizontal branches having numerous short spur branches. The bark is flaky and gray when young, but becomes dark gray-brown, thick, and fissured into irregularly heavy ridges and blocks. Leaves are elliptical to obovate to 5 in. (13 cm) long and 3 in. (7.5 cm) wide, somewhat leathery, smooth-edged, glossy green above, paler and often hairy beneath, turning brilliant scarlet in the autumn. The flowers are tiny, hairy and greenish, male and female on separate trees, opening in the spring. Male flowers are gathered into small heads on a long stalk; female flowers are borne in clusters of two to six. The oblong fruit is a blue-black, thinly succulent,

With age black tupelo tends to develop a flat-topped crown.

south to eastern Texas and east to southern Florida. It is found in a variety of hardwood and pine forest habitats as a late successional understory or canopy tree. Being only somewhat shade-tolerant, it is often replaced by climax canopy trees that are more shade-tolerant as saplings. It prefers deep, moist to wet, slightly to strongly acidic, loamy to clayey loam soils along river and stream valleys, swamps, bogs, lower slopes, and uplands. It has an obligate need for moist to wet soil and will not tolerate drought. Soil that is not acidic enough will often result in chlorotic foliage.

A graceful large tree, black tupelo will reach 100 ft. (30 m) under good conditions. It forms a single, generally short trunk which penetrates to the top

KEY FEATURES

Nyssa sylvatica

Form:	Large tree with dense, conical crown tending to be flat-topped; **branches tending to be horizontal**
Trunk:	Single, straight; penetrating high into the crown
Bark:	Dark gray-brown, thick, furrowed into blocky ridges
Twig:	Slender; pale brown, sometimes hairy
Leaves:	Elliptical, smooth-edged; somewhat thick and leathery, **lustrous bright green above, turning scarlet**
Flower:	Inconspicuous; male and female on separate trees in spring
Fruit:	Usually **paired**, small, **succulent, berrylike, blue-black** in the autumn

but sour-tasting drupe, often borne in pairs, to 0.5 in. (1.2 cm) long, ripening in autumn; the pit inside is a slightly 10-ribbed stone. Black tupelo has a deep tap root.

Black tupelo makes a superb specimen shade tree, especially in naturalized settings, most particularly adjacent to ponds or streams. Its summer and autumn foliage color, combined with its form and size, create a beautiful effect. Because it is tap-rooted, it must be transplanted when young on soils that are moist and slightly acid. Alkaline soils will cause disfiguring chlorosis of the leaves and poor yellow autumn color. It makes a good residential street tree provided it is not subjected to pollution; it also benefits from some protection from winter winds. It is not prone to many insect pests or diseases. Birds and small mammals relish the fruit, and a good honey can be made from the flowers. Its wood is hard, strong, heavy, and close-grained, and is of commercial importance.

Osmanthus americanus (L.) a. GRAY
Oleaceae (Olive Family)
Devilwood

Devilwood ranges along the Atlantic seaboard from southeastern Virginia to central Florida, and westward into southeastern Louisiana. It is a fairly shade-tolerant understory tree of several forest habitats along swamp, river and stream valleys and upland slopes. Although it prefers moist, well-drained, slightly acid loams, devilwood can also be found on sandy soils where the water table is high.

A small evergreen tree to 30 ft. (9 m), devilwood has a single- to multistemmed trunk supporting a open, loose and narrow crown of slender red-brown twigs. It is often encountered as a shrub, particularly in less favorable locations. The bark is gray and splits into thin scales, revealing an inner bark of dark red. The evergreen leaves are paired on stout leafstalks, narrowly elliptical, thick, leathery, shiny dark olive green above, paler below. Flowers appear in late winter and early spring. They are small, white to yellowish, fragrant, and clustered in the leaf axils, male and female flowers usually on separate trees. The elliptical, dark blue fruit is about 0.75 in. (2 cm) long, and is a thin-fleshed drupe with a large stone, persistent on the tree through the winter.

Devilwood makes a handsome small tree, all the more so for its fragrant flowers. It is not widely used or available, but has considerable merit, especially for

Usually a small multistemmed tree, devilwood is often maintained as a large shrub for it fragrant flowers.

naturalizing. It has a tendency to be open-crowned, but this can be improved through yearly pruning.

Ostrya virginiana (MILL.) K. KOCH
Betulaceae (Birch Family)
Ironwood, American Hophornbeam

A widespread tree in eastern North America, ironwood ranges from Cape Breton south to northern Florida, westward to eastern Texas, and north to southeastern Manitoba. It is a very shade-tolerant species of many hardwood forest habitats, preferring the understory position along the upper slopes of

Immature male catkins of ironwood are typically borne in threes at the ends of fine branches through the winter.

river, stream, and ravine valleys, and on drier uplands and ridges. Ironwood can be found on a range of slightly acid to slightly alkaline soils, from sandy loams to heavy clays, provided drainage is good. It is common as a late successional to climax understory tree and may be found singly, in small groups or extensively in almost pure stands.

Ironwood makes a small tree to about 50 ft. (15 m). In youth its crown is conical but becomes more rounded with age, with wide-spreading branches that end in a delicate reticulation of slender branches. The trunk is generally single, often burled with age or developing a sinewy character. The gray-brown bark develops early, fissuring finely into thin vertical scales which lift at top and bottom, and flake off easily. The soft-textured leaves of ironwood are borne alternately in two rows along the twigs. They are generally elliptical, widest at the middle, coming to a sharp point, to 5 in. (12 cm) long by 2 in. (5 cm) wide, doubly and finely toothed along the margins. The color is a mid-green above, slightly paler and often hairy below, turning yellow in the autumn. Male and female flowers are not very noticeable and are borne in separate clusters opening in the spring. Male flowers are found in small catkins, usually three at the end of a twig, and are visible from early autumn until early the following spring when they elongate to release pollen. Female flowers are clustered in separate small clusters. The fruit is 2 in. (5 cm) long, growing in a

Ironwood makes an excellent smaller shade tree with a dense, rounded crown.

KEY FEATURES

Ostrya virginiana

Form: Small tree with rounded crown

Trunk: Single, straight, generally penetrating the crown

Bark: Thin, pale brown, **shallowly fissuring into, narrow, thin, short, exfoliating scales**

Twig: **Fine and slender**; shiny red-brown; **buds angled away from twig**

Leaves: Elliptical **sharp-pointed, double-teeth**; short, hairy leaf-stalk; **many parallel veins**; turning yellow

Flower: Inconspicuous; male and female on the same tree in same-sex catkins

Fruit: Small nutlet in an **inflated, light brown paper sac**, collected in a **pendant cluster**

pendant, vaguely conelike cluster of pale brown, papery sacs, each one containing a small, brown, oval nutlet. Overall, the fruit resembles a hop. Ironwood is a deeply tap-rooted tree.

Although never showy, ironwood makes a fine smaller shade tree suitable for many landscape uses, not the least of which is as a residential-scale shade tree. It is not prone to diseases or insect pests, except perhaps when severely stressed by soil compaction or flooding. It is also very wind-firm. Its winter aspect offers a subtle charm, especially if the delicate net of fine twigs and branches can be seen against the sky. Its tap root can make transplanting difficult, but when done as a small tree in the early spring the shock is lessened. The wood is very hard and dense, and has been used for items that must take a blow.

Oxydendrum arboreum (L.) DC.
Ericaceae (Heather Family)
Sourwood, Sorrel Tree, Lily of the Valley Tree

Sourwood ranges from southwestern Maryland to northwestern Florida, west to Louisiana and north to southeastern Pennsylvania, with scattered populations in southern Indiana and Illinois. It is a shade-tolerant tree of oak and pine forests, preferring upland ridges and slopes above rivers and streams facing south and west. It is usually found on moist, well-drained, deep, acidic soils ranging from coarse sandy loams to clayey loams.

A small tree to 50 ft. (15 m), or rarely half again

Crimson autumn foliage together with clustered strands of whitish-gray fruit are characteristic of sourwood.

as large, sourwood forms a single, straight trunk, penetrating high into the conical to rounded crown of wide-spreading slender branches and twigs. The brown-gray bark is thick, and deeply fissured into scaly ridges. Its sour-tasting leaves are narrowly elliptical, to 7 in. (18 cm) long and about a third as wide, very finely toothed, shining yellow-green above, paler below, turning bright red in the autumn. The white flowers are borne in midsummer, in pendant 10 in. (25 cm) clusters, the flowers arranged along one side of the stalks, reminiscent of lily-of-the-valley in their arrangement, shape and size. The fruit is a small, finely hairy gray capsule, narrowly oval, five-celled, and splitting open in the autumn to release many tiny seeds. The fruits are arranged pointing upright along a pendant stalk and are retained after opening into the winter. The root system of sourwood is deeply lateral.

Sourwood is valued as a an attractive ornamental specimen tree on suitably acid soil. Its flowers, leaves and form make it appealing in all seasons. It associates and performs very well with pines and oaks, as well as ericaceous plants such as rhododendrons and azaleas. Its is not frequently bothered by diseases and is resistant to insect pests. Its root system can make it difficult to transplant, however. Its flowers also yield a choice honey.

The narrow, leathery, shiny green leaves of red bay may be used to flavor food.

Persea borbonia (L.) SPRENG.
Lauraceae (Laurel Family)
Red Bay, Shore Bay

Red bay is distributed along the Atlantic coast from southern Delaware south throughout Florida and west along the gulf coast to eastern Texas. It can be found in a variety of mixed forest communities along the edges of swamps, river, and stream valleys, sandy uplands, and dune communities. It prefers moist, even wet, moderately acidic soils, and is somewhat shade-tolerant, but intolerant of drought.

Forming a mid-sized evergreen tree sometimes as high as 60 ft. (18 m), but often shorter, red bay has a straight single trunk supporting a dense crown. Its red-brown bark furrows into scaly broad vertical ridges. Its leaves are narrowly elliptical, to 6 in. (15 cm) long by a third as wide, leathery, with the edges curled tightly under, bright shiny green above, paler below with white or rusty-colored hairs. They are aromatic when bruised. The flowers are borne in spring and are quite tiny, light yellow, clustered together in a ball at the end of a long stalk at the base of a leaf. The shiny, blue-black, sour-tasting fruit is round, to about 0.75 in (1.8 cm) in diameter, with a thin pulp and single seed; it matures in autumn.

Red bay makes a handsome evergreen tree on moist soils, but requires some room to develop well. Its leaves can be used to flavor cooked foods such as

KEY FEATURES

Picea breweriana

Form:	Large, coniferous evergreen with pyramidal crown of conspicuous, **weeping branchlets**
Trunk:	Single, straight, penetrating crown; branches close to ground
Bark:	Smooth, gray to purple-gray, fissuring and scaling with age
Twig:	**Branchlets conspicuously pendulous**
Leaves:	Thick, blunt-pointed, dark green above, generally lustrous, and white banded below
Cone:	Red-brown, cylindrical, medium-sized, with rounded, smooth-edged scales

They are about 1 in. (2.5 cm) long, thick, blunt-pointed, dark green above, generally lustrous, and white banded below. Emerging new growth is pale green and beautifully offset against the darker foliage on mature trees. The mature, red-brown female cones are cylindrical, up to 5.5 in. (14 cm) long by 0.75 in. (2 cm) wide, but usually smaller, and have rounded, smooth-edged scales.

In its native habitat, Brewer spruce provides shelter and food to a variety of birds and small mammals. It plays a useful role in maintaining high-altitude watersheds and controlling avalanche erosion. Undoubtedly its major importance commercially is as an ornamental tree. Because the weeping habit is slow to develop on seedling-grown stock, it is often grafted from vigorous strong shoots, which will more quickly develop the very attractive weeping pattern. It is particularly pleasing with snow in the winter, or the new growth emerging in spring. Care needs to be taken, however, to site trees where they will have room to develop. Crowding, or being overtopped by deciduous trees, will ruin the form. They are still not overly common in cultivation, and the oldest cultivated trees are only a third to less than half the size of trees in their natural habitat.

Picea engelmannii (PARRY) ENGELM.
Pinaceae (Pine Family)
Engelmann Spruce, Mountain Spruce, Columbia Spruce

Engelmann spruce is found from central British Columbia and adjacent Alberta south through west-central Washington and Oregon, and along the Rockies into Colorado, with local, high-mountain populations into Arizona and New Mexico. It prefers

A dense, narrow, conical crown of blue-green needles is typical of Engelmann spruce.

high elevations, often in pure stands or mixed with other conifers, occasionally forming part of the alpine tree line. It is, however, also found at lower elevations, in cool valleys and north-facing slopes mixed with subalpine conifers, birches and aspens. It is shade-tolerant and a long-lived climax forest tree. It is commonly found on a variety of well-drained, acid soils.

Reaching 115 ft. (35 m), Engelmann spruce forms a majestic tree with a straight ascending trunk supporting a dense, narrow, conical crown, with lower limbs descending. The bark is initially red-brown, thin and scaly, but becomes light gray-brown and fissures into thin, loose, coarse scales. The fine needles, from about 0.75 to 1.0 in. (1.5 to 2.5 cm) long, are borne in spruce fashion and are blue-green, frequently powdered white, squarish, somewhat flexible, blunt to sharp-pointed, and tending to point forward along the twig. The mature, tan-brown female cones are also borne in typical spruce fashion. They are 3 in. (7.5 cm) long, with papery scales and wavy margins, ripening in the autumn and shedding their winged seeds throughout the winter. The root system of Engelmann spruce is composed of fibrous, wide-spreading laterals.

Engelmann spruce is an important timber and pulp tree in the northern portion of its range. It is also grown as a large ornamental tree for landscape purposes, and several silver-needled cultivars are available. It is susceptible to several insect pests and diseases, and is prone to windthrow. The Navajo used its branches in sweat lodges and for ceremonial purposes, and made various everyday implements from its wood.

Picea glauca (MOENCH) VOSS
Pinaceae (Pine Family)
White Spruce, Canadian Spruce, Skunk Spruce, Cat Spruce

A northern transcontinental tree, white spruce extends from Newfoundland to interior British Columbia and most of Alaska, from the limit of

The narrow, conical, blue-green crown of white spruce is an icon of many winter landscapes.

trees in the north, southward of Lake Superior and into New England. There are isolated populations along the Rockies in Montana, and in the Black Hills of South Dakota and Wyoming. White spruce is a shade-tolerant dominant climax tree throughout most of its range, associating with a variety of other conifers and northern deciduous trees. In the southern parts of its range it is also a pioneer species on old fields with other trees. It is found on a wide variety of soils, from well drained to poor, strongly acid to alkaline, provided there is sufficient moisture.

White spruce grows to 100 ft. (30 m) with a single trunk supporting a narrow conical crown of horizontal branches. The bark is gray-brown, thin and scaly;

KEY FEATURES

Picea pungens

Form:	Large coniferous evergreen tree; dense, conical to columnar
Trunk:	Single, penetrating the crown; lower limbs to the ground
Bark:	Flaky, thin, almost papery scales; red-brown to purple-brown
Twig:	Stout, **grooved, orange-brown** to **yellow-brown**
Leaves:	Stiff, very sharp-pointed, **silvery green** becoming green to **blue-green** with age
Cone:	Light buff to tan: **papery, flexible scales** having **wavy, somewhat bluntly toothed margins**

Normally having a fairly wide, conical crown, red spruce becomes windswept in exposed settings.

affect its appearance. It is also popular as a Christmas tree. In the Midwest and on the Plains it has been used in windbreaks and shelter belts. Many songbirds and small mammals eat the seeds, and larger mammals browse the foliage.

Picea rubens SARG.
Pinaceae (Pine Family)
Red Spruce, Eastern Spruce, Yellow Spruce, He-balsam

Red spruce is found from eastern Ontario to Nova Scotia southward through New England, and along the Appalachians into western North Carolina and eastern Tennessee. It is a shade-tolerant, long-lived tree of cool moist upland sites, often in pure stands but also associating with other climax forest trees such as sugar maple, white pine, yellow birch, balsam fir and fraser fir. It prefers cool, moist, well-drained, somewhat acid soils, often on rocky terrain.

Reaching 80 ft. (24 m), red spruce forms a rather open conical crown, sometimes narrow, sometimes wide. Its bark changes from a somewhat shedding red-brown in youth to thick, deeply furrowed, platy red-black at maturity. Needles are borne in typical sprucelike fashion, to 0.75 in. (18 mm) in length, stiff, sharp-pointed, shiny yellow-green, often pressed forward along the hairy twig. The mature female cones are 2 in. (5 cm) long, cylindrical, red-brown, with stiff scales having a smooth or rough margin. They shed seeds in the second year, and bear heavily in alternate years, or less frequently. The root system of red spruce is shallow and fibrous.

The wood of red spruce is used commercially for lumber and pulp. It is used for reforestation projects and occasionally for landscape applications, although not extensively, despite forming a handsome tree. Spruce beer was made from the young foliage, and chewing gum from the resin. It is prone to windthrow, particularly when open grown. Many small birds and mammals eat the seeds and larger mammals forage on the branches in winter.

Picea sitchensis (BONG.) CARRIERE
Pinaceae (Pine Family)
Sitka Spruce, Coast Spruce, Tideland Spruce

Sitka spruce is found along the Pacific coast from Kodiak Island, Alaska, to northern California, inland along streams and rivers for about 90 miles (150 km). It grows in pure stands or with other conifers and deciduous trees of the temperate rainforest. It prefers deep, well-drained gravelly soils, and a humid, cool atmosphere.

Typically growing to 195 ft. (60 m), Sitka spruce is the world's largest spruce and can attain even greater heights. It is also very long-lived, to 800 years, forming a massive trunk, frequently buttressed at the base, supporting a somewhat open elongated columnar crown with the main limbs horizontal and secondary branches often drooping. The needles are borne in typical spruce fashion, but are triangular in section, and flattened above, somewhat pressed forward along the top of the twig. They are 1.25 in. (3.9 cm) long, sharp-pointed, stiff and yellow-green above with two white-dotted bands below. The ripened female cone is typically sprucelike, to 4 in. (10 cm) long, light yellow-tan, with thin, loose and brittle scales having a wavy, irregularly toothed outer margin. They open in autumn to release their seeds over several months. The root system of Sitka spruce is fibrous, shallow and wide-spreading.

A long-lived tree, Sitka spruce grows to enormous heights on a straight massive trunk.

Sitka spruce is an important timber and pulp tree of the Pacific Northwest. It provided much of the timber for World War II aircraft, including the Mosquito. It is currently important in the making of musical instruments. Sitka spruce is widely used in reforestation projects, both in western North America and western Europe. Because of its size it is not used for landscape applications, although a few dwarf cultivars are available, and reputedly make appealing, slow-growing small trees.

Windswept whitebark pine is typically found at the upper limits of the tree line.

tions, reaches 50 ft. (15 m), but more often is a windswept tree or shrub to about 20 ft. (6 m). The crown is open, somewhat globular in youth, becoming very irregular with age. Branches are stout and dense with needles. The bark is smooth dark gray becoming fissured and scaly with age, turning red-brown. The blue-green to gray-green needles are borne in clusters of five, packed densely along the stems. They are stiff, pointed, about 1.5 in. (4 cm) long, curved along the stem in the first year, speckled with white resin, and retained for up to 40 years. The mature female cones are oval, to 4 in. (10 cm) long, red-brown, each stiff, thick scale with a sharp, narrow, bristle-like prickle. Bristlecone pine has a deep tap root.

The ripe female cones are purple-brown, globular, to 3.25 in. (8 cm) long, with thick scales, only barely opening. The cones drop off and are picked apart by birds and mammals seeking the hard, large, wingless seeds. Whitebark pine has a deep, wide-spreading root system.

Whitebark pine tends to survive fire better than other high-altitude trees, and is important in the maintenance of mountain watersheds, as well as habitat for mammals and birds. The seed may be eaten by humans. It has a rugged aesthetic that suits its habitat, but this does not carry over into commercial landscape applications.

Pinus aristata ENGELM.

Pinaceae (Pine Family)

Rocky Mountain Bristlecone Pine, Colorado Bristlecone Pine

Bristlecone pine ranges at high altitude throughout western Colorado, northern Arizona and northern New Mexico. It is found in dry, exposed conditions on very well-drained, sandy to gravelly, infertile soils on rocky outcroppings, ridges, cliffs, ridges and slopes, scattered with high-altitude pines, firs and junipers.

An extremely long-lived tree (2,000-plus years), bristlecone pine potentially, in protected condi-

Rocky Mountain bristlecone pine is extremely long-lived and with age develops an irregular open crown having some dead branches.

Surprisingly cold-hardy, bristlecone pine is planted as a slow-growing picturesque ornamental tree far beyond its native range, thriving as far north as northeastern Iceland. It is suitable for small gardens, particularly rockeries. It is an important habitat tree for birds and small mammals, providing both food and shelter. The needles of bristlecone pine are tart and somewhat bitter-tasting, but can be used to flavor human foods.

Pinus arizonica ENGELM.
Pinaceae (Pine Family)
Arizona Pine

Sometimes considered a variety of ponderosa pine, Arizona pine varies in features of the needles and mature female cones, as well as having a more southerly distribution. It is found in southeastern Arizona, southwestern New Mexico and adjacent Mexico as far south as San Luis Potosi. It is found as scattered individuals mixed with other montane conifers and broadleaved trees or in pure stands. It prefers deep, acidic, sandy to clayey loam soils, moist to dry, along west and south-facing slopes.

Arizona pine reaches 100 ft. (30 m) on a straight trunk supporting a conical to open, rounded, wide-spreading crown of stout branches. The bark is rough and scaly when young, but becomes deeply fissured into irregular, flaky, dark red-brown to orange-yellow plates. The needles are borne in bundles of three, four or five. They are stiff, dark green, to 8 in. (20 cm) long and much thinner than those of the ponderosa pine. The ripened female cones are conical to oval, and are much shorter than those on the ponderosa pine, to about 3.5 in. (9 cm) in length. They also bear a sharp-pointed recurved prickle, much more pronounced than on the cones of ponderosa pine. Arizona pine has a deep tap root and moderately deep-penetrating laterals.

Arizona pine is a valuable habitat tree for mammals and birds. The seeds are eaten by songbirds and upland game birds and small mammals. Larger mammals such as deer browse the foliage. The trees provide both protection from heat and nesting for

Arizona pine typically develops a high, open, rounded crown of stout branches.

a variety of birds. Arizona pine is also valuable in controlling erosion. It is not commercially available, except perhaps locally.

Pinus attenuata LEMM.
Pinaceae (Pine Family)
Knobcone Pine

Closely related to the Monterey pine, knobcone pine differs in overall size, habit and the characteristics of the cone. Its distribution is also much more extensive than the Monterey pine, occurring inland from southwestern Oregon to northern Baja California. It has a preference for dry hilly sites in full sun, and occurs in a range of woodland and chaparral habitats.

Knobcone pine's tendency to fork its branches is just visible on this young tree.

Knobcone pine reaches a potential height of 80 ft. (24 m) under ideal conditions, but is usually less. It is fast-growing in youth, and has a tendency to fork, producing two or three ascending trunks. The crown is broadly conical, but becomes irregular if it is on several trunks. The bark is thin and gray on young trees, fissuring and scaly when older. The gray-green needles are up to 7.5 in. (18 cm) long, slender, stiff and borne in bundles of three. The ripened female cones are conical, paler yellow-brown than the cones of Monterey pine, and somewhat larger, to 8 in. (20 cm) in length and a quarter as wide. They are borne in whorls and persist for many years. The cone scales on the outward-facing part of the cone are distinctly conical in shape, not rounded as in the Monterey

pine, with a pointed tip; on the inward-facing part of the cone, the scales are flat-pointed.

Knobcone pine provides both shelter and food to a variety of birds and mammals, which eat its seeds and nest in its branches. It is not an extensively planted landscape tree but makes a fast-growing, appealing tree for naturalized settings.

Pinus balfouriana GREV. & BALF.
Pinaceae (Pine Family)
Foxtail Pine

Foxtail pine has a restricted distribution, being found only in the Klamath mountains of northern California at high altitudes. It is found in dry, exposed conditions on very well-drained, sandy to gravelly, infertile soils on rocky outcroppings, ridges,

The new female cones (tip of upper left branch) of foxtail pine are smaller than the nearly ripened ones of the previous year.

Bright yellow male cones of foxtail pine are borne at the base of newly emerging growth.

cliffs, ridges and slopes, scattered with high-altitude pines, firs and junipers.

A potentially large tree in sheltered conditions, foxtail pine can reach 80 ft. (24 m) with a broad, dense, conical crown of upswept branches, making it larger than either Rocky Mountain bristlecone or Great Basin bristlecone, to which it is closely related. It is often windswept, stunted and gnarled at high elevations and consequently smaller. It has gray cinnamon-brown bark, furrowed and ridged vertically. Its dark green needles are borne in bundles of five,

---

KEY FEATURES

Pinus balfouriana

Form:	Moderately large coniferous tree with broad, dense, conical crown of upswept branches
Trunk:	Single, straight, penetrating the crown
Bark:	Gray or cinnamon-brown bark, furrowed and ridged vertically
Twig:	Stout **orange-brown, hairy**
Leaves:	Dark green needles in **bundles of 5 (4)**, stiff, sharp-pointed, slightly curved; **retained to 20 yrs**
Cone:	**Oval to elliptical, purple-brown to red-brown, scales bearing a short prickle**

---

occasionally four, just over 1.0 in. (2.5 cm) long, stiff, sharp-pointed, slightly curved and retained for up to 20 years. There may be a waxy bloom over the inner surfaces of the needles. The ripened female cones are oval to elliptical, purple-brown to red-brown, to 5.5 in. (14 cm) long, with the scales bearing a short prickle. The seeds are distinctive in being patterned light and dark.

Foxtail pine is cultivated as a slow-growing ornamental landscape tree, its long retention of needles giving the tree a denser appearance than most of the larger pines. It makes an interesting single specimen for residential properties, or in small groups for larger sites. Given its site preferences in the wild, it is highly unsuitable for dense, poorly drained, or wet soils, performing far better on rapidly drained, infertile sandy soils. It is a valuable tree in its natural habitat in providing shelter and seed to a wide variety of birds and small mammals. It is also valuable for providing control of soil erosion and in watershed management.

Pinus banksiana LAMB.
Pinaceae (Pine Family)

Jack Pine, Scrub Pine, Gray Pine, Banksian Pine

Jack pine is widely distributed in northern North America from the lower Mackenzie River valley in the Arctic east to Nova Scotia and south into New Hampshire, northern Indiana and Minnesota. A colonizer of poor-quality sites after fires, it often forms pure stands, or is mixed with other colonizing tree species. It is eventually replaced by shade-tolerant species that emerge from under its canopy and shade it out. It has a strong preference for poor, acidic, well-drained, coarse-textured soils, often growing on thin soils on rocky, rugged terrain and on permafrost.

Jack pine grows to about 70 ft. (21 m), and under good conditions forms an open, conical crown. In exposed or difficult conditions, however, it is gnarled and stunted with a highly unkempt-looking crown. The bark is red-brown and scaly when young, becoming thick, gray, and furrowing into irregular ridges and plates. Needles are bundled in pairs, with

An open irregular crown is fairly typical of jack pine.

a persistent sheath at the base, distinctly yellow-green, finely toothed, stiff and sharp-pointed. They spread widely apart and are often slightly twisted. The cones are 3 in. (7.5 cm) long, irregularly shaped, often lumpy, or curved and pointing forward along the stem in clusters of two or three, red-brown when mature and retained closed for up to 20 years. The root system is moderately deep and wide-spreading, occasionally with a tap root.

The wood of jack pine is used for general construction purposes, and pulp. It is widely used for shelter belts, windbreaks and mass planting on poor sandy soils. It makes a poor ornamental, except in its natural setting, where in its gnarled aspect it conveys a sense of rugged durability. It provides useful cover and browse for deer and other mammals. Kirkland's warbler, an endangered species, nests only in young pure stands of jack pine no higher than 20 ft. (6 m) and in excess of 75 acres (30 ha).

Pinus cembroides ZUCC.
Pinaceae (Pine Family)
Mexican Pinyon, Mexican Nut Pine

Mexican pinyon extends into the United States from Mexico to southeast Arizona, southwestern New Mexico and western Texas. It is found in association with other pinyons and junipers on hot, dry, well-drained, rocky to silty soils between 4,500 and 6,500 ft. (1,370 and 1,980 m) on mountain slopes and mesas.

Usually reaching between 16 and 26 ft. (5 and 8 m), Mexican pinyon has the potential in cultivation to reach 60 ft. (18 m). It forms an irregularly rounded dome of a crown on a short trunk. Its bark is scaly silver-gray furrowing to reveal a red-brown underbark. It bears its needles in bundles of three, occasionally two, with a small, curled sheath, which is shed after one year, at the base of the bundle. The needles are 2.5 in. (6.5 cm) long, stiff, sharp-pointed, and dark green. The mature female cones are red-brown to yellow-brown, broad and globular, 1.6 in. (4 cm) long by 2.2 in (5.5 cm) wide, resinous, with a small number of scales. The essentially wingless seeds are the largest of the pinyons, about 0.6 in (1.4 cm) in diameter and have a distinctive pink interior.

The seeds of Mexican pinyon have a sweet, oily, nutty flavor and are highly esteemed raw or roasted. They are gathered and sold throughout the range of the tree in Mexico and the Southwest. Birds and small mammals also eat the seed, and the tree itself

Mexican pinyon develops a rounded domed crown; the seeds from the ripened female cones are edible.

provides protection from wind and heat. It is slow-growing, but makes an attractive tree for appropriate soil conditions.

Pinus chihuahuana ENGELM.
Pinaceae (Pine Family)
Chihuahuan Pine

Often treated as a variety of smooth-leaf pine (*Pinus leiophylla*), Chihuahuan pine extends from northern Mexico into southeastern Arizona and southwestern New Mexico, while smooth-leaf pine does not. It is found in association with pinyons and junipers on hot, dry, well-drained, rocky to silty soils between 4,500 and 6,500 ft. (1,370 and 1,980 m) on mountain slopes and mesas. After fire it is able to sprout from the stump.

Chihuahuan pine reaches about 80 ft. (24 m) forming a high rounded crown on a relatively short trunk. The bark is brown-black, fissuring into scales and revealing a red-brown underbark in the grooves between scales. The needles are 4 in. (10 cm) long, smooth, stiff, pale green, waxy, and borne in bundles of three, or occasionally four or five. The ripened female cones are 2.5 in. (6.25 cm) long, egg-shaped, light chestnut brown, and contain tiny nutlike seeds. They mature in the third year after being formed and are retained on the tree for many years.

Occasionally grown as a slow-growing ornamental in suitable conditions, Chihuahuan pine is rarely encountered outside its native habitat where it provides shelter from heat and wind to numerous bird species and mammals. The seeds are also eaten by a variety of birds and small mammals. Fine specimens can be seen at the Chiricahua National Monument in southern Arizona.

Pinus clausa (CHAPMAN ex ENGELM.) VASEY ex SARG.
Pinaceae (Pine Family)
Sand Pine, Scrub Pine, Spruce Pine

Sand pine has a restricted and disjunct distribution of two varieties. The Choctawhatohee race is found along the Gulf Coast of northwestern Florida and adjacent Alabama. The Ocala race is distributed across the central Florida Sandhills. As the common name suggests, sand pine prefers sandy, acid, well-drained, nutritionally poorer soils. It is shade-intolerant and if not subjected to fire is gradually replaced by shade-tolerant trees that grow up through its canopy and shade it out. The two varieties are ecologically distinct in that the cones of the central Florida variety remain closed until released by fire, and thus it tends to form even-aged stands. The northwest variety releases its seeds as cones mature, forming more varied-age stands.

Sand pine potentially reaches heights of 70 ft. (21 m), but is often less than this, and has an open, rounded or flattened crown. Its bark is initially smooth gray, but later develops long, narrow, scaly

The slender, waxy, light green needles of Chihuahuan pine are also quite stiff.

The Choctawhatohee race of sand pine typically grows in uneven-aged stands, as shown here.

ridges, dark red brown to gray in color. Its dark gray-green needles are borne in bundles of two, and are slender, to 3.5 in. (8.5 cm) long, slightly twisted and parted, stiff and sharp-pointed. The ripened female cones are yellow-brown, narrow, oval, to 3.5 in (8.5 cm) long, pointing down, with the scales having a prickle. They are clustered in twos or threes and are either retained closed for many years or open at maturity to release the seed, depending on the variety.

Sand pine provides browse and seed for a variety of mammals and birds, as well as shelter. It is useful for reclaiming sandy, degraded sites and for windbreaks and shelter belts. It is not noted for being an aesthetically pleasing pine.

Pinus contorta LOUD.

Pinaceae (Pine Family)
Lodgepole Pine, Sierra Lodgepole Pine, Shore Pine, Mendocino Shore Pine

This is a highly variable species of pine, with four distinct subspecies. The two shore pines are located along the Pacific Coast, Mendocino shore pine being restricted to the county after which it is named. The other shore pine is found from southeastern Alaska to northern California. The lodgepole pines are interior, Sierra lodgepole pine being native from the Cascades of southwestern Washington through the Sierra Nevada and into northern Baja California. The lodgepole pine proper is widely distributed throughout the Rockies from the Yukon to Arizona. These pines occur on a wide variety of soils, from rocky coastal outcropping and sand dunes in the case of the shore pines to moist or dry sands and loams for the lodgepole pines. They all can be found on boggy soils. The lodgepoles are adapted to fire by retaining their cones closed until the seeds are released by the heat of forest fire. Then they rapidly germinate in high densities to colonize the burnt-over area. Thus they form large, even-aged pure stands. The shore pines in contrast are far less dependent on fire to propagate themselves and are

An upright narrow crown is typical of the lodgepole subspecies of Pinus contorta.

thus more likely to be found as scattered individuals or in small groups of less even age.

The lodgepole pines reach heights of 100 ft. (30 m) on very slender, straight trunks, bearing high, narrow, conical crowns. Shore pines are smaller, to 50 ft. (15 m), with crooked trunks bearing irregular, open crowns, often windswept. The bark is fairly thin, gray, and fissuring into fine scales to expose new orange-brown underbark. The green to yellow-green needles are borne in pairs with persistent bundle sheaths. They are 3 in. (7.5 cm) long in the lodgepole pines, shorter in the shore pines, twisted, stiff and sharp-pointed, but they do not spread apart as in the sand and jack pines, which are closely related. The mature female cones are oval, purple-brown, to 2.5 in. (6.0 cm) long, with recurved prickles on the thick scales, usually borne in clusters of two or three, pointing out from the twig. On lodgepole pines they remain closed until heated by fire or less often by direct, hot sunlight. On shore pines, they open more readily to sunlight.

Lodgepole pines were used to support the lodges or tepees of the Native peoples on the prairie. They are also harvested for their lumber, which is widely used in construction, for poles, and railway ties, as well as for pulp. The shore pines have been used to create shelter belts on barren, particularly wet and peaty soils. All these pines are susceptible to several destructive insect pests and diseases, and none of them are used for residential landscape purposes.

Pinus coulteri D. DON
Pinaceae (Pine Family)
Big-cone Pine, Coulter Pine

Found throughout the mountains and coastal ranges of central and southern California into northern Baja California, big-cone pine is found as scattered individuals mixed with other montane conifers and broadleaf trees or in pure stands. It prefers well-drained, deep, acidic, sandy to clayey loam soils, moist to dry, along west and south-facing slopes, but will also be found in fairly extreme, dry, hot conditions.

Although it has the potential to reach 80 ft. (24 m), big-cone pine is much more often only half of that, due to poor conditions, with a somewhat irregular, open, conical crown. The bark is gray when young, but becomes purple-brown to black with age, fissuring into broad scaly ridges. Its stiff, grey-green to blue-green leaves are borne in bundles of three, and are up to 12 in. (30 cm) long and slender. The ripened female cones are the most massive of the world's pines, weighing up to 5 lb. (2.25 kg), with a length of almost 14 in. (35 cm). They are light brown to yellow-brown, with very sharp, forward-pointed spines on the scales. The edible seed is also large, to 0.8 in. (2 cm) in diameter.

Big-cone pine provides shelter, browse and seed for a wide variety of birds and mammals. It is also

The ripened cones of big-cone pine are the most massive in the world.

an attractive landscape tree through all its life stages. In cultivation, it is adaptable to various soil conditions, and makes an open conical crown with bold foliage. It requires space to develop, so is more suitable to parklike settings rather than the typical residential site.

Pinus echinata MILL
Pinaceae (Pine Family)
Short-leaf Pine

Short-leaf pine is found from southeastern New York and adjacent Pennsylvania to northern Florida, west to eastern Texas, and north into southern Missouri. It is often found in pure stands or with other pines and oaks in a variety of forest habitats. It is often a colonizer of old fields. It prefers deep, dry, well-drained, sandy or silty loams.

Reaching 100 ft. (30 m), short-leaf pine forms a straight trunk supporting a narrow to broad open

In maturity, a broad open crown is fairly characteristic of short-leaf pine.

crown. Young trees retain the ability to sprout from the trunk after a fire or cutting. It has a red-brown bark furrowed into flat, vertical irregular plates. Its dark blue-green needles are borne in bundles of two, or occasionally three, and are up to 4.5 in. (11.5 cm) long, thin, and flexible. They are retained for up to four years, and at times will develop on the main trunk. The mature female cones are dull brown, to 2.5 in. (6.5 cm) long, narrowly conical, with thin scales bearing a small prickle. The cones open at maturity to release seed but remain attached to the tree for some time. Short-leaf pine develops a deep tap root.

Short-leaf pine is a major timber and pulp tree, its wood finding uses in a large variety of construction products, veneers, interior and exterior finishes, and furniture, to name a few. It is also widely planted in reforestation projects. It is important in providing habitat for many birds and mammals. It is not common in cultivation, however, as there are many other pines of more visual interest.

Pinus edulis ENGELM.
Pinaceae (Pine Family)
Two-needle Pinyon, Rocky Mountain Pinyon, Pinyon

Two-needle pinyon ranges throughout the Southwest, from eastern Utah and Colorado to Arizona, New Mexico and western Texas. It is found in pure stands or in association with other pinyons and junipers, particularly Utah juniper, on hot, dry, well-drained, rocky to silty soils between 4,500 and 6,500 ft. (1,370 and 1,980 m) on mountain slopes and mesas.

Although slow-growing, two-needle pinyon makes an attractive evergreen with a dense crown.

Mature and immature female cones of a two-needle pinyon; most commercial "pine nuts" come from this species.

KEY FEATURES

Pinus edulis

Form: Small, coniferous evergreen with dense, compact, irregularly domed crown

Trunk: Single, **often crooked**, short

Bark: Scaly, silver-gray, furrowing to reveal red-brown underbark

Twig: Stiff; stout; **orange** when young, turning a **blue** color; **bloomed reddish so as to appear plummy**

Leaves: Stiff, sharp-pointed, dark green on the outside, lighter on the inside

Cone: Red-brown to yellow-brown, **broad and globular**; small number of scales with raised outer surface and a tiny prickle; **large, edible, essentially wingless, dark brown seeds**

Two-needle pinyon is slow-growing and long-lived, eventually reaching heights of 35 ft. (11 m). It forms a dense, compact, irregularly domed crown on an often crooked trunk. Its shoots are stiff, orange when young, turning a blue color and bloomed reddish so as to appear plummy. The bark is scaly silver-gray, furrowing to reveal a red-brown underbark. It bears its needles in bundles of two, occasionally one or three, with a small, curled sheath at the base of the bundle. The needles are 2.4 in. (6 cm) long, stiff, sharp-pointed, and dark green on the outside, lighter on the inside. The mature female cones are red-brown to yellow-brown, broad and globular, 1.2 in. (3 cm) long by up to 2.75 in. (7 cm) wide, with a small number of scales having a raised outer surface and a tiny prickle. The essentially wingless, dark brown seeds are quite large, about 0.6 in. (1.4 cm) in diameter.

Two-needle pinyon is the source of most of the native "pine nuts" that are commercially available. They are produced by the trees in bumper crops on an irregular basis. The wood is also desirable as an aromatic firewood. In its native setting, birds and small mammals also eat the seed, and the tree itself provides protection from wind and heat. Wood rats have been recorded storing up to 30 lbs. (13.6 kg) of the seed in their caches. Two-needle pinyon is slow-growing, but makes an attractive tree for appropriate soil conditions.

Pinus elliottii ENGELM.

Pinaceae (Pine Family)

Slash Pine, Yellow Slash Pine, Swamp Pine

A large and fast-growing tree, slash pine ranges along the eastern coastal plain from southern South

An important timber tree, slash pine is a fast-growing tree widely used in plantations.

female cone is a shiny chocolate brown, narrowly oval, to 6 in. (15 cm) long, with the cone scales having a short stout prickle, and opening on the tree at maturity to release the seeds.

Slash pine is an important timber tree of the Southeast, and is often grown far beyond its native range in forest plantations for its wood. It makes a quick landscape tree, and is popular as both a specimen and for shade, but should be sited with care since it is shade-intolerant, and makes a large tree quickly. It is a very appropriate tree for naturalizing. Many small birds and mammals eat its seeds and shelter or nest in it. In Florida, it is the favored nesting tree of the bald eagle.

Pinus engelmannii CARR.

Pinaceae (Pine Family)

Apache Pine, Arizona Longleaf Pine, Engelmann Pine

Apache pine has a limited distribution, being found along the Continental Divide in the extreme southwest of New Mexico and in adjacent southeastern Arizona and northern Mexico south to Zacatecas. It is sometimes considered a variety of the ponderosa pine, which it resembles. It is found as scattered individuals mixed with other montane conifers and broadleaf trees or in small pure, open stands. Its seedlings spend a few years in a "grass" stage, similar to the southeastern longleaf pine. It prefers deep, acidic, sandy to clayey loam soils, moist to dry, along west and south-facing slopes between 5,000 and 8,200 ft. (1,525 and 2,500 m).

Growing to about 70 ft. (21 m), Apache pine has a conical, dense crown in youth, becoming wide, open and columnar with an irregular top at maturity. The bark becomes rough and fissured into large dark brown to black-grey plates, yellowing with age. Its somewhat shiny green leaves are up to 15 in. (38 cm) long, borne in bundles of three, occasionally two or five, and are stiff or drooping. The ripened female cones are borne in pairs or triplets, occasionally in groups of five, and are ochre-brown, oval, to 7 in. (18 cm) long, with small persistent prickles on the scales.

Carolina to southern Florida and west just into southeastern Louisiana. It is mostly found in pure stands as a shade-intolerant pioneer tree of burned sites, but is occasionally found mixed with broadleaved trees in later stages of forest succession. It prefers low-lying areas along the edges of swamps and ponds, as well as poorly drained ground, especially acid, sandy soils. It can be found colonizing old fields, or occasionally localized on upland sites with poor drainage.

Slash pine grows to 100 ft. (30 m), with a straight high trunk supporting a crown that is initially dense, narrow and conical, becoming somewhat open and rounded with age. The bark is orange-brown, becoming gray-black then purple-brown, furrowing into large scaly plates. The 12 in. (30 cm) long needles are a somewhat glossy green, stout, stiff and borne in bundles of two or three. The mature

Apache pine characteristically develops a very open, columnar crown with maturity.

The inner bark of Apache pine was eaten as a food supplement by Native peoples and the resin was used to waterproof wicker water-bottles. Many small birds and mammals eat the seeds and shelter from sun and wind in its canopy. It is uncommon enough that it is not commercially exploited for its wood. Although not often encountered, it makes a very bold, commanding tree in cultivation.

Pinus flexilis JAMES
Pinaceae (Pine Family)
Limber Pine, Rocky Mountain White Pine

Limber pine has an extensive distribution along the Rocky Mountains from southwestern Alberta south into northern Mexico. It occurs primarily as single trees or in open, small copses on dry, rocky, exposed sites and steep slopes, usually with other montane conifers and deciduous broadleaved trees. Limber pine is found at high elevations, from 7,500 to 12, 000 ft. (2,285 to 3,660 m).

A slow-growing and long-lived tree, limber pine potentially reaches heights of 40 ft. (12 m) in the wild, although in the protection of cultivation it may reach twice that height. Its crown is conical in youth, but more open, irregular and windswept with age, often retaining lower limbs that extend outward farther than the tree is high. The young branches are extraordinarily tough and pliable, and can be bent and knotted. The bark is smooth and pale gray when young, becoming shallowly fissured into fine, scaly, gray-brown plates with age. Its 4 in. (10 cm) long, slender, dark green needles are faintly lined in white, borne in bundles of five, and tightly clustered towards the tips of the current season's growth The mature, tan-brown female cones are narrowly oval, to 8 in. (20 cm) long, with thin scales, slightly thickened, and sometimes reflexed at the tip. They open on the tree to release the nearly wingless seed in autumn and then drop during the winter. Limber pine has a deep tap root and wide spreading deep laterals.

Many small birds and mammals eat the seeds of limber pine, and deer browse on the foliage. It is an

With age, limber pine develops an open, irregular, and windswept crown.

important habitat tree at high elevations. It is used for reforesting avalanche paths, and in watershed management at high altitudes. It is available commercially for landscape applications, and several cultivars, with either bluish foliage or dwarf form, can be found.

Pinus glabra WALT.
Pinaceae (Pine Family)
Spruce Pine

Spruce pine is found along the coastal plain from southern South Carolina to northern Florida and west into southeastern Louisiana. It is an uncommon tree, found singly in combination with other conifers and broadleaved trees of mixed swamp forests. It prefers acidic, moist to wet soils, and is somewhat tolerant of shading.

Growing to 90 ft. (27 m), spruce pine forms a narrow, elongated crown with branches growing out horizontally. Unusually for a pine, though not

Spruce pine often develops branches growing strongly outward horizontally.

uniquely, it forms minor branches between major whorls, like a spruce. Its bark is smooth and gray when young, becoming fissured into dark gray scaly ridges. The needles are up to 4 in. (10 cm) long, borne in bundles of two, slender and dark green. The ripened female cone is dull red-brown, narrowly oval, to 2.5 in. (6 cm) long, with thin scales having a deciduous prickle. They are borne nearly stalkless, tending to point back along the branch or downward, and may or may not open at maturity.

Spruce pine is sometimes harvested for pulpwood or lumber, and is occasionally used ornamentally for landscape purposes on suitably moist soils. Its seed is eaten by a variety of birds and small mammals.

Pinus jeffreyi BALF.
Pinaceae (Pine Family)
Jeffrey Pine

Jeffrey pine occurs from southwestern Oregon south through the Sierra Nevada into western Nevada and adjacent California, and south into northern Baja California. It has been included as a variety of ponderosa pine by some authorities. It is most often found as scattered individuals mixed with other montane conifers and broadleaf trees or in small pure, open groves. It prefers deep, acidic, sandy to clayey loam soils, moist to very dry, along west and south-facing slopes.

A large tree, growing to 130 ft. (40 m), Jeffrey pine forms a single trunk supporting a conical to columnar crown with an irregular rounded top when mature. Its twigs are stout, gray-green and bloomed violet becoming orange-brown. The bark is dark gray-black, developing fine deep fissures. Its stout, bluish-green needles are about 10 in. (25 cm) long and are borne in bundles of three. They have a fruity vanilla-like flavor. The mature female cone is light buff-gray to red-brown, about 10 in. (25 cm) long, ovoid when closed, broadly conical with a flat base when open. The cone scales have a prominent recurved prickle.

Jeffrey pine is a majestic and striking tree for the combination of bloomy shoots, long, stout, blue-green foliage, dark bark and sheer size. In cultivation

An enormous tree, sugar pine can reach heights of 240 ft. (73 m), although it is usually less than that. It forms a straight, high trunk, free of branches, supporting a conical crown of wide-spaced horizontal branches. The twigs are at first downy with red-brown hairs, but become smooth and orange. The bark in youth is gray-green, smooth and thin, but becomes darker gray and thick on older trees furrowing into scaly ridges. Its stout, twisting needles are about 4 in. (10 cm) long, borne in bundles of five, and are deep green on the outer surface, blue-white on the inside. They tend to press forward along the shoot and persist on the tree for two or three years. The ripened, brown female cone is large, often up to 21 in. (53 cm) long, narrowly cylindrical, relatively thin-scaled, without prickles, hanging down at the tips of branches.

Jeffrey pine is sometimes found growing in open pure stands.

it seems not to live as long as in its native habitat, and it requires careful siting with respect to soil in order to allow it to develop. Its cones are gathered and sold as ornaments, particularly at Christmas. It provides valuable habitat and seed for small birds and mammals, and is useful in watershed management and erosion control.

Pinus lambertiana DOUGL.
Pinaceae (Pine Family)

Sugar Pine

Sugar pine ranges along the Pacific Coast from southwest Oregon through California and into northern Baja California. Unlike other western pines, it has a strong affinity for moist, well-drained, acidic soils, particularly favoring north and east-facing mountain slopes. It is the world's largest pine with the longest cones.

The world's largest pine, sugar pine also has the world's longest pine-cones.

scales, which are somewhat reflexed at the edge when open. They are pendulous at the tips of branches, open when ripe, later falling off. The root system of the western white pine is wide-spreading and fibrous.

Western white pine has been badly ravaged by white pine blister rust, which can easily kill young trees. Programs to develop resistant stock have been developed, but the tree is also susceptible to several other diseases and bark beetles as well. Native peoples used the bark and resin for various medicinal purposes. The wood has been used for carving and a variety of interior trim finishings, and doors. In its natural habitat it provides shelter and seed for many birds and small mammals. If kept free of disease, it makes a beautiful, majestic tree, suitable for larger sites, but it is uncommon.

Pinus muricata D. DON
Pinaceae (Pine Family)
Bishop Pine

A rare plant, Bishop pine occurs on just seven sites along the California coast from Humboldt to Santa Barbara counties. It displays considerable morphological variation between populations, and the pine known as *P. remorata*, found on Santa Cruz and Santa Rosa Islands, may be a variety. It is also found in Baja California and on Cedros Island off the Mexican coast. Bishop pine is found growing on

A short trunk and broadly domed crown are typical of Bishop pine.

poor, acidic, sandy soils. It is highly adapted to fire and depends upon it for regeneration.

Potentially growing to 100 ft. (30 m), Bishop pine is usually considerably less high, with a single trunk supporting a broadly domed to narrowly columnar crown. The twigs are orange-brown, and the gray-brown bark is furrowed deeply into long, vertical plates. The 6 in. (15 cm) long, stiff needles are green to dark blue-gray, borne in bundles of two, rarely three, and are densely crowded on the twigs. The mature female cones are dark matte brown, conical, to 3.5 in. (9. cm) long and about half as wide, with sharp, often recurved prickles in the outer scales. The cones are usually borne in clusters, pointing back along the shoot or downward, and can be retained closed for as long as 70 years.

Bishop pine has been used to some extent on infertile sandy sites for reforestation, but this use hasn't become extensive. It is not widely available for landscape use. In its native habitat it provides nesting and shelter to a number of species of birds and small mammals.

Pinus palustris MILL.
Pinaceae (Pine Family)
Longleaf Pine, Southern Yellow Pine, Longleaf Yellow Pine

Longleaf pine is distributed along the coastal plain from southeastern Virginia to central Florida and west into eastern Texas, primarily below 600 ft. (180 m). It may often be found in pure stands, but also in small groves and individually in a variety of forest habitats at low elevation. It strongly prefers deep, dry, well-drained, acidic, infertile, sandy soils. It is shade-intolerant, and has an extensive seedling "grass" stage of several years as an adaptation to fire.

Somewhat slow-growing, longleaf pine reaches 100 ft. (30 m), forming a long, straight, branch-free trunk supporting a high, small, open and irregular crown of wide-spreading branches. It has very stout twigs and distinctive, enormous buds having reflexed white scales that provide some protection against fire. The bark is initially rough gray but

Long-leaf pine typically forms a long, straight, branch-free trunk, supporting a high, small, open crown.

becomes deeply furrowed into orange-brown scaly plates. The flexible, drooping, dark green needles are up to 18 in. (45 cm) long, and borne in bundles of three, arranged densely on the twigs. The ripened female cone is brown, narrowly conical, to about 10 in. (25 cm) long, each scale with a stout, sharp prickle. Longleaf pine forms a deep tap root during the "grass" stage, during which the shoot remains very short.

Longleaf pine is prized for its quality and is the major source of timber for naval stores worldwide. The wood is used in construction, for poles and for pulp. It is also "tapped" for its resin and the manufacture of turpentine. Because of its "grass" stage, a seedling that is kept containerized and then grown on to larger size often suffers later, usually by failing

to produce an adequate tap root. The tree is thus prone to windthrow. Consequently, longleaf pine is not often commercially available as an amenity tree.

Pinus ponderosa LAWSON
Pinaceae (Pine Family)
Ponderosa Pine, Western Yellow Pine

Ponderosa pine ranges from south-central British Columbia south throughout virtually all the western states into Mexico, and as far east as South Dakota. It is found in pure stands at lower elevations where forest fires occur frequently, but also exists in small open groves or individually mixed with

Ponderosa pine typically forms a columnar open crown, and may be found growing in open mixed forest.

Distinctive flat, yellow-gray, platy bark is indicative of ponderosa pine.

other conifers in open forest at higher elevation. It prefers deep, acidic, sandy to clayey loam soils, moist to very dry, along west and south-facing slopes. It is intolerant of shade.

Growing to 130 ft. (39 m), ponderosa pine can be larger on favorable sites, and can live up to 500 years. It forms a straight trunk supporting a crown that is

---

KEY FEATURES

Pinus ponderosa

Form:	Very large, coniferous evergreen tree; pyramidal, becoming columnar with an irregular top when older
Trunk:	Single, penetrating the crown; **lower portion free of branches**
Bark:	Rough, **purple-gray and scaly**; fissures into broad flat plates **turning distinctive yellow-brown**
Twig:	Stout, smooth, **green-brown**; eventually turning **red-brown**
Leaves:	Needles borne in **bundles of 3** (2 or 5), stiff, sharp-pointed, gray-green to yellow-green
Cone:	Narrowly oval when closed, **shiny red-brown**; scales having **thickened tip and sharp prickle**

---

pyramidal in youth, becoming columnar with an irregular top when older. The bark on younger trees is rough, purple-gray and scaly. As it matures, the bark develops deep fissures and broad flat plates, at first pink-gray or red-brown, but turning a distinctive yellow-brown with age. Its needles are generally about 10 in. (25 cm) long, although the variety growing east of the Rockies tends to have much shorter needles. They are borne in bundles of three, or rarely two or five, depending on the variety, and are stiff, sharp-pointed, gray-green to yellow-green. The bundles are densely packed and press forward along the shoot. The sheath at the base of the bundles persists after the needles drop, making the twig rough. The mature cones of ponderosa pine are narrowly oval when closed, shiny red-brown; the scales have a thickened tip and sharp prickle. They are often borne in clusters of three, and open on the tree to become a conical shape, dropping the seeds in the autumn. The cones fall later in the winter, often leaving some scales still attached. Ponderosa pine has a tap root and moderately deep laterals.

The wood of ponderosa pine is widely used for a variety of interior finishings, in cabinetry and for boxes and crates. It provides very valuable habitat to a wide variety of birds and mammals providing protection from heat and wind. Deer browse its foliage, bark and twigs; birds and small mammals eat the seeds. It is grown in windbreaks and shelterbelts in the Midwest and to some extent as a landscape tree, although it is really only suitable for larger sites. It is prone to a very large number of insect pests, and several diseases.

Pinus pungens MICHX. f.
Pinaceae (Pine Family)
Tablemountain Pine, Hickory Pine, Mountain Pine

Restricted primarily to the Appalachians from Pennsylvania south, barely into northern Georgia, tablemountain pine occurs locally in the District of Columbia, Delaware and New Jersey. It prefers

Found along ridges and slopes at high elevation, tablemountain pine forms a rounded to irregular crown of stout, very tough, horizontal branches.

higher elevations where it can be found in either pure stands or mixed with other pines along ridges and slopes. It prefers dry, coarse soils, from gravel to sand, poor, well-drained and acidic.

Tablemountain pine is a small tree, to about 40 ft. (12 m). In cultivation it can reach about twice this height. It forms a single straight trunk supporting a low, rounded to irregular crown of stout, very tough, horizontal branches. Unusually for a pine, it also forms small sets of branches between the main whorls. The thick bark is fissured, scaly and dark brown. Its dark green to yellow-green, 2 in. (5 cm) needles are borne in bundles of two, seldom three, and are stiff, stout, twisted, and smell of lemon when bruised. The lustrous, light brown ripened female cones are oval, to 3.5 in. (9 cm) long, borne in clusters of up to four, and often pointing backward or downward. The cone scales are thick and have a prominent, sharply pointed prickle; they only partially open when ripe, the cone being retained for many years on the tree.

Although an attractive tree when young, tablemountain pine is not often encountered in cultivation as an amenity tree. It is a useful tree for erosion control of barren soils on mountain slopes, and in providing habitat for a variety of birds and mammals. Its wood is not extensively used on a commercial basis.

Pinus quadrifolia PARL. ex SUDWORTH
Pinaceae (Pine Family)
Parry Pinyon, Four-needle Pinyon

Parry pinyon has a limited distribution, being found in southern California into northern Baja California. It is found in small open groves or in association with other pinyons and junipers, on hot, dry, well-drained, rocky to silty soils between 2,000 and 8,000 ft. (610 and 2,440 m) on mountain slopes and mesas.

While Parry pinyon can make a tree to 33 ft. (10 m) it is rarely this high in the wild. It forms a short trunk supporting a low, rounded crown, less dense than most other pinyons. It has orange-brown shoots covered in fine hair. The bark is initially smooth and gray but develops to become fissured, scaly, and red-brown. Its bright green to blue-green needles are typically borne in bundles of three or

Parry pinyon forms a rounded crown, less dense than other pinyons.

The saplings in the understory of pitch pine will eventually replace the pines unless fire occurs.

the trunk after a fire, forming multistemmed, shrubby growth. It also occurs mixed with other trees in open woodland. Pitch pine prefers poor, well-drained, dry, acidic, deep, sandy soils, and is shade-intolerant.

Short-lived and rapid-growing, pitch pine reaches 65 ft. (20 m), forming a short trunk supporting a rounded to irregular crown of wide-spreading branches, and producing several whorls of branches a year, as well as clusters of densely packed branchlets on the trunk. The bark is red-brown to gray-black, furrowing into irregular scaly plates. Its dark gray-green to yellow-green needles are borne in bundles of three, and are up to 5 in. (13 cm) long, thick, stiff, sharp-pointed and twisted. The ripened yellow-brown female cones are conical, to 2.75 in.

(7 cm) long, the tips of cone-scales thickened and bearing sharp, recurved spines. The cones are produced from a very young age, remain on the tree for many years, opening either at maturity, irregularly, or staying closed until opened by fire. The root system consists of a tap root that can reach down 9 ft. (3 m), and grow below the water table.

Pitch pine was once a source of resin, turpentine and tar. Knotty wood, rich in resin, was used for torches. It is particularly valuable in reforestation of barren, dry, sandy sites. It is prone to a number of diseases and insect pests, and is not highly regarded as a landscape ornamental, except perhaps in a natural setting such as Cape Cod. Birds and small mammals eat the seeds and deer browse the foliage.

Pinus sabiniana DOUGL.

Pinaceae (Pine Family)

Digger Pine, California Foothills Pine

Digger pine is endemic to California, distributed through the coastal ranges and the Sierra Nevada mountains. It is found as scattered individuals mixed with other montane conifers and broadleaf trees or in pure stands. It thrives on a wide range of sites, from moist or dry, well-drained, deep, acidic, sand to heavy clay, along west and south-facing slopes. It is also to be found in fairly dry, hot conditions, and is shade-intolerant.

Digger pine grows to 65 ft. (20 m) forming a sparse, open crown. The shoots are relatively slender, green with a white bloom in the first year, becoming purple-brown. The bark becomes purple-brown to black with age, fissuring into broad scaly ridges. Its flexible, gray-green to blue-green leaves are borne in bundles of three, and are up to 12 in. (30 cm) long, slender and drooping. The ripened female cone is dark brown, oval, to 10 in. (25 cm) long and slightly less than half as wide, on a long, curved stalk, with the scales bearing a stiff, often curved or S-shaped, sharp, clawlike spine. The seed is large, to 1 in. (2.5 cm) in diameter.

Digger pine provides shelter, browse and seed for

The slender drooping needles of digger pine are blue-green, creating a fine-textured crown.

An open irregular crown and crooked stout branches are typical of pond pine.

a wide variety of birds and mammals. The Digger First Nation relied on its seeds as a dietary staple. It is also an attractive landscape tree, changing its aspect from fairly dense when young to quite open as it matures. In cultivation, it is adaptable to various soil conditions, and of a height suitable to a variety of landscape uses from residential amenity tree to open, parklike groupings.

Pinus serotina MICHX.
Pinaceae (Pine Family)
Pond Pine, Marsh Pine, Pocosin Pine

Occasionally treated as a subspecies, or variety, of pitch pine, pond pine differs in its preference for wetland sites and in some morphological features. It ranges from southern New Jersey and adjacent Delaware south into western and central Florida. It is often found in pure stands along swamps, ponds and shallow stretches of water, or on moist, poorly drained, sandy, acidic soils. It is fire-dependent and will sprout from the base of the stem as either seedling or established tree. It also is shade-intolerant.

Pond pine reaches 70 ft. (21 m), forming an open, rounded to irregular crown. It has stout and often crooked branches. The bark is red-brown to gray-black, furrowing into irregular scaly plates. Its yellow-green needles are borne in bundles of three, and are up to 8 in. (20 cm) long, slender, somewhat flexible, sharp-pointed and twisted. The ripened shiny yellow female cones are conical, to 2.5 in. (6 cm) long, the tips of cone-scales thickened and bearing a weak prickle. The cones remain on the tree for many years, staying closed until opened by fire.

Pond pine is rarely cultivated, but is an important wetland tree, quickly colonizing fire-damaged sites, minimizing erosion, maintaining water quality and providing food and habitat for a wide variety of wetland birds and mammals.

Pinus strobiformis ENGELM.
Pinaceae (Pine Family)
Southwestern White Pine

Southwestern white pine ranges primarily in northern Mexico, but also occurs in the United States

Southwestern white pine forms a columnar open crown of dark green to blue-green foliage.

12 in. (30 cm) long, with thick scales reflexed at the tips. The cone opens on the tree to release the seed, which is about 0.6 in. (1.5 cm) long by 0.4 in. (1 cm) wide, with a rudimentary wing.

Rarely cultivated, southwestern white pine makes an attractive tree suitable for large, parklike settings. Native peoples within its range gather and eat the seed. In its natural habitat it provides shelter and seed for many birds and small mammals.

Pinus strobus L.
Pinaceae (Pine Family)
Eastern White Pine

Eastern white pine is found in east central North America, from extreme southeast Manitoba east to Newfoundland south through New England and into the Appalachians to extreme northern Georgia, and west south of the Great Lakes into northeastern Iowa. It is usually found as individual trees, and small to extensive groves mixed with a variety of deciduous hardwoods and other conifers. It may also occur as large pure stands. It is moderately shade-tolerant as a sapling and can persist for one or two decades in the understory of open woods, emerging into the canopy whenever an opening appears. Mature, thick-barked trees tend to be resistant to fire and perpetuate the local presence of the species after burning. Eastern white pine prefers moist, well-drained,

along the Mexican border. It is closely related to both the limber pine and the Mexican pine (*P. ayacahuite*), and is sometimes treated as a variety of the latter. It occurs primarily as single trees or in open, small copses on moist, sheltered sites, on rich, acidic, well-drained soils in valleys and ravines.

Southwestern white pine grows to a potential height of 100 ft. (30 m), but is usually about 70 ft. (21 m). It forms a conical to columnar crown of horizontal spreading branches. The shoots are covered in a red-brown pubescence, but become smooth and waxy. Its bark is gray-white, but becomes fissured into dark brown ridges with age. Needles are bluish-green to dark green, slender, borne in bundles of five, and are up to 5 in. (12 cm) long. The mature female cones are dark brown, narrowly oval to cylindrical,

Eastern white pine in settings like this one have high aesthetic value, and are deeply loved.

The slender blue-green needles of eastern white pine are retained for only two years; its cones are long and slender, with the tips of scales often gummy with resin.

acidic sandy soil, often on slopes, especially north-facing ones in the south of its range, as well as on rocky outcroppings. Typical of most pines, it forms an extensive symbiotic relationship with soil microrrhyzae (a fungus) that increases its water and nutrient uptake-capacity in poor, drier soils. In return the fungus is provided with carbohydrate largely in the form of sugar from the pine.

Historically, white pine was commonly found growing to 150 ft. (45 m). However, it has been heavily harvested since colonial times and now it is rarely found larger than 100 ft. (30 m). It grows with a straight trunk supporting an initially conical open crown of whorled branches. The crown becomes more irregular in maturity, with a number of stout horizontal branches, and an often flat-topped "banner" swept in the direction of the prevailing wind, particularly in the region of the Great Lakes. In forest conditions it is often free of branches for up to two-thirds of its length. The bark is initially a smooth slaty green-gray, becoming dark gray-brown and deeply fissured into thick vertical narrow to broad rough ridges. Its blue-green needles are fine-toothed, borne in bundles of five and are soft, fine and flexible, to 5 in. (13 cm) in length. The bundle sheath is quickly deciduous and the needles drop after the second year. The ripened, yellow-brown female cone is cylindrical, to 8 in. (20 cm) long, slightly curved, with thin scales that open on the

tree in autumn to release the winged seed before dropping off during the winter. Eastern white pine forms deep, wide-spreading lateral roots.

Once prized for use as ships' masts, the soft wood of eastern white pine is still extensively used for a great many products, ranging from trim, doors, millwork, dimension lumber, paneling and pulp to the manufacture of industrial patterns, toys and novelties. It is extensively used in forestry projects and is well loved as an amenity tree in residential, park and recreational settings. It makes a magnificent formal evergreen hedge, but is suitable to large sites only. Care should be taken with existing mature eastern white pine not to disturb the microrrhizal relationship with the roots by changing either the ground elevation or drainage pattern anywhere near the tree, or by fertilizing. Eastern white pine is sensitive to pollution, salt, drought and soil compaction, as well as susceptible to white pine blister rust and other diseases and insect pests, all of which limit its landscape usefulness on urban sites. Its seed is edible.

KEY FEATURES

Pinus strobus

Form:	Large coniferous evergreen; irregular, open crown in maturity, flat-topped "banner" with age
Trunk:	Single, straight, penetrating crown; often free of lower branches
Bark:	Dark gray-brown; deeply fissured into thick vertical narrow to broad rough ridges
Twig:	**Fine, flexible, smooth**, slaty gray-green
Leaves:	**Blue-green** needles finely toothed; in **bundles of 5**; soft, fine, flexible; dropping after **second year**
Cone:	Yellow-brown; **fairly long**; cylindrical, **slightly curved, thin scales** opening to release winged seed

Pinus taeda L.
Pinaceae (Pine Family)
Loblolly Pine, Bull Pine, Rosemary Pine, Oldfield Pine

Native to fifteen states in the American Southeast, loblolly pine ranges from southern New Jersey to central Florida, west into eastern Texas, and north from the Gulf coast into extreme southern Tennessee, Arkansas and extreme southeastern Oklahoma. It grows along river and stream floodplains into uplands on moist, poorly drained ground. It prefers deep, acidic, moist to wet, poorly drained soils, from sandy loams to clay. However, it is quite adaptable to drier, better drained soils as well. It is a common and aggressive colonizer of old fields and disturbed, especially moist ground, often forming extensive, fast-growing pure stands. Unlike other colonizing species of pine, however, it is not fire-adapted and is relatively shade-tolerant.

Loblolly pine grows very quickly, and may reach 100 ft. (30 m), although it is commonly less. It forms an open, lax pyramidal crown in youth, developing a clear trunk at maturity with a rounded, somewhat open crown of spreading branches. In pure stands, its trunk is often clear of branches for a considerable length. The bark is black and scaly when young, becoming dark gray to red-brown in maturity and fissuring into variably sized scaly plates and ridges. Its yellow-green needles are borne in bundles of three, very rarely two, and are somewhat stiff but

This picture shows male cones of loblolly pine, ready to shed pollen, and the emerging candle of new growth.

Loblolly pine is characteristically associated with river and stream floodplains.

slender, to 9 in. (23 cm) long and finely toothed. The ripened light brown female cones are conical to 6 in. (15 cm) long, nearly stalkless, with a raised thickening on the back of the scale, on which sits a sharp-pointed prickle. The cones open at maturity to release the seed but otherwise remain on the tree for some time. The root of loblolly pine is initially a tap root, but this is abandoned generally in favor of wide-spreading laterals.

Loblolly pine is widely grown in the Southeast in forest plantations for lumber and pulp. Although relatively coarse visually, it is useful in landscaping applications. In its younger stages it can provide quick screening, and in its later stages visual structure, to a landscape design. It has fragrant resinous foliage, which lends further sensory appeal. It will

KEY FEATURES

Pinus taeda

Form: Large coniferous evergreen with open, lax pyramidal crown becoming rounded, somewhat open

Trunk: Single, straight, penetrating the crown; free of branches in lower portion at maturity

Bark: Black and scaly, becoming dark gray to red-brown; fissuring into variably sized scaly plates and ridges

Twig: **Slender, glossy; olive-brown turning yellow-brown to red-brown**

Leaves: Yellow-green needles in bundles of 3 (2); somewhat stiff but slender; finely toothed, to 9 in. (23 cm) long

Cone: Light brown; conical; **nearly stalkless**; raised thickening on back of scale with a sharp-pointed prickle

transplant easily, but care should be taken not to use pot-bound plants. Such plants tend to have considerable difficulty establishing a wind-firm root system, and because they grow rapidly they often blow over within a few years of planting. Discretion is also advisable before using loblolly pine as screening near areas where it may become invasive.

Pinus torreyana PARRY ex. CARR
Pinaceae (Pine Family)
Torrey Pine, Soledad Pine

Torrey pine is endemic to California, and has an extremely restricted distribution. It is found on Santa Rosa Island and two cliff sites near the mouth of the Soledad River in San Diego County. It is found as scattered individuals in exposed situations or mixed with other montane conifers and broadleaf trees. It grows on a range of hot sites, from moist to dry, well-drained, acidic, sands to clayey soils, along west

and south-facing slopes. It is also shade-intolerant.

Torrey pine reaches a height of about 50 ft. (15 m) in the wild, but is usually less. It has a narrow, conical crown in youth, which becomes more rounded and open at maturity. The shoots are stout and green with a whitish bloom at first, becoming pale purple and ultimately very nearly black. The bark becomes red-brown and deeply fissured into broad scales. Its stout, gray-green to blue-green needles are borne in bundles of five, and are about 13 in. (33 cm) long. The yellow-brown mature female cone is oval, to 6 in. (15 cm) long, borne on a long, curved stalk, and bears small, short, stiff prickles on the scales. The edible seed is up to 1 in. (2.5 cm) in diameter.

In its natural setting Torrey pine provides shelter, browse and seed for a wide variety of birds and

Torrey pine is usually found singly, in exposed situations, where it develops an irregular crown.

mammals. It is also an attractive landscape tree, resembling a smaller version of Digger pine. However, it requires a more sheltered position in cultivation. It is adaptable to various soil conditions, and of a height suitable to a variety of landscape uses from residential amenity tree to open, parklike groupings.

Pinus virginiana MILL.
Pinaceae (Pine Family)
Virginia (Scrub) Pine, Jersey Pine, Spruce Pine, Poverty Pine

Closely related to jack pine, Virginia pine is found at fairly low elevations from Long Island to extreme

Like jack pine, to which it is closely related, Virginia scrub pine develops an open irregular crown.

northeastern Mississippi and northeast into southern Indiana. It prefers clays and clay loams, but will grow on well-drained sandy loams and poor, eroded soils as well. It can be found in pure stands, colonizing old fields and derelict agricultural lands. Being shade-intolerant, it is invariably replaced by later successional and climax hardwood trees, and can occasionally be found in later stages of its life cycle mixed with these trees.

Virginia pine reaches 60 ft. (18 m), developing an open, broad, flat-topped, occasionally thin-looking and irregular crown of straggling, outstretched limbs. On harsh sites, it is often shrublike. The brown-gray bark is thin, smooth and somewhat flaking in youth, fissuring into scaly plates and ridges as it ages, eventually becoming shaggy. Its dull gray-green needles are borne in bundles of two, with a persistent bundle sheath, 1.5 to about 3 in. (4 to 7.5 cm) long. They are stout, stiff, sharp-pointed, divergent and twisting, and carried for up to four years. The lustrous, red-brown, mature female cones are very nearly stalkless, narrowly oval to about 2.75 in. (7 cm) long, with a raised thickening on the scales and sharp, long, slender prickles. They are borne in pairs, sometimes in clusters of four, opening in the fall of the second year to release seeds, but remaining attached afterward.

Virginia pine provides protective cover and food to a variety of birds and mammals. Its chief non-habitat value is as a pioneer cover on degraded and impoverished soils in preparation for more desirable habitat and commercial tree species.

Pinus washoensis MASON & STOCKWELL
Pinaceae (Pine Family)
Washoe Pine

A rare and highly localized tree, Washoe pine is found in Washoe County, Nevada, and Warner County in adjacent California. Some authorities believe it should be considered a subspecies of Ponderosa pine, to which it is even more closely related than it is Jeffrey pine, which it strongly

An open columnar crown on a straight trunk is typical of Washoe pine.

resembles. It is most often found as scattered individuals mixed with other montane conifers and broadleaf trees or in small pure, open groves. It prefers moist to very dry, deep, acidic, sandy to clayey loam soils along west and south-facing slopes.

A large tree, growing to 130 ft. (40 m), Washoe pine forms a single trunk supporting a conical to columnar crown with an irregular rounded top when mature. Its twigs are stout, orange-brown becoming gray-white. The bark is dark gray-black, developing fine deep fissures. Its stout, bluish-green needles are about 6 in. (15 cm) long and are borne in bundles of three. The mature female cone is light buff-gray to red-brown, about 4 in. (10 cm) long, ovoid when closed, broadly conical with a flat base

when open. The cone scales have a prominent recurved prickle.

Washoe pine is an interesting tree for the combination of pale shoots, blue-green foliage, almost black bark and sheer size. In cultivation it seems slow-growing and requires careful siting with respect to soil in order to allow it to develop. It provides valuable habitat and seed for small birds and mammals, and is useful in watershed management and erosion control.

Planera aquatica (WALT.) GMEL.
Ulmaceae (Elm Family)
Water Elm, Planer Tree

Water elm is an uncommon tree found on the coastal plain from southeastern North Carolina to northern Florida and west into east Texas, as well as up the Mississippi River valley into extreme southern Illinois. It is found in a range of wetland and floodplain habitats, usually as a single tree widely mixed with other hardwoods. It prefers moist to wet alluvial soils, particularly those flooded annually by rising rivers and streams.

A small tree, to 40 ft. (12 m), water elm forms a single, relatively short trunk supporting a broad, wide crown of ascending main limbs. The mature pale gray-brown bark is thin and scaly, shedding in sizable sheets, revealing a red-brown underbark. Its

The mature bark of water elm is thin and scaly, shedding to reveal a reddish-brown underbark.

rough-surfaced, dull green leaves reveal many elm-like features; they are about 2.5 in. (6 cm) long and slightly less than half that wide, oval, short-pointed, with the base of the blade rounded, but unequal to either side of the leaf-stalk. The leaf-margin is bluntly wavy-toothed, each tooth ending in a gland. The one-seeded fruit is oddly shaped; it is about 0.25 in. (0.6 cm) long, pale brown, with many irregular protuberances or warty outgrowths covering it. It is dry at maturity in the spring, and is shed without splitting open.

Water elm is a botanically interesting tree, related to the elms and hackberries. It makes a dense-crowned smaller tree on moist to wet soils, but performs badly if subjected to drought. It is not commonly used as an amenity tree, although it is useful for providing species diversity in naturalization projects in floodplain situations.

Platanus occidentalis L.
Platanaceae (Planetree Family)
Sycamore, American Sycamore, American Planetree

Sycamore ranges widely throughout eastern North America from extreme southwestern Maine west through southwestern Ontario to extreme eastern Nebraska, south to central Texas and east to extreme northwest Florida. Isolated populations can be found in northeastern Mexico. It can be found in association with many floodplain hardwoods in a variety of habitats, most commonly as isolated individuals. It strongly prefers deep, rich, moist soils ranging from sandy to silty loams that are neutral to slightly alkaline, along rivers, streams, shallow lakes and swamps. However, it commonly colonizes well-drained abandoned fields in more upland locations, provided there is an adequate source of groundwater. It is moderately shade-tolerant and can persist for a time as a sapling in the forest understory.

A fairly long-lived tree, to 350 years, sycamore also grows quickly, reaching 100 ft. (30 m), occasionally half again as large. Its trunk becomes very

A short trunk and wide-spreading crown of stout limbs is typical of open-grown sycamore.

massive, to over 10 ft. (3 m) in diameter, and rises straight, penetrating high into the crown. It develops a broad, open, often irregular crown of massive, crooked and spreading limbs. The bark is at first smooth, mottled white, gray, brown and green, peeling off when white in irregular, stiff, thin patches to reveal the other colors. Eventually the bark becomes deeply fissured into wide scaly gray-brown ridges. The leaves of sycamore are large, to about 8 in. (20 cm) long, often wider, sometimes larger, very coarsely toothed, with three or five pointed lobes. When three-lobed the base is flat; when five-lobed, concave. The base of the leaf-stalk is hollow and covers a conical bud on the twig. Around the twig where the leaf attaches, a large, toothed, leafy stipule is often present in the spring but dries up and falls in the summer. When emerging, the leaves are covered in a plush rusty pubescence that easily comes off. The summer color is bright green, becoming tan-brown in autumn. The flowers of sycamore are not particularly notable: the female flowers are clustered in a tight sphere, pendulous, on a long stalk, on branches separate from the similarly arranged male flowers. The fruit is a large, firm, single spherical aggregation, about 1 in. (2.5 cm) across, of tightly packed tan nutlets, which hangs from a long stalk, and slowly disintegrates in late winter and early spring. The root system of sycamore is shallow and wide-spreading.

Sycamore characteristically develops peeling, multihued bark.

KEY FEATURES

Platanus occidentalis

Form:	Large deciduous tree with broad, open, often irregular crown of massive, crooked and spreading limbs
Trunk:	Single, **becoming very thick**, straight, penetrating high into the crown
Bark:	Smooth, **mottled white, gray, brown and green**; **fissuring** into wide scaly gray-brown **ridges**
Twig:	Stout, smooth, green becoming red-brown; zigzag; **buds conical**; no terminal bud
Leaves:	Large, **densely downy** when young; **3 or 5-lobed**; coarsely toothed; **stalk with a hollow base**
Flower:	Not showy, in **tight round single pendant clusters**; male & female in separate clusters on same plant
Fruit:	**Pendant, hard, dry, spherical cluster**

Sycamore in its maturity is a commanding tree, much admired, and sometimes as much despised. It makes a magnificent shade tree on appropriate large sites, and its mottled bark, often described as looking like "camouflage," is very appealing, especially in winter when the leaves are gone. In landscape applications, however, it is a very messy plant, since it is constantly shedding something of itself, and requiring clean-up. It is also prone to the disease anthracnose, which badly blights the leaves and makes them unsightly. In its natural setting its trunk becomes hollow and provides nesting for a number of birds and mammals. It is also notable for being one of the parents of the even more admired, and probably not so much despised, London plane.

A riparian tree, western sycamore typically develops a leaning trunk.

Platanus racemosa NUTT.

Platanaceae (Planetree Family)

Western Sycamore, California Sycamore

Western sycamore is endemic to California, and can be found from Baja California north to the Sacramento Valley and up into the foothills of the Sierra Nevada. It is found below 4,250 ft. (1,300 m), and is associated with riparian woodland habitat, preferring well-drained, moist sandy soils. It is a mid-successional canopy tree in open woodlands along river terraces above the flood level.

A long-lived tree, western sycamore reaches 100 ft. (30 m), usually having multiple trunks, often leaning or partially on the ground, and a high, wide-spreading crown. The bark is mottled white, brown and pale green, like that of the sycamore, but does not generally develop the fissured mature bark of the sycamore. Its leaves are smooth-edged, sometimes remotely toothed, with five long-pointed lobes, reminiscent of a maple leaf, from 3 to about 9 in. (7.5 to 23 cm) long and wide, bright green in summer, becoming tan-brown in autumn. They are otherwise similar to the sycamore. Likewise, its flowers and fruits resemble those of the sycamore, but the female flowers and fruits are borne in three to seven spherical clusters attached to a single long stalk. Western sycamore has shallow, wide-spreading roots.

Western sycamore is invaluable in maintaining riparian habitat for many small birds and mammals,

Arizona sycamore is often found as a tree of two or three stems, often with one stem partially decumbent on the ground near a stream.

as well as in erosion control and watershed management. It is used as a shade tree, and along streets in the Southwest as well, but it requires a fair amount of clean-up maintenance as it sheds bark, leaves, fruit and dead twigs regularly.

Platanus wrightii S. WATS.
Platanaceae (Planetree Family)
Arizona Sycamore

Arizona sycamore ranges from central to southeastern Arizona, into southwestern New Mexico, and south into northern Mexico. It is commonly found along streams in valleys and ravines, on deep, rich, moist soils ranging from sandy to silty loams that are neutral to slightly alkaline, at elevations between 2,000 and 7,000 ft. (610 to 2,130 m). It associates with other trees and shrubs of riparian habitats.

Potentially reaching 80 ft. (24 m) on a single trunk with an open, wide-spreading crown, Arizona sycamore is more often found as a tree of two or three stems, often with one or more of them partially decumbent on the ground near a stream, usually to about 50 ft. (15 m). Like the sycamore, it has mottled white, brown and pale green bark, but does not generally develop fissured mature bark. Its leaves are remotely toothed or smooth-edged, with five or seven long-pointed lobes, reminiscent of a maple leaf, from 3 to about 9 in. (7.5 to 23 cm) long and wide, bright green in summer, becoming tan-brown in autumn. They are otherwise similar to the sycamore. Likewise, its flowers and fruits resemble those of the sycamore, but the female flowers and fruits are borne in two to four spherical clusters attached to a single long stalk. Arizona sycamore has shallow, wide-spreading roots.

Arizona sycamore is invaluable in maintaining riparian habitat for many small birds and mammals, and for erosion control and watershed management. It is used as a shade tree, and in the Southwest as a street tree, but requires a fair amount of clean-up maintenance as it sheds, bark, leaves, fruit and dead twigs regularly.

THE POPLARS (*POPULUS*)
Willow Family (*Salicaceae*)

The poplars are a genus of about 35 species of trees found in the temperate regions of the Northern Hemisphere. Of these, eight are native to North America. As a group, the poplars often occur in pure stands, occasionally even-aged, or mixed with other deciduous trees and conifers. They generally prefer moist, well-drained soils. Some are found along the edges of wetlands and others occur in riparian habitats. They are intolerant of shade, fast-growing and short-lived, tending to colonize sites disturbed to mineral soil. Several species sucker from the root and form clonal colonies, and all have root systems that spread widely. Most species are usually replaced by longer-lived, shade-tolerant trees.

Normally medium to large trees, poplars may be smaller on less favorable sites. They tend to have a single, relatively slender trunk. The young

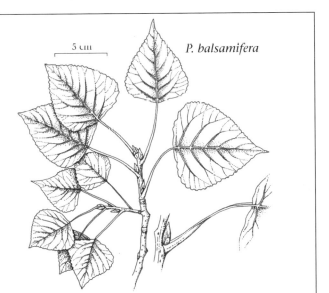

5 cm   *P. balsamifera*

Poplars have triangular-shaped leaves with more or less pronounced toothed margins. In some species, the leaf stem is flattened at right angles to the blade.

bark is thin and smooth later becoming thick and furrowed. Several species have large resinous buds. The leaves are borne alternately along the twigs, and are generally more or less oval with teeth along the edges, and generally long leaf-stalks, which are flattened in some species. Appearing before the leaves unfold, the flowers of poplars are tiny, without petals, and are unisexual, male and female flowers gathered into same-sex clusters on separate trees. The clusters are catkinlike and pendulous, a single stem having numerous, almost stalkless, individual flowers. On female trees the flowers are followed by small, oval, green capsules, strung like beads along a pendulous stem. They mature as the leaves are fully grown in early summer, and split open into two, three or four parts to release their cottony seeds.

Poplars are commercially important for their wood, which is used in the manufacture of a variety of items. Their wood is particularly valued for pulp. Because of their fast growth they are often planted as a crop for harvest. Some species are planted in windbreaks, shelterbelts and as amenity shade trees. Their tendency to develop widely spreading roots and to sucker requires care in siting them, in order to avoid septic beds and drains, as well as sewers and water lines which they can badly clog. In their natural settings, poplars are useful for retaining disturbed riparian soils. A variety of mammals and birds also eat the buds, twigs and seeds.

Populus angustifolia JAMES
Salicaceae (Willow Family)
Narrowleaf Cottonwood, Narrowleaf Balsam Poplar

Narrowleaf poplar ranges from southern Alberta and extreme southwestern Saskatchewan south throughout the American Southwest and into northern Mexico. It is a colonizer tree of riparian habitats, particularly on sandy soils, after floods. It prefers coarse, wet to moist soils, and is shade-intolerant. In the southern portion of its range it is usually found at higher elevations, from 4,000 to 8000 ft. (1,220 to 1,440 m).

Narrowleaf poplar is a colonizer tree of riparian habitats, forming a slender trunk supporting a narrow, rounded crown.

Fast-growing, short-lived, and potentially reaching 50 ft. (30 m), narrowleaf poplar is occasionally higher, and often much shorter. It forms a slender trunk supporting a narrow, rounded crown of slender branches, green turning yellow-brown in the first year, becoming bright ivory-white in the second. It may also appear more shrublike, sprouting from the trunk if the crown is somehow damaged. The bark is initially smooth, yellow-green to white-green, becoming gray-brown and deeply furrowed into flat, forking vertical ridges at the base of the trunk. Its leaves, resembling those of a willow, are narrowly elliptical, to 4 in. (10 cm) long, finel toothed, firm, bright shiny yellow-green above, paler below with a short, stiff, round leaf-stalk. The flowers are typically poplarlike catkins, opening in the spring. The fruit is also poplarlike, shedding the cottony seed in late spring. Narrowleaf poplar has wide-spreading shallow roots.

Narrowleaf poplar is an important colonizer of flood-disturbed riparian habitat, and as such is useful in erosion control and watershed management. A wide variety of birds and mammals eat the young shoots, resinous buds, catkins and bark. It also makes a useful, small, albeit short-lived, shade tree in the Southwest, and is planted around houses and as a street tree. Its wood is occasionally used as fuel and fence posts. Its inner bark was used by Native peoples of the Plains to prevent scurvy, and its young, supple branches were used to make baskets.

Populus balsamifera L.
Salicaceae (Willow Family)
Balsam Poplar, Tacamahac

Balsam poplar ranges from Newfoundland to the arctic slope of Alaska, from the limit of trees in the north southward into the Dakotas and locally just south of the Great Lakes Basin, with scattered populations across the Great Plains eastward into Pennsylvania and New York. It is common primarily in transition zones between boreal forests and tundra or prairie, often forming pure stands or co-dominating with other trees. It prefers gravelly or silty soil with abundant soil moisture along rivers, streams, lakes and swamps. It is an early pioneer tree of disturbed wet sites, and is shade-intolerant, eventually being shaded out by climax hardwoods or conifers.

Balsam poplar quickly reaches 30 to 100 ft. (9 to 30 m), forming a straight trunk and open, narrow crown of stout ascending branches. Its bark is smooth pale brown becoming fissured into flat, scaly gray ridges. The buds are relatively large and sticky from a yellow resin that is quite fragrant in the spring or after rain. The leaves are oval to cordate, to 5 in. (13 cm) long by half as wide, minutely wavy-toothed and pointed at the tip, lustrous green above, paler, almost whitish below, with an irregu-

lar rusty stain, and borne on a somewhat hairy round leafstalk with two glands at the base of the leaf-blade. Its flowers are borne in typical poplar fashion, male and female catkins on separate trees in early spring. The small capsular fruit is also typical of poplars, egg-shaped and pointed-tipped, splitting in two to release many cottony seeds. The roots of balsam poplar tend to be shallow, and to sucker forming a colony.

Balsam poplar is not a common amenity tree, although on the Great Plains where there is adequate soil moisture it makes a useful shade tree. It is an important riparian tree for stabilizing riverbanks and providing habitat and food resources for a wide variety of mammals and birds. It is particularly suitable for landscape restoration where soil water is adequate. Its wood is valued for high-grade paper and crates, as well as veneer, lumber, pulp and particleboard. However, it is not extensively harvested.

Populus deltoides MARSH.
Salicaceae (Willow Family)
Eastern Cottonwood, Eastern Poplar, Plains Cottonwood

Eastern cottonwood extends from extreme southwestern Quebec through the lower Great Lake Basin, northwest to southern Alberta, south to western Texas and east to northwestern Florida. It is usually divided into three distinct geographical subspecies. Eastern cottonwood is common in small pure stands or mixed with other riparian trees on moist to wet soils of various fertility and texture along seasonally flooded streams, rivers, and ditches. It is a pioneer tree of flood-exposed soils, intolerant of shading, and dependent on seasonal flooding to maintain its populations. In the absence of flooding it is replaced by more shade-tolerant species.

An extremely fast-growing tree to 100 ft. (30 m), eastern cottonwood varies widely in height depending on the subspecies. In the open, it develops a short massive trunk supporting a large, wide-spreading open crown of stout branches. In pure stands the trunk is higher and the crown smaller and rounded. Its bark is initially smooth, yellow-green

Balsam poplar usually forms a straight trunk and an open crown of stout ascending branches.

The leaves of swamp cottonwood have long leafstalks and blades almost as broad as they are long.

Florida to Louisiana, and up the Mississippi watershed to southern Michigan and northern Ohio. It is found along the low, wet borders of swamps, rivers, and streams (not in the permanently submerged soil), associating with other swamp trees, or in small stands. It is a short-lived colonizing tree with a preference for clay soils, intolerant of shade, and usually replaced by more shade-tolerant, longer-lived trees. It is classified as rare species by the U.S. Fish and Wildlife Service.

Attaining a height of about 80 ft. (24 m), swamp cottonwood forms a straight trunk supporting a narrow, open, rounded crown of stout branches and twigs, covered with white hairs when young. Its buds are large and resinous. The bark is smooth, thin and green-gray when young, becoming brown and furrowed into irregular, vertical, scaly ridges. Leaves are broad and ovate, to 7 in. (17.5 cm) long and almost as wide, gradually narrowing toward the tip, somewhat rounded at the tip, cordate at the base, with fine, incurved teeth, densely white-haired when emerging, becoming smooth and dark green above, pale and often downy below; borne on slender, rounded leafstalks. The flowers and fruits are typical of poplars, the seed germinating only on exposed wet sandy soil soon after it is shed in spring, before the leaves are fully developed. The root system of swamp cottonwood is shallow and wide-spreading.

Swamp cottonwood is very occasionally planted as a shade tree. It is of some importance in the nat-

ural maintenance of wetland habitats, because it colonizes exposed wet ground quickly from seed. It is more difficult to propagate from cuttings than eastern cottonwood, and does not sucker as readily. It is used in wetland restoration in locally appropriate areas. To wildlife it is of minor importance, because of its relative rarity. Similarly, it is of secondary importance for its wood, and where harvested is often graded and used as eastern cottonwood.

Populus tremuloides MICHX.
Salicaceae (Willow Family)
Quaking Aspen, Trembling Aspen, Golden Aspen, Popple

Having the widest range of any tree in North America, quaking aspen extends from Newfoundland to Alaska, and south from the northern limit of trees in two directions. In the west it follows the western mountains southward into California, Arizona, New Mexico and Trans-Peco Texas, and further into Mexico. In the east it skirts south of the Great Lakes from Iowa to New Jersey. It is absent from the Southeast and much of the Great Plains. Quaking aspen may be found growing in even-aged pure stands or mixed with other trees in a wide variety of forest types. It grows on many types of soil where water is not limited, and mean July temperatures not in excess of 75°F (24°C). It prefers nutrient-rich,

Quaking aspen often develops a spreading clonal colony from root sprouts.

well-drained, fine-textured soils such as silty clay loams derived from igneous rock such as basalt, or from limestones, with high organic content, where the water table is between 2 ft. (0.6 m) and 8 ft. (2.4 m). In elevation it occurs between sea-level and 3,000 ft. (910 m) in the north, and between 6,500 ft. (1,980 m) and 10,000 ft. (3,050 m) in the south. Quaking aspen is a short-lived, rapidly growing, colonizing tree of disturbed sites, and is shade-intolerant. Depending on conditions of soil, light and plant competition, it will develop a spreading clonal colony from root sprouts. Depending on plant community dynamics, colonies of quaking aspen may be replaced either by slower-growing, shade-tolerant trees where soil water is abundant, or grasses and forbs where water is limited; it may also persist as a stable cover until natural decline. Individual stems in a clonal colony are generally short-lived. In the east clonal colonies generally last about 60 years, while in the west they reach about 150 years and occupy larger areas. Some reach several thousand years of age. One male clonal colony in the Wasatch Mountains of Utah covers 17 acres (43 ha) and has an estimated age of one million years. It is, as yet, the world's most massive and oldest living organism.

Quaking aspen usually reaches about 50 ft. (15 m) in height, although twice this is possible, with a slender trunk supporting a narrow, pyramidal to rounded crown of relatively slender, smooth branches. Its bark is white-green, thin and smooth for a long time, eventually becoming dark gray, thick and furrowed. Leaves are thin, up to 3 in. (7.5 cm) long, roundly ovate, with an abruptly pointed tip and fine teeth, smooth green above, paler below, turning golden in the autumn. They are borne on long, slender, flattened leafstalks, which allow the leaves to tremble in the slightest breeze. The flowers and fruit are typically poplarlike. The root system is very wide-spreading and shallow, with sinker roots extending down to 10 ft. (3 m).

Quaking aspen is a much admired tree, appreciated in its natural habitat and planted as a fast-growing small shade tree. However, when stressed

KEY FEATURES

Populus tremuloides

Form:	Narrow, pyramidal to rounded crown
Trunk:	Slender
Bark:	**White-green, thin and smooth** for a long time, eventually becoming dark gray, thick and furrowed
Twig:	Slender, **smooth, red-brown**
Leaves:	**Roundly ovate**, abruptly pointed tip and fine teeth, smooth green above, paler below, turning golden
Flower:	**Dioecious, in catkins**
Fruit:	**Cluster** of small, **green, oval capsules**

environmentally, it is particularly prone to several diseases and insect pests. It makes an excellent wind- and firebreak. It is an important habitat and food-source tree to a wide variety of birds, particularly ruffed grouse, and mammals, notably beavers. It often plays a crucial role in the cycling of nutrients in forests. It is important in watershed management, facilitating groundwater recharge and modulating stream flow, and is used in landscape restoration and reclamation. Its wood is used for a wide variety of products from lumber, plywood and chipboard to excelsior, matches, furniture, boxes and crates. Because it does not splinter, it is suitable for benches and play structures. Whole trees can be chipped and processed into animal feed and biomass fuels.

Populus trichocarpa HOOK.
Salicaceae (Willow Family)
Black Cottonwood, Balsam Cottonwood, California Poplar

Black cottonwood ranges from Kodiak Island, Alaska, south into the mountains of southern California and northern Baja California. It extends

Usually found along the bottomlands of rivers and streams, black cottonwood turns rich gold in autumn.

usually located in riparian habitats along the bottomlands associated with rivers and streams, or on lower mountain slopes. It strongly prefers moist, well-aerated, nutrient-rich, slightly acidic soils, and is intolerant of shade, poorly oxygenated or brackish water, and drought. Black cottonwood is a fast-growing, short-lived colonizing species, which depends upon periodic soil disturbance to maintain its dominance. Without such disturbance it is usually replaced by longer-lived, slower-growing, shade-tolerant trees.

Black cottonwood reaches 100 ft. (30 m) in the north interior part of its range, and 200 ft. (60 m) in northern California. It forms a single, straight trunk supporting a narrow, oval, open crown of stout branches and large resinous buds, fragrant in the spring. Its young bark is thin, smooth, light gray to yellow-green, becoming darker gray and deeply furrowed into irregular, vertical ridges. Leaves are oval, to 6 in. (15 cm) long by half as wide, minutely wavy-toothed and pointed at the tip, lustrous green above, paler, almost whitish below, and borne on a somewhat hairy leafstalk with two glands at the base of the leaf-blade. Flowers and fruits are typical of poplars. The root system of black cottonwood tends to be deep and wide-spreading.

Black cottonwood provides valuable habitat for many birds and mammals, and bees use the resin as an anti-infectant in their hives, and to seal the remains of dead intruders such as mice, preventing decay and damage. Its wood is valued for fine paper, pulp, lumber, veneer, plywood, boxes and furniture. The Native peoples used all parts of the tree, especially the resin for medicinal remedies.

inland to southwestern Alberta, and south through Montana, Idaho and Utah into Nevada. Along the coast it forms large stands, often pure, or associated with other coastal forest trees. Inland it is generally found associated with canopy coniferous trees. It is

THE PLUMS AND CHERRIES (*PRUNUS*)
Rose Family (*Rosaceae*)

About 200 species of plums and cherries occur throughout the Northern Hemisphere, mostly in temperate regions. Of these, fewer than 30 are native to North America. They vary from largely shrubby species to forest trees, and there are

many that straddle the boundary between the two. Only eight species, which tend more consistently toward the tree form under good conditions, are discussed in this book. The tree species are often found along forest and wood edges, in hedgerows and along fence lines, and are commonly among the first trees to colonize abandoned fields or disturbed ground where soil and climate are favorable. Some species occur in small

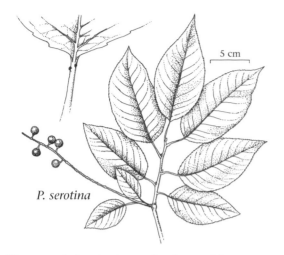

P. serotina

Plums and cherries have simple, oval leaves, usually with teeth along the margin. Two glands sometimes mark the leafstalk near the blade.

pure stands, but most often they are found mixed with other trees. The plums and cherries are fairly adaptable to soils that are well-drained and moist, and not too acidic. Some prefer cool soil, and some tolerate drier soil or short periods of summer drought. The native species discussed here are shade-intolerant, although seedling black cherry will persist for several years in shade. They are also fast-growing and short-lived, usually displaced by longer-lived, shade-tolerant trees.

Except for black cherry, which can be a large tree, the native species of plums and cherries are smaller trees, often multitrunked, with light oval-shaped to rounded crowns. Their leaves are arranged alternately along slender twigs, and are simple, mostly elliptical or oval, with small teeth along the edges, and often a pair of glands on the leafstalk below the leaf-blade. They often exhibit good autumn colors. The flowers of the native species discussed here are borne in the spring, and are five-petalled, white, sometimes fragrant depending on the species, and arranged in various kinds of small clusters. Each flower, has male and female parts in it. After flowering, the fruit develops and ripens in late summer and autumn. It is either a small plum or a cherry. Many are edible, although some are highly astringent. Several species contain high levels of hydrocyanic acid, which is noticeable in the smell of bruised tissues or cut bark.

Only the black cherry has wood that is commercially important. But several others are used as small ornamental landscape trees either for their flower and autumn foliage color, or for their evergreen foliage. The fruit of the plum species is locally important. These trees are variably susceptible to several diseases, notably fire blight, and insect pests can be troublesome as well. However, they are valuable in providing shelter and food to a wide variety of wildlife, and are characteristic of many rural landscapes.

Prunus americana MARSH.
Rosaceae (Rose Family)
American Red Plum, Wild Plum

Found from extreme southeastern Saskatchewan, eastern Montana and North Dakota, south to Oklahoma, east to northwestern Florida, north to New Hampshire, American plum generally skirts south of the Great Lakes, except for southwestern Ontario north of Lake Erie. It is found in a wide variety of open plant habitats, and along the borders of woods and forests, and in old abandoned pastures. It prefers moist, well-drained, sandy, rich loams along valleys and stream banks, but may also be found on drier, upland sites and mountain slopes. It is short-lived and shade-intolerant, and is usually replaced by larger, canopy trees.

American plum attains a height of about 30 ft. (9 m), on a short, crooked trunk, supporting an irregular, broad crown of stiff upright branches. It is often also found as a large shrub. Its bark is scaly and dark brown; its hairless, slender twigs are light brown, often ending in a spine. Leaves are elliptical, to 4 in. (10 cm) long by 1.75 in. (4.5 cm) wide, long-pointed at the tip, with fine, sharp-pointed double teeth, the veins sunken, matte green above and paler below. The white, plumlike flowers are borne before the leaves in spring in small clusters of up to five,

The white flowers of American plum emerge in dense clusters just ahead of the new leaves.

each about 1 in. (2.5 cm) across. They are followed by small red-skinned plums, about 1.0 in. (2.5 cm) across, having sour juicy yellow flesh and large flattened stones. The root system of the American plum is fibrous and shallow.

American plum is widely grown for its fruit and a number of cultivated varieties are available. In flower it also makes a pleasing small tree, and is much more resistant to diseases than many other plums and cherries. It is a valuable habitat tree to a variety of birds and mammals who eat the fruit or browse the foliage and twigs. It has also been used in soil stabilization projects, since it will spread via root sprouts.

Prunus caroliniana AIT.
Rosaceae (Rose Family)
Carolina Cherry Laurel

Carolina cherry laurel extends along the Atlantic and Gulf coastal plains from southeastern North Carolina south to central Florida and west to eastern Texas. It is found along the edges of forests and as an understory tree in mixed hardwood forests, often forming dense thickets. It is widely cultivated, and where escaped may be found along fencelines, where birds roost. It prefers moist, well-drained, rich soils, but is otherwise adaptable. Being fairly shade-tolerant, it generally becomes established as a late successional tree and persists in the understory of canopy trees as they shade it.

Carolina laurelcherry is popular in landscaping because of its glossy evergreen leaves and spring flowers.

Reaching to about 40 ft. (12 m), Carolina cherry laurel is frequently shrubby. But as a tree it forms a single trunk supporting a dense, evergreen crown of spreading branches, often irregular and weedy-looking. The bark is thin, smooth and gray, becoming fissured on very old trunks, and smelling distinctly of maraschino cherries when cut. Leaves are evergreen, elliptical, to 4 in. (10 cm) long by 1.5 in. (4 cm) wide, thickened, with the edges slightly turned under, smooth, glossy green above and paler below, aromatic when crushed, bitter-tasting and poisonous to livestock. The flowers are very tiny, arranged densely in a cluster along a stem, and borne in the spring. The fruit is a plum to about 0.5 in. (12 mm) in diameter, elliptical, with a thick shiny black skin, thin inedible dry pulp and large stone, maturing in the autumn and persisting through the winter. Its root system is shallow and fibrous.

Carolina cherry laurel is widely planted as an evergreen, broadleaved ornamental. Its use should be tempered, however, since it can be weedy and unkempt-looking without pruning, and is invasive from seeds spread by the many birds that eat its fruit. It is also poisonous in all its parts, due to hydrocyanic acid. In its natural setting it provides shelter and food to a wide variety of birds.

Dark green leaves and a profusion of white flowers in spring typify Canada plum.

Prunus nigra AIT.
Rosaceae (Rose Family)
Canada Plum

Canada plum is distributed mainly in northern New England, southwestern Quebec, southern Ontario, Michigan, Minnesota, Wisconsin and southern Manitoba. Sporadic populations are also located in Illinois, Indiana and Ohio. It is associated with a variety of forest habitats, frequenting moist, well-drained soils of river and stream valleys, along the edges of woods and in hedgerows. It is a short-lived species, with some tolerance for shade. It is usually replaced by longer-lived, more shade-tolerant canopy trees.

As a small tree, Canada plum reaches about 25 ft. (7.5 m); however, it often tends to sucker from the root in exposed conditions and form dense, shrubby thickets. It develops a short trunk supporting a narrow, irregular to rounded crown of several major limbs and stout dark brown branches. Its light brown-gray bark darkens with age, and is scaly and thin. Thorn twigs are present, usually with a bud at the tip. The leaves are elliptical, up to 5 in. (12 cm) long and about half as wide, broadest at the middle, with a long narrow point, coarse gland-tipped double teeth and paired glands at the base of the leaf-blade, dark green above, paler and often hairy beneath. The fruit is a plum to about 1.25 in. (3 cm) long with a red to yellow skin, yellow edible pulp and large stone. The root system of Canada plum is shallow, wide-spreading and freely suckering.

Canada plum is uncommon in cultivation, although one cultivar, Princess Kay, with double fragrant flowers, is commercially available. A few cultivars have also been developed for fruit production. Native peoples harvested and dried the fruit for winter use. In its native setting, Canada plum is eaten by a variety of birds and small mammals.

Prunus pensylvanica L. f.
Rosaceae (Rose Family)
Pin Cherry, Wild Red Cherry, Fire Cherry, Bird Cherry

Pin cherry is found from Newfoundland west into central British Columbia, and from the upper Mackenzie River Valley of the Northwest Territories to south of the Great Lakes and east into New

Common in hedgerows, pin cherry is usually a small, suckering, multistemmed tree.

England. It ranges sporadically throughout the Great Plains, and south of its main range in the east, especially along the Appalachians into northern Georgia. Found in a wide variety of forest communities, particularly those appearing after fire or logging, pin cherry is also common along rural fencelines and in hedgerows. It is widely adaptable to various soil types, provided drainage is adequate. It is flood- and shade-intolerant and is an early pioneer tree eventually shaded out by slower-growing, shade-tolerant climax trees.

Though often shrublike, pin cherry grows to 30 ft. (9 m) as a tree, forming a single short trunk supporting an open, narrow to rounded crown of horizontal branches. Its bark is initially smooth, thin and reddish brown-gray, but becomes fissured into gray scaly irregular plates; it is also aromatic when cut, and bitter-tasting. The leaf is lance-shaped, to 4.5 in. (11 cm) long and about a quarter as wide, with a long pointed tip, finely sharp-pointed teeth, and two glands below the base of the leaf-blade on the leafstalk. The summer color is shiny green above and paler below, becoming yellow-orange in autumn. The white cherrylike flowers are about 0.5 in. (12 cm) across and borne in clusters of up to five in the spring with the emerging leaves. The fruit is a small red cherry to about 0.25 in. (6 mm) across with a thin sour pulp and large stone. The root system of pin cherry is shallow, wide-spreading and prone to suckering.

Pin cherry is a valuable early colonizer of fire-disturbed or logged sites, quickly establishing itself and minimizing soil erosion, water runoff and nutrient loss. Its fruits are eaten by a wide variety of birds and mammals. Its wood is not considered economically important, nor is it planted as an amenity landscape tree. However, it is used as a grafting understock for sour cherry.

Prunus serotina EHRH.
Rosaceae (Rose Family)
Black Cherry

Black cherry has a wide distribution from Nova Scotia west through southwestern Quebec and

In the open, black cherry forms a wide, irregular crown on a short single trunk.

The flowers of black cherry are borne in many-flowered clusters in late spring after leaf emergence.

southern Ontario to Minnesota south to eastern Texas and east to central Florida. Several geographic varieties occur in Trans Pecos, Texas, New Mexico and Arizona, as well as central Mexico and Guatemala. It occurs as scattered individuals mixed with a variety of other hardwoods throughout its range. It prefers moist, well-drained, slightly acidic soils out of river and stream floodplains. Black cherry is shade-intolerant and regarded as a gap-phase species. Seedlings can persist in the understory for about five years, and if an opening appears in the canopy, these seedlings will rapidly grow and fill the gap, overtopping the saplings of slower-growing shade-tolerant species. Thus it is rarely present in the canopy of mature forests. In secondary forests, it may be fairly common in mid-succession, sometimes forming pure stands before the climax trees emerge from below its canopy and shade it out.

At its tallest, black cherry reaches 120 ft. (36 m), generally forming a single straight trunk. In a forest setting its trunk is high, supporting a narrow oval crown, while in the open its trunk is shorter and broader, and the crown is wider, and more irregular. Its bark is initially thin, smooth and dark red-brown to almost black, becoming fissured and irregularly scaly, but remaining thin. It develops an appearance of having been fire-scorched, and when cut has a cherrylike odor and bitter taste. Leaves are elliptical to 5 in. (13 cm) long by 2 in. (5 cm) wide, with a pointed tip, fine incurved blunt-pointed teeth and one or two deep red glands at the base of

the blade on the leafstalk. The leaves are glossy green above, paler below, with persistent white- to orange- to rust-colored hairs along the mid-rib, becoming yellow to yellow-red in the autumn. They are also cherry-scented and bitter-tasting when crushed. The white, cherrylike flowers are small, to about 0.375 in. (10 mm) in diameter and borne in many-flowered clusters along a drooping stem in late spring, well after the leaves begin to emerge. The

KEY FEATURES

Prunus serotina

Form:	Narrow oval crown
Trunk:	Single straight
Bark:	Initially thin, smooth and dark red-brown to **almost black, becoming fissured** and irregularly scaly
Twig:	Slender
Leaves:	Elliptical, 1 **or 2 deep red glands at the base of the blade on the leafstalk, cherry-scented**
Flower:	White, borne in **many-flowered clusters along a drooping stem** in late spring
Fruit:	Small cherry, **dark red turning black with a somewhat bitter, juicy** and edible pulp

Coastal Douglas fir has a narrow crown and sheds lower limbs as it grows, to create a high branch-free trunk.

Idaho northward; southward it is more scattered and restricted to mountain topography. Both varieties are found in a wide range of forest types, primarily in association with other coniferous trees, but also with some deciduous trees; both grow on a variety of soils, and will tolerate dry conditions, but prefer moist, well-aerated, deep, nutrient-rich soils, with an acidity between pH 5 and 6. Coast Douglas fir prefers a moist, mild maritime climate and grows between sea level and about 5,000 ft. (1,525 m) in the north, while in the south both lower and upper altitude limits increase. It will also not tolerate temperatures below 14° F (minus 10° C) for more than a week. Rocky Mountain Douglas fir occurs at low to middle elevations and is more frost-hardy. While both varieties are long-lived and may become the dominant climax forest tree, this tendency is more common for the Rocky Mountain Douglas fir. Coast Douglas fir is more likely to be a successional species. Usually, it is either replaced in the long run by more

shade-tolerant trees, or disturbed by fire or logging, after which it re-establishes itself in even-aged stands. On drier sites without disturbance it can form climax forest.

Douglas fir is a medium to large tree. The coastal variety grows to about 250 ft. (76 m), while the Rocky Mountain variety reaches about 120 ft. (36 m). In the open, young trees retain their branches close to the ground, while in forested settings the lower limbs are very gradually shed to create a straight massive trunk and high, relatively narrow, pyramidal crown. The bark on young trees is gray, thin and smooth, spotted with resin blisters, but becomes very thick, deeply furrowed and corky. Needles are yellow-green, to about 1 in. (2.5 cm) long, set spirally

The distinctive cones of Douglas fir have prominent trident bracts poking between the scales.

KEY FEATURES

Pseudotsuga menziesii

Form: Conical, somewhat open
Trunk: Straight, penetrating crown
Bark: Gray, thin and smooth, spotted with
         resin blisters, becoming very thick,
         deeply furrowed and corky
Twig: Slender with **sharp-pointed
         slender red-brown buds**
Leaves: **Yellow-green**, set spirally around
         the branches
Cone: Red-brown, hanging downward with
         exserted trident bracts associated
         with each cone scale

around the branches. The mature, red-brown female cones are 2 to 4 in. (5 to 10 cm) long, and are primarily borne on the tips of higher branches and hang downward. They have exserted trident bracts associated with each cone scale, giving the cone a bristly appearance. The root system of Douglas fir is shallow, and wide-spreading.

Douglas fir is the most utilized timber tree in North America, particularly the coastal variety. It is used for dimensional lumber, plywood, timbers and pilings, posts, poles, flooring, veneer, pulp and furniture. It is also extensively grown for reforestation, as a landscape amenity tree, in mass plantings, for windbreaks and as a Christmas tree. Native peoples used the wood of Douglas fir for many everyday implements, and the resin in the preparation of medicinal salves. In its natural setting it provides shelter for many mammals and birds. In the coastal forests it is also an important host for epiphytic mosses, ferns and lichens. Its seed is an important source of food to many small mammals, which cache whole cones, as well as to many birds.

Ptelea trifoliata L.
Rutaceae (Rue Family)
Hop Tree, Wafer Ash, Stinking Ash, Water Ash

Hop tree has a widespread, discontinuous distribution, extending from extreme southwestern Ontario through western New York to New Jersey and south into Florida, west to Texas and north to southern Wisconsin. In addition, there are local populations west from Texas into Arizona and north to southern Utah. Hop tree is found as a small understory tree or edge tree of forests and woods in a number of hardwood forest types. It has a strong preference for moist to dry, well-drained, neutral sandy loams to

Usually a multistemmed small tree, hoptree develops waferlike green-white fruits in the autumn.

coarse gravelly soils, on upland sites. It is tolerant of shade but not flooding.

Growing to 20 ft. (6 m), hop tree forms a single, short, often crooked trunk supporting a narrow to rounded crown of twisting interwoven branches. It also occurs at times as a large shrub. The bark is dark gray-brown, thin, usually somewhat scaly, and very aromatic, smelling somewhat skunklike when cut or bruised. The leaf is also aromatic when bruised and comprises three elliptical, smooth-edged leaflets, each about 2 in. (5 cm) long, joined at a common point at the end of a long leafstalk. Leaves are hairy when young, becoming smooth dark green above, paler below, and turning yellow in the autumn. The flowers are borne in clusters at the ends of twigs in spring and are green-white, tiny and not visually notable. The fruit is a 1-inch (2.5 cm) disk-shaped samara, waferlike, with a central body surrounded by a papery wing. It is initially white-green but becomes dry and yellow-brown, persisting on the plant until late autumn. The root system of the hop tree is variably shallow to deep-rooted.

Hop tree is often grown as a small tree or large shrub for shady places. Its odor when bruised is considered by most people to be rank, which limits its usefulness. The bitter flavor of the fruits led to its use as a hops substitute by early pioneers.

THE OAKS (*QUERCUS*)
Beech Family (*Fagaceae*)

The oaks comprise a large and important genus, numbering over 200 species thoughout the world. They include mostly trees, along with some shrubs. They are by and large Northern Hemisphere plants, being found in temperate regions, as well as tropical areas of southeastern Asia, Central and South America. There are between 75 and 80 species native to North America, with about 40 to 45 that are trees. The oaks interbreed fairly freely where their ranges overlap, and this has contributed for a long time to the difficulty in determining the limits of some species. As a result, the exact number recognized as species has been changing over the years, and this process is still continuing. The horticultural trades have yet to fully adopt some of the changes in status, and this adds to the confusion.

The native tree oaks occur in a variety of habitats from the borders of swamps to dry uplands, from areas with cold winters or hot summers to those with maritime or subtropical conditions. Most, but not all, prefer deep, moist, well-drained soils, often fairly acidic and nutrient-deficient. They are rarely encountered in pure stands, being more commonly mixed with other hardwoods and, in some habitats, with conifers such as pines. Many,

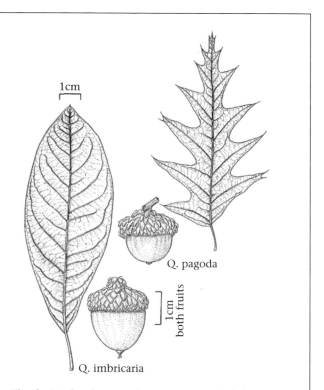

1cm

Q. pagoda

1cm both fruits

Q. imbricaria

The fruit of oaks are always acorns. Oak leaves vary from smooth-edged and simple to pinnately lobed and toothed.

but not all, are fairly shade-tolerant as saplings, and can persist in the forest understory until gaps appear in the canopy that they can exploit. A large number of the native tree oaks appear later in the successional process, and some persist and become a characteristic tree of climax forests.

A significant number of the native tree oaks are majestic and tall with wide-spreading crowns when open-growing. There are others that, while definitely trees at maturity, are shabby in comparison. They all tend to be rather twiggy, but somehow on the larger, more stately trees, this lends additional character. The same characteristic on the less appealing oaks only seems to emphasize their sometimes unkempt appearance. Still, every oak has its aficionados, and this is part of their power over the human imagination. The bark of the tree oaks is usually rugged, fissured and often thick. Leaves are borne alternately on the twig, but tend to be clustered, along with buds, toward the tip of the current season's growth. Leaves are evergreen to near-evergreen in some species, and belatedly deciduous in many others. The shape of oak leaves is highly variable from species to species, and there is a strong tendency in some species for juvenile leaves to be visually distinct from mature leaves. Many species have pinnately lobed leaves with coarse, bristle-tipped teeth, but some have simple, smooth-edged and narrowly elliptical leaves; and then there are those whose leaves strongly resemble those of other species, such as the chestnuts, willow and maple. The flowers of the oaks are characteristically tiny, unisexual, and without petals. They usually appear as the leaves are beginning to unfold in the spring. Male and female flowers appear on the same tree, the male flowers attached to long, slender, pendulous stems gathered into clusters, and the females borne solitary or in clusters elsewhere on short, stout stalks. Female flowers give rise later in the autumn to acorns the size, shape and color of which are characteristic of the species. Acorns have a "cap" of many tiny, partially or entirely fused bracts, which are also characteristic of the species. Oaks typically have deep root systems, often being tap-rooted.

Oaks are one of the few groups of trees which command human attention as much for their symbolism as for their economic value. A byword for strength, durability, integrity and longevity, the oaks have been esteemed, and in the past held divine in many cultures. The genus name, *Quercus*, derives from a word for lightning-bolt, in reference to tap-rooted oaks being preferentially struck by lightning, the sacred weapon of many sky-gods. Mythology aside, several of the larger native tree oaks are highly valued for the quality of their wood, which is used in a large array of products. The bark and leaves of some have been used in tanning, and a few have edible acorns, although some need to be leached of their tannic acid. Many of the native tree oaks are also valued as landscape amenity trees, for shade, and specimens, particularly on larger sites. A few are suitable urban street trees. Those with evergreen foliage are valuable for providing year-round interest and there are several that have good autumn foliage color. Several of the oaks are useful to slope and soil retention because of their deep root systems The acorns of the more common oaks are a very important food for a large number of birds, including waterfowl, as well as many mammals, and the trees themselves provide cover and nesting to many animals.

Quercus alba L.
Fagaceae (Beech Family)
White Oak, Stave Oak

White oak ranges from southeastern Minnesota eastward to southwestern Maine, with an extension along the St. Lawrence River into southeastern Quebec, south to northwestern Florida and west into eastern Texas. It is largely absent from the lower Mississippi River floodplain and delta, as well as from the coastal areas of the Gulf of Mexico. It is a dominant tree in many hardwood plant communities. In the south it occurs at times in pure stands, but northward this becomes increasingly rare. While it grows best on deep, well-drained, moist loams, white oak is found on a wide variety of soils, including gravelly and rocky soil, provided it is deep and well-drained. It is tolerant of drought, but not of wet ground or

In the open, the trunk of white oak is short and thick, supporting a wide-spreading, dense crown.

wide straight trunk. In the open the trunk is shorter and thick, supporting a wide-spreading, dense crown of stout limbs. In forested settings, the trunk is slimmer, and the crown higher, smaller and more compact. Its light gray bark is fissured shallowly into wide, long, vertical, scaly or platy ridges. Leaves are classically oaklike, to about 9 in. (23 cm) long and about 4 in. (10 cm) wide, with lobes and sinuses rounded, with a few shallow, rounded teeth, bright green above, whitish-haired beneath, turning subtle shades of red-purple-violet in the autumn before turning brown. As with many oaks, the leaves persist well into winter on young trees, while on older ones, only a few leaves cling in the interior of the canopy. The flowers and fruits are typical of oaks. The egg-shaped acorn is about 1.25 in. (3 cm) long with a shallow cap of warty, light gray scales, produced abundantly on a five-year cycle. The root system of white oak is primarily a deep tap root, with strong deep laterals often developing as well.

White oak has been an important economic tree since colonial times. Once extensively used in shipbuilding, it is currently the major source of wood for whiskey barrels. It is valued in the manufacture of furniture, flooring, paneling, veneer and caskets as well. Although slow-growing and difficult to transplant, it is prized as an amenity landscape tree, both for its stately form and for its autumn foliage color. Native peoples used the acorn as a food source after leaching out the bitter tannins, and made a

flooding. In the north it may be found from sea level to about 500 ft. (150 m), while in the south it will reach 5,900 ft. (1,800 m), although it generally becomes scrubby by 4,500 ft. (1,375 m). White oak is a long-lived species which establishes itself after disturbances, such as fire, in mid- to late succession. In the north on moist sites it is usually replaced by sugar maple and other climax trees capable of reproducing in the shade of the canopy. Seedlings of white oak itself cannot persist under these conditions. However, replacement of white oak by climax trees is very slow because of the long lifespan of the oak. In oak-hickory forests of the south, white oak is a dominant climax species, in association with other trees.

Living to 600 years, white oak is a slow-growing, large tree, reaching 100 ft. (30 m) it height, with a

The leaves of white oak have rounded lobes and sinuses with few, if any, rounded teeth.

topical medicinal oil from pressing them. Many birds and mammals eat the acorns, and deer and other browsers eat the twigs of saplings. Small mammals and birds nest in the branches and take advantage of the persistent leaves for autumn and winter cover.

KEY FEATURES

Quercus alba

Form:	Wide-spreading, dense crown of stout limbs
Trunk:	Single, stout
Bark:	Light gray bark is fissured shallowly into wide, long, vertical, scaly or platy ridges
Twig:	Somewhat slender, red-brown to olive-brown, **rounded buds clustered towards the tip**
Leaves:	**Lobes and sinuses rounded**, with few shallow, rounded teeth, **whitish-haired beneath**
Flower:	Monoecious, male flowers in slender stringy catkins, female flowers in tiny clusters
Fruit:	Egg-shaped acorn with a **shallow cap of warty, light gray scales**

Quercus austrina SMALL
Fagaceae (Beech Family)
Bluff Oak

Bluff oak has a distribution restricted to the southeast coastal states, from North Carolina south to Florida and west to Mississippi. It is found in several hardwood forest habitats, mixed with other hardwoods. As the common name suggests, it has a preference for growing on bluffs and benches above river floodplains on deep, moist, rich, well-drained soils. As a sapling it is tolerant of the shade of other trees, but becomes shade-intolerant at maturity.

Faster-growing than white oak, bluff oak reaches about 70 ft. (21 m), forming a relatively short trunk supporting a rounded, broad crown of spreading branches. Its bark is gray and fissured shallowly into wide, long, vertical, scaly or platy ridges. The leaves are very similar to those of white oak, except they are slightly smaller, to about 8 in. (20 cm) long, with five elongated, round-tipped lobes and shallower sinuses, dark green above and lighter below, turning red-brown in the autumn and remaining on the tree into winter. Flowers and fruit are typical of oaks. The tan-brown acorns are borne either singly or in pairs and are egg-shaped, sometimes slightly hairy at the base or tip and with a gray cap covering about a third or somewhat more of the acorn. Bluff oak is deep-rooted.

Because it is never abundant, bluff oak is not commercially harvested. It is grown locally, however, and used as a mid-sized shade tree for deep, moist soils. In its natural setting it provides shelter for many small birds and mammals, and its acorns are also an important source of late-season food for them.

Developing a broad rounded crown, bluff oak is useful as a landscape shade tree.

The first hints of scarlet color appear in the round, open crown of scarlet oak.

Quercus douglasii HOOK. & ARN.
Fagaceae (Beech Family)
Blue Oak, Iron Oak, Mountain Oak, Mountain White Oak

Endemic to California, blue oak almost entirely surrounds the Central Valley in the lower slopes of the Coastal Ranges and the Sierra Nevada. It is found in several forest, shrub and chaparral plant communities. Sometimes it forms open pure stands, but it can also co-dominate plant communities with other trees. Blue oak may be found on a variety of soils, but in general it prefers shallow, infertile, warm, dry, well-drained gravelly loam to gravelly clay loam. Blue oak is relatively short-lived, to about 100 years, shade-intolerant, but very drought-tolerant, shedding its leaves when soil moisture is limiting. It grows in plant communities regularly subjected to fire-disturbance and regenerates afterwards.

Blue oak reaches about 65 ft. (19.5 m), forming a generally short, straight trunk supporting a wide-spreading, irregular to rounded canopy of twiggy branches. Its gray bark is thin and flaky, fissuring shallowly to form small irregular plates. The blue-green, thin, stiff leaves are small, to 4 in. (10 cm) long and 1.75 in. (4.5 cm) wide, and variable in form, from elliptical to oval to four- or five-lobed, the lobes abruptly pointed, with pointed shallow sinuses between them. The flowers and fruit are typical of oaks. The elongated acorn is borne in pairs or sometimes in threes, and is variable in size and shape, from elliptical and broad to narrow, with a shallow warty cap. The root of blue oak is a deeply penetrating tap root, sometimes with a few deep laterals.

Blue oak is an important habitat tree, providing shelter for and being browsed by deer and other wildlife. Its acorns are consumed by a large variety of birds and small mammals. Being tap-rooted, it is important in preventing soil erosion on sloping land. It is also a valued amenity tree for shade, due to its form, size, and leaf color, although it is prone to a number of insect pests and diseases. Native peoples ground acorns into a meal after leaching them of tannic acids, which were used to dye baskets.

the autumn. Flowers and fruits are typically oaklike, the egg-shaped acorn having two to four faint ridges and a cone-shaped cap covering a third to a half. Acorns take two years to ripen. Scarlet oak has a deep tap root with few lateral roots.

Because of its fast growth, broad open form and superb autumn color, scarlet oak is widely planted as an amenity tree in parks, along streets and on residential properties. It is, however, prone to a variety of insect pests and diseases, and should be pruned to remove failing growth. Its acorns are eaten by many types of birds and mammals, and old trunks and dead snags are a favored nesting site for cavity birds. The wood is not regarded as highly as other oaks, but is harvested, sold and used as red oak.

Blue oak often forms open pure stands with wide-spreading, irregular to rounded canopies.

The wood is not of major importance, although it is hard. The natural regeneration of blue oak is currently in decline, and several factors are believed to be responsible.

Quercus ellipsoidalis E.J. HILL
Fagaceae (Beech Family)
Northern Pin Oak, Hill's Oak, Jack Oak

The range of northern pin oak extends from extreme southwestern Ontario to extreme northwestern Ohio, southeast to extreme northern Missouri, and north to extreme southeastern North Dakota. It is found in a upland deciduous forest throughout its range, and occurs in either pure stands or in association with other hardwoods, particularly oaks, and conifers, especially pines. It strongly prefers dry, well-drained, acidic, sandy soils with little by way of an organic top layer. It is very shade-intolerant, and will not perpetuate itself on a site without disturbance. It is usually replaced by other oaks and shade-tolerant climax trees.

Northern pin oak reaches about 70 ft. (21 m) forming a single, usually short trunk supporting an irregular narrow crown of low-hanging branches, often persisting for long periods of time as dead stubs. The bark is dark gray-brown, fissuring shallowly into narrow platy ridges exposing a pale yellow inner bark. Its leaves are up to 5 in. (13 cm) long by 4 in. (10 cm) wide, generally elliptical in shape, with five to seven lobes having a few bristle-tipped teeth and deep rounded sinuses between them. They are glossy on both surfaces, green above, paler below, turning scarlet, then brown, yellow or purple-brown in the autumn, and often attached into winter. The flowers and fruit are typical of oaks. The acorn is roundish to elliptical, about 0.75 in. (2 cm) long, almost half enclosed by a deep cap, and maturing in the second year. The root of pin oak is a deeply penetrating tap root supported by a few deep laterals.

While suited to amenity landscape applications, northern pin oak has not been extensively used for

Northern pin oak forms an irregular crown of low-hanging branches, with leaves turning purple-brown in the autumn.

this. It has strong potential for stabilizing poor, dry soils, in the arid conditions to which it is well adapted. Its acorns are eaten by several kinds of birds and small mammals. Kirkland's warbler, a federally endangered bird species, nests in trunk cavities of northern pin oak. The wood is used to some extent in the manufacture of furniture, flooring and interior finishes.

Quercus engelmannii GREENE
Fagaceae (Beech Family)
Engelmann Oak, Mesa Oak

Engelmann oak is restricted to extreme northern Baja California and extreme southwestern California, including the Channel Islands. It is found in a limited number of plant habitats, chiefly oak woodland, savannas and chaparral in valleys, or on mesas at low elevations. It occurs in open pure stands, or mixed with coast live oak. Its distribution has been greatly affected by development in southern California and the best remaining stand is near Temecula in the Nature Conservancy's Santa Rosa Plateau preserve. It strongly prefers well-drained, warm, dry, sandy loams. Engelmann oak, being fire-adapted and shade-tolerant as a seedling but intolerant at maturity, forms a dominant tree in habitats prone to fire disturbance.

A semi-evergreen tree, Engelmann oak will sometimes lose its leaves in dry summers. It usually

The leaves of Engelmann oak are small, stiff, and gray-green, varying from elliptical to oval in shape, sometimes with sharp teeth or lobes.

attains about 60 ft. (18 m) forming a spreading, irregular, open crown. Its gray-green stiff leaves are small, to about 2 in. (5 cm) long and about 1.5 in. (3 cm) wide, somewhat variable in shape, from elliptical to oval to sharply and coarsely toothed (or lobed). The flowers and fruit are typically oaklike, the acorns maturing in one year. It is a deep-rooted tree.

Engelmann oak is used neither commercially for its wood nor extensively as a landscape amenity tree. However, its use in naturalization is being promoted. In its natural setting it provides shelter to a variety of animals and its acorns are consumed by both birds and small mammals. Deer and cattle browse on it. These pressures, combined with development and the need for specific weather conditions, particularly adequate levels of soil moisture at the right time, have resulted in poor natural reproduction. Consequently Engelmann oak, although still relatively abundant, is listed in California as a threatened species.

Quercus falcata MICHX.
Fagaceae (Beech Family)
Southern Red Oak, Spanish Oak, Red Oak

Southern red oak is found from Long Island, New York, south to northern Florida, west to the Brazos River in eastern Texas, and north to southern Missouri. It is notably uncommon on the coastal plain, except in the north Atlantic states, and rare in the Mississippi bottomlands. It is a common tree in a variety of hardwood forests, associating with other oaks and pines. It strongly prefers dry, warm, well-drained, sandy, loamy or clay soils on upland sites, frequently on slopes facing south or west. It is mildly tolerant of shade when a sapling, and is a late colonizer after disturbance, often replacing pines in the absence of fire, and persisting as a co-dominant canopy tree in the climax forest.

Living to about 150 years, southern red oak reaches up to 80 ft. (24 m) relatively quickly, forming a single, straight trunk supporting a large, rounded, open crown of wide-spreading large

Southern red oak forms a single, straight trunk, supporting a large open crown of wide-spreading branches.

of growth. However, it is prone to a number of diseases and insect pests when wounded, over-mature or grown on unsuitable soils. It is important in providing habitat to wildlife, and the acorns are an important food source to a very large number of mammals and birds, particularly game birds.

Quercus garryana HOOK.

Fagaceae (Beech Family)

Oregon Oak, Garry Oak, Brewer Oak, Pacific Post Oak, White Oak

Oregon oak is found from extreme southwestern British Columbia, south through western Washington and Oregon to the coastal ranges and Sierra Nevada into southern California. Except in British Columbia and Puget Sound in Washington it is generally found inland from the coast. Oregon oak is found in a large number of plant communities, both deciduous and coniferous forests as well as chaparral. It generally prefers somewhat acidic, clay soils but is otherwise adaptable to gravelly or sandy loams. It can be found on poor, exposed and drought-prone sites as well as poorly drained soils that have a high water table or are prone to seasonal flooding. It is somewhat shade-tolerant, particularly as a sapling, and will reproduce under its own shade, but not that of conifers. Long-lived to 500 years, it is regarded as a climax canopy tree on fire-disturbed sites or in dry areas unsuitable to conifers, but elsewhere is replaced by shade-adapted conifers.

Reaching 90 ft. (27 m), Oregon oak forms a straight single trunk supporting a rounded crown of stout, crooked, spreading branches. Its bark is thin, scaly, and gray when young, developing into squarish blocks with age. Leaves are up to 5.5 in. (12 cm) long and 3.5 in. (9 cm) wide, round-lobed, widest at the middle lobes, glossy, very dark green above, yellow-green below with soft brown hair, turning yellow-brown in the autumn. Flowers and fruit are typical of oaks. The acorns are borne in pairs or trios and are about 1.25 in. (3 cm) long, egg-shaped, with a pointed tip and rough cap, turning brown when ripe. The root system is a well-developed tap root supported by deep laterals.

branches. Its dark gray bark is furrowed in broad platy ridges. The leaves are generally elliptical, to 8 in. (20 cm) long by 6 in. (15 cm) wide, with usually one narrow elongated end lobe and one to three sickle-shaped lobes along each side, each lobe having one to three bristle-tipped teeth. The leaves are shiny dark olive-green above and paler below with soft, rust or grayish hairs, turning brown in the autumn. The initial tap root dies back and the laterals develop sinker roots.

Although rougher and more coarsely grained than its near relative, cherrybark oak, southern red oak is highly valued for factory lumber and timbers. It is widely admired and used as a landscape amenity tree for its size, attractive form and relatively quick rate

Oregon oak forms a straight trunk supporting a rounded open crown of crooked, spreading branches.

Oregon oak is particularly valued as a firewood, and has been used for a wide variety of wood products, but not extensively so. It also has high scenic value, although it is not much used in landscaping. It is valuable in watershed restoration work because its root system stabilizes soil on sloping ground. It is in decline throughout its range, in part because suppression of fire has led to its being displaced by conifers. It is the preferred nesting and forage habitat of a number of birds, especially acorn woodpeckers. Many small and large mammals also eat the acorns. Native peoples ground them to make a meal, after leaching them of tannic acid. The Salish also used the bark as part of a remedy for a number of ailments, including tuberculosis.

Quercus hemisphaerica BARTR. ex WILLD.
Fagaceae (Beech Family)
Darlington Oak, Laurel Oak

Darlington oak has been considered in the past as one of two varieties of laurel oak (*Quercus laurifolia Michx*). However, based on some anatomical distinctions and significant differences in site preferences, it is now considered by several authorities to be a distinct species. Its range extends from southeastern Virginia to southern Florida and west into the southeast corner of Texas along the Gulf coast. Isolated populations occur north of its main range but within the coastal plain states. It is found in a number of forest habitats associated with other hardwood, evergreen broadleaved trees and conifers, as well as in prairie. Moist to dry sandy soils are strongly preferred, particularly on low hills, hammocks and stable dunes. Although short-lived, Darlington oak is shade-tolerant, particularly as a sapling, and in the absence of fire disturbance will establish itself under the shade of other shade-intolerant trees. Eventually, it will emerge from under them, shade them out and become a component of the climax forest community.

A semi-evergreen tree, Darlington oak grows quickly to about 60 ft. (18 m), although 130 ft. (40 m) is not uncommon on good sites. It forms a dense, compact, rounded crown on a single trunk. Its smooth gray bark becomes shallowly and lightly furrowed

Darlington oak grows quickly to form a dense, compact, rounded crown of nearly evergreen foliage.

with age. The leaf form is variable between a juvenile form, occurring on saplings, root sprouts and low branches, and a mature form that is otherwise characteristic of the tree. The juvenile leaves are more irregularly shaped with wavy margins and shallow, variable lobes. The mature leaves are narrowly elliptical and smooth-edged. All leaves are dark glossy green above and lighter below. The flowers and fruit are characteristically oaklike, with the dark brown acorns small, spherical, and either short-stalked or stalkless. Darlington oak has a tap root, often supported by deep lateral roots.

Darlington oak is valued as an attractive amenity tree, and is widely planted for shade, as well as in allées and as a specimen. Its crisp, shiny, nearly ever-green foliage and dense canopy are particularly appealing. Its acorns are consistently produced, unlike many oaks, and being spring germinators are available to the many birds and mammals that depend upon them as winter food. Although the wood is dense and hard, it is not commercially valued.

Quercus imbricaria MICHX.
Fagaceae (Beech Family)
Shingle Oak, Laurel Oak

Shingle oak occurs from southern Iowa east to southern Michigan to eastern Pennsylvania, south to western North Carolina and west to northern Arkansas. Local populations are found in Louisiana and Alabama. It associates with other hardwoods, particularly post and black oaks, on deep, moist, strongly acidic, well-drained loams, from rocky uplands to low sandy hills to streambanks and floodplains. It is also found on other soils, but not those that are permanently excessively wet, or shallow, or too dense. It is moderately tolerant of both flooding and shade, and is resistant to drought. Shingle oak is a slow-growing, long-lived tree that develops in the understory of the climax forest, at times breaking through into the canopy.

Reaching up to about 60 ft. (18 m), shingle oak forms a large, rounded, open crown of strongly hor-

Shingle oak makes an excellent shade tree; the crown is conical in youth but becomes round with age.

izontal branches on a single trunk. Its light gray-brown bark varies between loose, thin scales and broad, scaly ridges, with shallow fissures. The leaves are elliptical to oval, about 6 in. (15 cm) long by a third as wide, with a smooth, sometimes undulating edge and a bristle at the tip, lustrous dark green above, softly hairy and gray-green below, turning yellow to red-brown in the autumn and tending to persist late into the season. The flowers and fruit are typically oaklike, the brown acorn being a little more than 0.5 in. (13 cm) long, often half-covered by the hairy cap, borne singly or in pairs on stout stalks, and maturing in the second year. The root system comprises a tap root supported by deep laterals.

Leaves of shingle oak are elliptical, with a smooth, sometimes undulating edge and a bristle at the tip.

Shingle oak is an adaptable and very attractive landscape tree. In the early phase of growth, when open-grown, it forms a handsome, symmetrical pyramidal crown. Eventually it develops a very appealing rounded crown. It is used as a residential shade tree and as a street tree. It is also planted in large park settings. It makes an excellent windbreak or visual screen because of its long leaf retention. In addition, it takes very well to pruning, and because it retains its foliage late into the season can be used to create a large hedge. It is more easily transplanted than many oaks and is not as prone to as many diseases and insects. Because it is tolerant of a variety of growing conditions, as well as salt and some pollution, it can be used in suburban settings, in landscape reclamation and for soil stabilization. Its only drawback is its slow growth rate. In its natural setting, the acorns are relished by many birds and small mammals, and it provides protective cover to large and small mammals as well as birds. Shingle oak has historically been used in the manufacture of shingles, for which it is still used today.

Quercus incana BART.
Fagaceae (Beech Family)
Bluejack Oak, Sandjack Oak, Cinnamon Oak, Upland Willow Oak

Bluejack oak ranges along the Atlantic and Gulf coastal plains from southeastern Virginia southward to central Florida and west into central Texas, and north into southeastern Oklahoma and southwestern Arkansas. It is found in several forest habitats along with other oaks and pines. Bluejack oak is restricted to dry, well-drained, finer sandy soils, downslope of ridgetops, with well-developed clay subsoils near the surface, along river terraces and uplands. Opuntia, a type of cactus, prefers the same growing conditions as bluejack oak. Opuntia is almost always growing close to it. Bluejack oak is moderately shade-tolerant and grows as an understory in open pine woods. In the absence of fire disturbance it generally dies out gradually and is only sparsely present in climax forests.

Occasionally a thicket-forming large shrub, bluejack oak forms a small tree, to an average height of 20 ft. (6 m). The blue-gray smooth bark becomes dark gray-black, thick, rough and furrowed into squarish plates. Its leathery leaves are distinctively shiny blue-green above and downy gray-green below, turning red-brown in autumn. They are oblong, to about 4 in. (10 cm) long and a quarter as wide, smooth-edged,

---

KEY FEATURES

Quercus imbricaria

Form: Large rounded, open crown of strongly horizontal branches

Trunk: Single, straight

Bark: Light gray-brown bark varies between being loose, thin scales and broad, scaly ridges with shallow fissures

Twig: **Slender, glossy, green-brown**

Leaves: **Elliptical to oval, smooth edge**, lustrous **dark green above**, softly **hairy and gray-green below**

Flower: Monoecious, male flowers in slender stringy catkins, female flowers in tiny clusters

Fruit: Brown acorn, often **half-covered by the hairy cap**, borne singly or in pairs on stout stalks

Bluejack oak forms a small tree with leathery, distinctively shiny blue-green leaves.

or on young vigorous branches slightly lobed, with a bristle at the tip. Flowers and fruit are oaklike, the brown, nearly round acorn being just over 0.5 in. (1.3 cm) long and half covered by the cap. They are normally borne in pairs and ripen in the second year. The root system is characteristically deep rooted, but may be shallow if lower soil levels are infertile.

Bluejack oak is an important component of longleaf pine/scrub oak communities, which support several rare species of animals, notably Sherman's fox squirrel, indigo snake, gopher tortoise, red-cockaded woodpecker, and scarab beetle. Numerous small and large mammals as well as birds eat the acorns, and many birds utilize its cover in the forest understory.

This particular plant community is ranked as threatened in Texas and vulnerable in Florida, and efforts are being made to reintroduce the native species of pine and oaks, bluejack among them. The wood of bluejack oak is not commercially important.

Quercus kelloggii NEWB.
Fagaceae (Beech Family)
California Black Oak, Black Oak, Kellogg Oak

California black oak is distributed from southwestern Oregon, just north of Eugene, to Baja California, where it is found in a few sparse populations. It favors the west slopes of the Cascade Ranges, the Sierra Nevada, and the Coast, Traverse and Peninsular Ranges, but may also be found sporadically on east-facing slopes. It is found in either pure stands, on sites where conditions are unfavorable to conifer growth or where there has been disturbance, or mixed with other oaks and conifers. California black oak has a strong preference for deep, well-drained, slightly acid loams, but can also be found on gravelly clay loams. However, it is never found on serpentine soils. It is long-lived, and moderately shade-tolerant when young, but requires full light at maturity. In habitats prone to regular fire or logging disturbance California black oak may become persistent and dominant. Otherwise it is gradually displaced by conifers.

Typically growing to 80 ft. (24 m), California black oak forms a short trunk supporting a broad rounded crown when growing in the open. In dense stands it develops a higher, slender trunk and a narrow, small crown that becomes wider and more irregular with age. Its initially thin smooth bark becomes thick and deeply furrowed into platy ridges. The leaves are dark shiny green above and pale yellow-green and often hairy below, up to 8 in. (20 cm) long, with generally five or seven well-developed, sharp-pointed, coarsely toothed lobes with deep sinuses. The flowers and fruit are typically oaklike. The dark brown acorn is up to 1.5 in. (3.5 cm) long by about half as wide, with a fringed cap covering about half of it. The root system of

California black oak, when open-grown, forms a short trunk supporting a broad rounded crown.

California black oak comprises one to several vertical roots reaching to bedrock, with large lateral roots extending horizontally off these.

California black oak is very highly valued as a landscape shade tree, and is widely planted for this purpose. It is prone to a number of insect pests and fungal diseases, particularly when stressed, and it's highly susceptible to fire. It is also used in both watershed management for slope stabilization and in wildlife habitat restoration to provide shelter and acorns. Native peoples preferred the acorn of this oak above all others for producing meal, and it has been suggested that it be reintroduced as a human food source since it is palatable and has a high oil content. The wood is also highly valued for a wide range of lumber products.

Quercus laevis WALT.
Fagaceae (Beech Family)
Turkey Oak, Catesby Oak, Scrub Oak

Turkey oak is distributed along the coastal plain from southeastern Virginia to central Florida and west into southeastern Louisiana. It is found in pure stands or associating with other hardwoods, notably oaks, and pines in several forest habitats. It has a strong preference for well-drained, strongly acidic, sandy soil, low in organic material. It is intolerant of salt spray and is not found on the coast, but in places near to it. Turkey oak is a short-lived, shade-intolerant tree and dominates on sites where there is frequent but not excessive fire disturbance. Without fire, it is eventually replaced by longer-lived, shade-tolerant mixed hardwood forest.

Generally a small tree to about 50 ft. (15 m), turkey oak is often more of a large shrub, and at time, on good sites, a larger tree. The trunk is short, supporting an open, irregular crown of crooked and gnarled branches. It develops a rather thick gray-black bark that is deeply furrowed into blocky ridges. Its leaves are quite variable in size and shape. They are basically triangular, spreading outward from a pointed base, ranging from 4 to 8 in. (10 to 20 cm)

Turkey oak develops a rather thick gray-black bark that is deeply furrowed into blocky ridges.

long, with three, five or seven narrow long lobes, each with up to three bristle-pointed, long-tipped teeth. They are shiny on both surfaces, yellow-green above, lighter with scattered rust-colored hairs in the axils of veins below, turning red in autumn and falling late in the year. They respond to sunlight by orienting themselves vertically and edge-outward, to minimize moisture loss. The flowers and fruit are characteristically oaklike. The brown, egg-shaped acorns are about 1 in. (2.5 cm) long, with a short-stalked, conical cap having hairy scales running down the inside surface. The root system is initially tap-rooted but becomes extensively lateral and spreading with age to exploit relatively distant sources of water and nutrient.

The hard, dense wood of turkey oak is chiefly used for firewood, and the bark and twigs are used in tanning leather. While not a majestic tree, some consider it appealing. The autumn foliage and twigs are gathered and dried for commercial use in autumn decoration. Turkey oak is an often important component of forested habitats, providing shelter and acorns for mammals and birds.

Quercus laurifolia MICHX.
Fagaceae (Beech Family)
Laurel Oak, Diamond Leaf Oak, Coastal Laurel Oak, Water Oak, Swamp Laurel Oak

Also botanically known by the name *Quercus obtusa*, as well as several others, laurel oak is very closely related to Darlington oak, from which it differs in some anatomical features and in site preferences. Its range extends from southeastern Virginia to southern Florida and west into the southeast corner of Texas along the Gulf coast. Isolated populations occur north of its main range, but within the coastal plain states. It may be found in forested wetlands along the edges of swamps between swamp plant communities and moist higher ground, often in pure stands. It prefers moist to wet, well-drained sandy soils, and will withstand deep, frequent flooding on sites that otherwise drain well. Although

Laurel oak, like Darlington oak, forms a dense, compact, rounded crown of nearly evergreen foliage.

short-lived, laurel oak is shade-tolerant, particularly as a sapling, and in the absence of fire disturbance will establish itself under shade-intolerant trees. Eventually, it will emerge from under them, and replace them, to become a component of the climax forest community.

A semi-evergreen tree, laurel oak grows quickly to about 80 ft. (24 m), although 145 ft. (43.5 m) is not uncommon on good sites. It forms a dense, broad, rounded crown on a single trunk. Its smooth gray-brown bark becomes rough and furrowed with age. The leaf is generally shiny on both surfaces, dark green above and lighter below, to about 5.5 in. (14 cm) long by 1.5 in. (4 cm) wide, narrow and oblong to lance- or diamond-shaped, generally straight edged and bristle-tipped, shedding in the early spring. The flowers and fruit are characteristically oaklike, with the dark brown acorns small, spherical, and either short-stalked or stalkless, maturing in the second year. Laurel oak has a tap root, often supported by deep lateral roots; in wet areas the roots are often buttressed for stability.

Like Darlington oak, laurel oak is valued as an attractive amenity tree, and is widely planted for shade, and as a specimen. It produces abundant acorns consistently, and being spring germinators, like Darlington oak, they are available to the many birds and mammals that depend upon them as winter food. Although dense and hard, the wood is not commercially valued.

Quercus lobata NEE
Fagaceae (Beech Family)
Valley Oak, California White Oak, Water Oak, Weeping Oak, Roble

Endemic to California, valley oak is found south from Shasta County throughout the central valley and the foothills of the Sierra Nevada and coastal ranges to Los Angeles County, as well as on Santa Catalina and Santa Cruz Islands. It is found in several forest habitats in association with a variety of hardwoods, particularly other oaks, and conifers. In particular, it dominates and is often the only tree in valley oak woodlands. It strongly prefers deep, rich, moist, loamy soils with a water table at about 33 ft. (10 m), but will tolerate more poorly drained soils. Valley oak is moderately shade-tolerant and long-lived. In valley oak woodlands and floodplain riparian woodlands it forms the climax canopy, while in other habitats it is usually replaced by mixed hardwoods or conifers unless there is fire disturbance.

Among the tallest North American oaks, valley oak typically reaches 80 ft. (24 m), but heights of 125 ft. (37.5 m) are found. It develops a very broad crown on a short wide trunk. Its bark is dark gray, thick and deeply furrowed into narrow ridges and blocks. The leaves are glossy dark green to yellow-green above, lighter gray-green below, about 4 in. (10 cm) long by 2 in. (5 cm) wide, with up to six

Valley oak develops a very broad, open, and irregular crown on a short wide trunk.

rounded lobes with rounded coarse teeth, widest towards the end. The flowers and fruit are characteristically oaklike. The acorns are long and slender, to 2 in. (5 cm) by 0.8 in. (2 cm) with a conical cap. The root is typically composed of several vertical roots with extensive horizontal root branches.

Valley oak habitats are critically important to the survival of several species of state and federally endangered animals. More birds are found in this habitat than in any other in California. The acorns are consumed by a large number of them, as well as by mammals, and many birds nest in the trees. Valley oak is increasingly used in the restoration of valley oak habitat and riparian woodland. The wood is used to a limited extent commercially, primarily for cabinetry. In the past it has been used for fuel and charcoal.

Quercus lyrata WALT.
Fagaceae (Beech Family)
Overcup Oak, Swamp Post Oak, Water White Oak

Found on the coastal plain, overcup oak ranges from Delaware south to northwestern Florida, west into eastern Texas, and up the Mississippi River valley into southern Indiana and Illinois. It is found in several wetland plant habitats with other hardwoods, sometimes in pure stands. It prefers seasonally inundated, wet clay soils of floodplains, streambanks and bayous. Overcup oak is relatively shade-tolerant and long-lived. On low-lying, wetter sites it is usually present in the climax forest canopy, but on drier sites is replaced by other hardwoods.

Overcup oak attains a height of about 90 ft. (27 m), with a relatively short, stout trunk supporting a rounded crown of much-branched, drooping limbs. The light gray bark is thick and fissuring into irregular, scaly or shaggy plates and ridges. Its leaves have five to eleven round to short-pointed lobes, and are relatively narrow, to 8 in. (20 cm) long and half as wide, usually wider towards the tip, with a pointed base to the leaf-blade. They are shiny dark green above, usually softly hairy and gray-green

Forming a dense rounded crown, overcup oak can make a suitable landscape tree.

below, turning yellow to red-brown in the autumn. The flowers and fruit are typically oaklike. The acorns mature in a single season, and are about 1 in. (2.5 cm) long, almost round and nearly totally enclosed in the somewhat warty cap, which is often fringed with long-pointed scales. Overcup oak has an initial tap root that is replaced by a wide-spreading lateral root system.

Occasionally used as a landscape amenity tree on appropriate soils, overcup oak is intolerant of drought and prone to many damaging insects and diseases, which limit its usefulness. Wood of the best trees is sold as white oak, and has been used for lumber and cooperage, but in general the wood is inferior to many other oaks. Although its acorns are eaten by wildlife, they are not preferred to those of other oaks. It is useful in the preservation of wetlands and seeding is the preferred method.

Quercus macrocarpa MICHX.
Fagaceae (Beech Family)
Bur Oak, Mossycup Oak

Bur oak occurs from southern New Brunswick westward to extreme southeastern Saskatchewan, south to southeastern Texas and northeast to Tennessee. Its range is more concentrated to the west, with the eastern portion consisting of more widely isolated populations. It is found in a large number of forest, savanna and prairie habitats with other hardwoods and conifers. It can be found growing from upland woods to river and stream valleys on a wide range of soils. Bur oak tends to prefer medium-textured soils over 20 in. (50 cm) deep that are moist and well drained. It is adaptable to acidic and alkaline soils. It is not often found on clay soils and is not very tolerant of flooding. It is shade-intolerant and fairly long-lived, to 300 years. Depending on the site, bur oak may be a component of the climax plant community, especially under drier conditions or fire disturbance. In other cases it is replaced eventually by other hardwoods.

Although sometimes a shrub on poorer soil, bur oak is more often a tree, up to 80 ft. (24 m), with a short stout trunk supporting a broad, open, rounded crown of wide-spreading, crooked, corky and coarse branches. Its light to dark gray bark is thick and deeply fissured into rough scaly ridges. The leaves tend to be variable but are most commonly up to 10 in. (25 cm) long and half as wide, with five to nine quite shallow, rounded lobes, widening considerably towards the broad tip, with deep sinuses at the midpoint, often nearly cutting the leaf in half. They are variably smooth to hairy on both sides, dark blue-green above and downy gray-green below, turning yellow-brown in autumn. Flowers and fruit are in the characteristic oak pattern. Acorns mature in a single

Bur oak has a short stout trunk supporting a broad, open, rounded crown.

season, and are large, to about 2 in. (5 cm) long and wide, elliptical in shape, and up to three-quarters enclosed in the cap, which usually has a pronounced fringe along the edge. Bur oak has a tough, deeply rooted, well-branched, spreading root system.

Tolerant of urban pollution, bur oak is widely planted as a bold shade tree where soils are appropriate. Its wide-spreading crown is particularly appealing and majestic with age. It is also extensively used in shelterbelts and landscape reclamation. In its natural setting it provides shelter and food to many birds and mammals.

Quercus marilandica MUENCHH. (Q. neoashei Bush)
Fagaceae (Beech Family)
Blackjack Oak, Scrub Oak, Barren Oak, Black Oak, Jack Oak

Blackjack oak ranges from Long Island south to northwestern Florida, west to southeastern Texas, and north to southeastern Iowa. It is notably absent from the Mississippi River valley and delta. It is found in a wide array of habitats with other hardwoods, particularly other oaks, and conifers, especially pines. It characteristically occurs on dry, infertile soils ranging from clays to sands overlaying clay, to gravels, on flats and dry slopes and ridges, often facing south or west. Although slow-growing and long-lived, blackjack oak is shade-intolerant. On the poor dry sites it prefers it often forms the dominant understory component of the climax habitat, as it does in sites where fire is a regular disturbance. Otherwise it is usually replaced by shade-tolerant trees.

On very poor sites more of a shrub, blackjack oak will usually reach 50 ft. (15 m) under good conditions, forming a short trunk and a low, rounded to irregular canopy of crooked branches, which persist on the tree long after they have died. The black bark is thick and deeply fissured into rough, wide, platy ridges. Its somewhat thickened, roughly triangular leaves are up to 5 in. (13 cm) long and nearly as wide, with a very narrow base widening prominently toward the tip, where there are usually three broad, shallow, bristle-tipped lobes. They are yellow-green

Blackjack oak typically has a short trunk and irregular canopy; leaves have three broad, shallow lobes.

and shiny above, brownish-haired and lighter yellow-green below, turning yellow-brown in autumn and clinging to the tree well into winter. The flowers and fruit are typical of oaks. Its acorn matures in the second year, and is up to 0.75 in. (19 mm) long, elliptical and about half enclosed in a thick, rust-brown, conical cup. Blackjack oak has a tap root.

Blackjack oak has limited use in human commerce. It is not commonly cultivated, although it makes a wind-firm, drought- and salt-resistant tree. Its high susceptibility to disease, slow growth rate and lack of strong aesthetic appeal limit its use as an amenity tree. Its wood is mainly used for railway ties, fence posts and charcoal. In its natural setting, the acorns are an important food source for birds and mammals, and it provides shelter as well.

Quercus michauxii NUTT.

Fagaceae (Beech Family)

Swamp Chestnut Oak, Basket Oak, Cow Oak

Swamp chestnut oak occurs along the coastal plain from Maryland south to northern Florida and west into eastern Texas, as well as north along the Mississippi and Ohio river valleys into southern Indiana. It occurs with other hardwoods and pines in a number of upland forest habitats. It prefers sites along river bottomlands, streambanks and swamp edges on moderately well-drained silty clay and clay loams. Swamp chestnut oak is a long-lived, slow-growing, flood- and shade-tolerant tree, characteristic of climax forest canopies on sites briefly flooded in the spring.

Swamp chestnut oak develops a narrow to rounded compact crown of shiny dark green leaves.

Reaching about 80 ft. (24 m) swamp chestnut oak develops a narrow to rounded compact crown. The light gray bark is furrowed into scaly plates. Its leaves are elliptical to 9 in. (23 cm) long by 5.5 in. (14 cm) wide, with an abruptly pointed tip and up to 14 pairs of lateral veins, each ending in a forward curving tooth, giving a wavy effect to the leaf margin. Leaves are shiny dark green above, softly hairy and gray-green below, turning dark red-brown in the autumn. Flowers and fruit are characteristically oak-like. The egg-shaped acorns mature in a single season, and are up to 1.25 in. (3 cm) long, with a third covered by a thick cap. Swamp chestnut oak is reported to be tap-rooted.

Swamp chestnut oak is rarely used as an amenity landscape tree. The wood is highly valued in the production of flooring, furniture barrels and wooden containers of all kinds. Thin splints of the wood have been used to make sturdy baskets. The acorns are large, sweet and relatively low in tannic acid, and may be eaten raw. Many birds and mammals, including cattle, consume large amounts of them as well.

Quercus muhlenbergii ENGELM.

Fagaceae (Beech Family)

Chinquapin Oak, Yellow Chestnut Oak, Chinquapin Oak

Chinquapin oak is distributed from western Vermont west through southern Ontario to Wisconsin, south to southwestern Texas, adjacent New Mexico and northern Mexico, and east to northwestern Florida. Except for in northwestern Florida, it is absent on the Atlantic and Gulf coastal plains and Piedmont, and uncommon in Pennsylvania and New England. It occurs mostly as scattered individuals with other hardwoods in a number of forest habitats on limestone outcroppings and rocky upland slopes. It is common on alvars, and strongly prefers well-drained, slightly alkaline soils derived from limestone that are often deficient in nutrients and low in organic matter, but can also be found at times on rich, slightly acid soils. It is somewhat

Chinquapin oak forms a very broad, round to somewhat irregular crown, even when young.

allel lateral veins ending in coarse, narrow, forward curving teeth. The leaves open fuzzy pink, become shiny blue-green above, very finely hairy and silvery white below, turning yellow-brown to red in autumn. Flowers and fruit are characteristic of oaks. The egg-shaped, brown to almost black acorn is about 0.75 in. (19 mm) long and half enclosed by the cap, maturing in one season. Chinquapin oak develops a root system of deeply penetrating laterals.

A very attractive amenity shade tree, especially with age, it deserves greater use than it has been accorded, especially since it is drought- and salt-tolerant, is adaptable to slightly acid or alkaline soils, and is not bothered by many diseases. Its wood is highly valued for cabinetry, furniture and containers. Its edible acorns are sweet and constitute a high-quality food for many birds and animals, particularly the red-headed and red-bellied woodpecker. In retaining its leaves into the late autumn and early winter it also provides late-season cover and shelter.

Quercus nigra L.
Fagaceae (Beech Family)
Water Oak, Possum Oak, Spotted Oak, Duck Oak, Orange Oak

Occurring on the coastal plain from New Jersey south to central Florida and west to eastern Texas, water oak also ranges up the lower Mississippi river valley to Missouri and Tennessee. It may be found in a number of lowland forest communities with other hardwoods and pines. It prefers, but is not restricted to, well-drained moist silty clay or loamy soils on the elevated margins of swamps, streams and rivers where it is seasonally flooded deeply for no more than a few weeks a year. Somewhat tolerant of shade when a seedling, Water oak is intolerant soon afterward, requiring full sun to sustain rapid growth. It is also short-lived and is considered a transitional tree in bottomland forest canopies, eventually being replaced in most instances by longer-lived, slower-growing, shade-tolerant hardwoods.

shade-tolerant as a seedling, but becomes intolerant with age. While long-lived, chinquapin oak is shorter-lived than many other upland oaks. On alkaline soils it is a climax forest understory tree, while on moist rich soils it is replaced by more shade-tolerant hardwood trees.

Reaching to about 80 ft. (24 m), chinquapin oak forms a very broad, round to somewhat irregular crown of large limbs on a short trunk when in the open. In closer quarters it will form a higher, straight trunk and dense, rounded, elmlike crown of slender branches. The bark is pale gray to silvery, thin, loosely scaly to shallowly fissured. Its leaves reach 9 in. (23 cm) long by 5.5 in. (14 cm) wide, and are oval to obovate, with a narrow base and up to 11 par-

With a conical to rounded crown of blue-green leaves, water oak makes a handsome shade tree for moister sites.

Water oak reaches about 100 ft. (30 m), forming a straight trunk supporting a conical to rounded crown of slender branches. Its smooth, gray bark becomes dark gray-black and fissured into narrow scaly ridges. The leaves are about 5 in. (13 cm) long and 2 in. (5 cm) wide, narrow at the base and widening out to become broadest very near the rounded and shallowly three-lobed tip, creating a wedgelike appearance. The leaves are dull blue-green above, paler below, turning yellow to yellow-brown and crimson late in the year. In the south they are semi-evergreen. Flowers and fruit are oaklike, the brown acorns being very nearly round, close to 0.75 in. (19 mm) long, with a shallow cap, and maturing in the second year. Water oak has a shallow, wide-spreading root system.

Although short-lived and susceptible to air pollution, particularly acid rain, water oak makes a handsome, bold amenity shade tree for moister sites. Its wood is not as highly regarded as that of upland oaks and is chiefly used as a veneer on plywood for produce containers. Its acorns, like those of most oaks, are consumed by a variety of mammals and birds, and it is also important in providing snags for cavity-nesting birds and habitat for the southern flying squirrel. Water oak is often used to restore bottomland hardwood forests as well.

Quercus pagoda RAF.
Fagaceae (Beech Family)

Cherrybark Oak, Pagoda Oak

Often considered a variety of southern red oak, cherrybark oak is chiefly distinguished by small differences in leaf shape and a large difference in site preference. Cherrybark oak is found from southeastern Virginia, south to northwestern Florida, west into eastern Texas, and north up the Mississippi river valley, although rare in the lower delta. It is a common tree in a variety of bottomland hardwood forests, usually occurring singly rather than in groves. It strongly prefers the better-drained, seasonally flooded, loamy soils of floodplains, but will also grow on moist upland sites. It is drought-intolerant and only mildly tolerant of light shade when a sapling, and is only occasionally a co-dominant canopy tree in the climax forest. More often it is replaced by other hardwoods.

Living to about 150 years, cherrybark oak reaches up to 130 ft. (39 m) quite quickly, forming a single, high, straight trunk supporting a large, rounded, open crown of wide-spreading large branches. Its bark is initially light whitish-gray and smooth, resembling cherry, becoming dark gray and furrowed in broad platy ridges. The leaves are generally elliptical with a broadly wedged-shade base, to 8 in. (20 cm) long by 6 in. (15 cm) wide, with usually

Cherrybark oak typically has a single trunk; a large, round canopy; and wide-spreading branches.

one narrow elongated end lobe and one to three lobes along each side separated by shallow sinuses, each lobe being set at right angles to the mid-rib and having one to three bristle-tipped teeth. The leaves are shiny green above and paler below with soft, rust or grayish hairs, turning brown in the autumn. The initial tap root dies back and the tree develops a wide-spreading lateral root system.

The wood of cherrybark oak is of very high quality and is used in the manufacture of furniture, interior finishes, and veneers. It is widely admired and used as an landscape amenity tree for its size, attractive form and fast rate of growth. However, it is prone to a number of diseases and insect pests when wounded, over-mature or grown on unsuitable soils. It is important in providing habitat to wildlife, and the acorns are an important food source to a very large number of mammals and birds, particularly game birds.

Quercus palustris MUENCHH.
Fagaceae (Beech Family)
Pin Oak, Swamp Oak, Water Oak, Spanish Oak

Round-crowned at maturity, pin oak develops an intense red-brown autumn color.

Pin oak is found from southwestern New England, west through extreme southwestern Ontario to northern Illinois, southwest to northeastern Oklahoma, and east to Virginia. It occurs primarily on the bottomlands of major rivers, and on moist uplands on moderately acid clay and clay loam soils. It may be found singly, mixed with other hardwoods in a variety of habitats, or in extensive pure to nearly pure stands. It is tolerant of winter flooding only, moderately tolerant of summer drought and intolerant of shade. It is moderately fast-growing and lives to about 175 years. Pin oak is often a transitional tree between early colonizers and the later climax canopy trees. However, with regular disturbance it can persist as a dominant tree by regenerating faster than other trees.

Topping out at about 90 ft. (27 m), pin oak forms a strong single trunk penetrating high into the broad, pyramidal crown. In forested settings the lower limbs die and eventually break off to leave short dead spurs. Its bark is initially smooth and dark gray but becomes shallowly fissured into broad, scaly ridges. The leaves are dark shiny green above, lighter below, turning red to brown in the autumn. They are about 5 in. (13 cm) long and 4 in. (10 cm) wide, with five to seven narrow lobes having only a few bristly teeth and deep rounded sinuses between them that reach almost to the mid-vein. Flowers and leaves are typically oaklike. The brown acorns mature in the second year, and are about 0.5 in. (13 cm) long, nearly round and about one-third enclosed in a very shallow cap. Having an initially well-developed tap root as a seedling, pin oak gradually changes to having a wide-spreading, fibrous root system.

Pin oak is a popular amenity shade tree having a pleasing form, fine-textured foliage attractive in all seasons, and a relatively rapid rate of growth. If care is taken to ensure it is planted on somewhat acidic soil it is generally pest- and disease-resistant. Its wood tends to be knotty and is used for fuel and construction timbers. Its acorns are an important food source for many mammals and birds, particularly migrating waterfowl. Pin oak is used in the restoration of bottomland forests as well as artificially created wetlands where it is intended to attract migrating waterfowl and provide them with food.

Quercus phellos L.
Fagaceae (Beech Family)
Willow Oak, Peach Oak, Pin Oak

Except for most of Georgia and adjacent Florida, and southern Louisiana where it is absent, willow oak occurs on the coastal plain from New Jersey south to northwestern Florida and west into eastern Texas. It also ranges up the Mississippi River to southern Illinois. It favors hardwood forest communities transitional between those on lowland sites and those on the uplands. Ideally it grows on deep, moist, somewhat acidic soils with more than 2 percent organic material and a water table in the growing season between 2 and 6 ft. (0.6 and 1.8 m). Willow oak is tolerant of winter flooding, but intolerant of shade beyond the seedling stage. It is relatively fast-growing and fairly long-lived. On sites with winter flooding it tends to become a component of the climax forest canopy, while on drier or wetter sites it is replaced by other hardwoods.

Willow oak reaches 80 ft. (24 m) on a straight, tall, slender trunk supporting a large, graceful, conical to rounded crown of slender branches. The smooth, gray bark becomes gray-black and roughly furrowed into narrow irregular platy ridges. Its leaves are narrowly elliptical, to about 4.5 in. (11 cm) long by about 0.75 in. (1.9 cm) wide, with a smooth, somewhat wavy edge and bristled tip. They are slightly lustrous and light green above, paler below, turning light yellow in the autumn. The flowers and fruit are characteristically oaklike. The brown acorn matures

A superb shade tree, willow oak forms a slender trunk, supporting a large, graceful, rounded crown.

in the second year, and is nearly round, to about 0.5 in. (13 cm) long, with a shallow cap. Willow oak has a root system that is fibrous and spreading, penetrating to the water table.

A favored amenity shade and street tree in the Southeast, willow oak easily transplants and grows quickly to provide a graceful and appealing crown in or out of leaf. It is prone to a few insect and disease problems as well as acid rain, so some care to monitoring is useful. Its wood is also valued for timber and pulp. It produces acorns abundantly and dependably every year, and these are eaten by many mammals and birds. Willow oak is also used in hardwood forest restoration in bottomlands, as well as around reservoirs with fluctuating water levels.

Quercus prinus L.

Fagaceae (Beech Family)

Chestnut Oak, Rock Oak, Rock Chestnut Oak, Tanbark Oak

Chestnut oak is found from extreme southwestern Maine west to northern Pennsylvania, southwest to southern Illinois, south to extreme northeastern Mississippi, east to northern Georgia and north along the Piedmont to Delaware. It is found in a number of different forest communities on rocky upland sites in association with other hardwoods and conifers or occasionally in pure stands. While it grows best on slightly acid, rich, well-drained, moist soils along streams and rivers, chestnut oak is more commonly found on dry, rocky infertile soil with low moisture-holding ability. It is intolerant of flooding

Chestnut oak makes an appealing landscape tree, especially on dry soil.

and moderately tolerant of shade, particularly as a sapling. It is slow-growing and long-lived. On the rocky slopes it prefers, chestnut oak is apparently a climax community tree, while on more lowland sites it is usually replaced by more shade-tolerant trees.

Reaching 80 ft. (24 m), chestnut oak develops an open, irregular and wide-spreading crown on a straight trunk. Its thick, gray bark becomes very deeply fissured into both broad and narrow ridges. The leaves are chestnutlike, but not spiny, to 8 in. (20 cm) long and half as wide, elliptical in general shape, broadest beyond the middle, with a bristled tip. There are up to 16 regularly spaced and shaped, incurved teeth along each side, with every tooth associated with a lateral vein. The leaves are lustrous yellow-green above, gray-green below, turning yellow to crimson in the autumn. Flowers and fruit are oaklike. The brown, egg-shaped acorns mature in the first year, and are about 1.25 in. (3 cm) long with a thin, slightly pointed cap of warty, hairy scales covering up to a third of the acorn. Chestnut oak initially has a tap root, but loses this in favor of laterals that extend well beyond the tree canopy to a depth of about 3 ft. (0.9 m); these laterals branch and rebranch to cover an area five times that of the canopy.

The wood of chestnut oak is graded, sold and used as white oak. The bark has a very high tannic acid content and is valued in tanning leather. It makes a very appealing shade tree, particularly for dry, rocky, infertile sites, but is not as extensively used as it might be. It has been used for mine reclamation. The large acorns, while produced infrequently, are relished by many birds and mammals.

Quercus rubra L.

Fagaceae (Beech Family)

Red Oak, Northern Red Oak, Eastern Red Oak

Red oak ranges from Cape Breton west to Minnesota, south to eastern Oklahoma, and east to Georgia. It is common in many forested habitats with other hardwoods and conifers, particularly pines. It is

Developing a round crown on a short trunk, red oak typically turns red to red-brown in the autumn.

often found in pure stands. It is characteristically located out of the floodplain but otherwise is found on moist to dry sites. While red oak grows best on deep, fertile, well-drained but moist, fine-textured soils, with a relatively high water table, it may be found growing on many other soils as well, from clay to gravel or stony, thin ground. It is a moderately shade-tolerant and long-lived tree. It generally is a mid- to late colonizer after disturbance, and persists well into the climax forest canopy, but is eventually displaced by more shade-tolerant trees in most but not all habitats.

The fastest-growing of the oaks, red oak usually attains a height of 90 ft. (27 m), but on good sites may reach 160 ft. (49 m). In the open it develops a short, stout trunk supporting a wide-spreading open and rounded crown of stout limbs. In forested settings it forms a tall, straight trunk with a large rounded crown. The bark is gray-brown with shallow vertical furrows and low flat wide ridges, but becomes checkered with age. Its leaves are generally elliptical to obovate, reaching 9 in. (23 cm) long by two-thirds as wide, with seven to eleven moderately sized, pointed lobes with a few irregular bristle-tipped teeth. They are a dull, smooth green above, lighter below, turning dark red-brown in the autumn. Flowers and fruit are characteristic of oaks. The egg-shaped acorn is just over 1 in. (2.5 cm) long with a shallow cap and bitter seed, turning red-brown and maturing in the second year. The root system of the red oak consists of a well-developed tap root with an extensively developed system of deep, spreading laterals.

Red oak is a cold-hardy, fast-growing, easily transplanted tree, widely used as a street and shade tree. It has a majestic form and generally colors very well in the autumn. Its wood is highly valued and used for many products including furniture, flooring, door sills, paneling, veneer, cabinetry, caskets, fence posts and railway ties. It is also used as firewood. Native peoples used to leach the tannic acid from the acorns and make a meal from them. They also used the bark in remedies for bowel problems. Many birds and mammals consume the acorns, and use the trees for nesting and protective cover. Red oak is used in the restoration of wildlife habitat and degraded sites, especially those with acidic soil conditions.

Red oak generally produces an abundance of acorns.

KEY FEATURES

Quercus rubra

Form: Wide-spreading open and rounded crown of stout limbs

Trunk: Stout, single to multiple

Bark: Gray-brown with shallow vertical furrows and **low flat wide ridges**, but becomes checkered with age

Twig: Slender, smooth, **red-brown, pointed buds** clustered at tips

Leaves: Elliptical, 7 to 11 **pointed lobes** with a few **irregular bristle-tipped teeth, turning dark red-brown**

Flower: Monoecious, male flowers in slender stringy catkins, female flowers in tiny clusters

Fruit: Egg-shaped acorn with a **shallow cap** and bitter seed, turning red-brown

Quercus stellata WANGEN.

Fagaceae (Beech Family)

Post Oak, Iron Oak

Post oak ranges from southeastern Iowa to southeastern Massachusetts, south central Florida and west to northwestern Texas. It occurs with a variety of other hardwoods, particularly other oaks, and conifers, notably pines. It is primarily found on dry uplands having southerly or westerly exposures, but may occur on well-drained soils near to streams. It prefers to grow on shallow, well-drained, coarse-textured, infertile soils, low in organic material, and with clay or bedrock near the surface. Post oak is long-lived and slow-growing, but shade-intolerant. On most moist sites it is eventually overtopped by other hardwoods and shaded out. On dry sites, its drought tolerance enables it to persists as a climax forest tree.

Closely related to the post oak, and often considered a variety of it, delta post oak, *Quercus similis*, differs primarily in site preferences and overall stature. It occurs in bottomlands from western Mississippi to eastern Texas and up the Mississippi river valley into southeastern Arkansas. It strongly prefers rich, moist, sandy loams on the highest ridges and terraces of river floodplains. Delta post oak is moderately shade-tolerant.

Reaching about 70 ft. (21 m) or occasionally larger, post oak may be shrubby on very difficult sites. It generally has a short stout trunk supporting a dense rounded crown. Its light gray bark is fissured into thin platy ridges. The leaves are slightly thickened, about 6 in. (15 cm) long by 4 in. (10 cm) wide with five to seven deep, broad rounded lobes, the middle two of which are much larger than the rest, suggesting a Maltese cross. The leaves are lustrous dark green above and slightly rough from scattered hairs; hairy and gray-green below. Fall color is orange above and violet below. Flowers and fruit are typically oaklike. The elliptical acorn is about 1 in. (2.5 cm) long, half enclosed in the cap, maturing brown in the first season. The roots of post oak are initially a thick tap root, but where there is clay in an undersoil, development is slow and restricted to the upper soil.

Post oak is used infrequently as a drought-tolerant shade tree. It is prone to diseases, particularly

The leaves of post oak have deep, broad, rounded lobes, the middle two much larger than the rest.

chestnut blight. Its main value economically is for posts, lathing, planks, flooring, siding and construction timbers. In its natural setting, post oak provides cover for many animals, particularly cavities for nesting. Its acorns are eaten by birds and mammals as well.

Quercus tomentella ENGELM.

Fagaceae (Beech Family)

Island Live Oak, Channel Island Oak

Island live oak is endemic to the Channel Islands of Santa Rosa, Santa Cruz, Santa Catalina and Guadaloupe of the coast of California and Baja California. It inhabits the moister, more protected

Island Live Oak is a stately tree in cultivation, having a rounded dense crown of evergreen leaves.

drainage courses in deep, narrow canyons and wind-swept slopes.

Potentially reaching about 65 ft. (19.5 m), island live oak is more often closer to 40 ft. (12 m), forming a single trunk supporting a rounded crown. The bark is thin, red-brown, and fissured shallowly into large scales. Its evergreen leaves are elliptical, sharp-pointed, often wavy, with variably coarse toothed edge, the upper surface shiny dark green, the lower densely and finely hairy. The flowers and fruit are typical of oaks, the acorn being borne singly or paired. It is oval, to 1.25 in. (3.0 cm) long, with a shallow, warty cap.

Island live oak is used as a stately amenity landscape and street tree, but is under threat on the Channel Islands from human development. It has hard durable wood, but is not commercially harvested. In its native setting it provides invaluable habitat to birds and mammals.

Quercus velutina LAM.

Fagaceae (Beech Family)

Black Oak, Yellow Oak, Yellowbark Oak, Quercitron Oak

Black oak extends from southeastern Minnesota through southern Ontario to southwestern Maine, south to northwestern Florida and west to central Texas. It is absent from the Gulf coastal plain and the lower Mississippi river valley. It is found in a number of forest communities associating with other hardwoods, especially oaks and conifers, predominantly pines, but occasionally it forms pure stands also. It is common on drier warmer southern and western slope aspects, but its best growth occurs in moist, rich, well-drained soils. Black oak is moderately fast-growing and moderately long-lived. However, because it is only moderately shade-tolerant as a seedling and needs light to progress to the sapling stage and beyond, it competes poorly with other hardwoods on moister sites, and is generally not present in the climax forest canopy. On the drier, warmer sites its drought tolerance enables

Although not often planted as an amenity tree, black oak forms a large, open, rounded crown when open-grown.

are either shallow, or deep and narrow, with a few bristle-tipped teeth at the ends of each lobe. They are shiny dark olive-green above, yellow green and often hairy-brown below, turning a dull red-brown in the autumn. Flowers and fruit are typically oak-like. The elliptical brown acorns mature in the second year, and are about 0.75 in. (19 mm) long and half covered by a thick cap, slightly pointed at the top and with rust-brown hairy scales fringing the edge. Black oak develops a deep tap root supported by deeply penetrating, wide-spreading laterals.

Black oak is not commonly planted as an amenity tree, largely because it is difficult to transplant and not as fast-growing as red oak. Its wood is graded, sold and used as red oak for use in furniture, flooring and interior finishes. Tannin is extracted from the bark for use in tanning, and a yellow dye may be extracted from the inner bark for use in dying natural fibres. Many birds and mammals eat the acorns of black oak, and it is an important tree for cavity-nesting birds. The management of black oak on sites where it competes with other more shade-tolerant, longer-lived species depends on the use of fire, advance regeneration from young stumps, and maintaining at least 20 percent light levels on the ground.

it to compete more effectively and it will establish itself in the climax canopy, especially in habitats prone to fire.

Reaching 80 ft. (24 m) black oak forms a single straight trunk supporting a large open rounded crown when growing in the open. In forest settings it is often free of branches for half its height and has a smaller oval crown. The ashy gray bark first develops shallow fissures and wide, flat ridges, but later becomes quite thick and unevenly furrowed into rough ridges and blocks, with a yellow bitter-tasting inner bark. Its leaves are up to 9 in. (23 cm) long and two-thirds as wide, with between seven and nine pointed lobes, separated by sinuses which

Quercus virginiana MILL.
Fagaceae (Beech Family)
Live Oak, Virginia Live Oak, Southern Live Oak, Bay Live Oak

Live oak ranges along the coastal plain from southeast Virginia south to southern Florida and west into central Texas. Local populations also occur in southwest Oklahoma and northeastern Mexico. This range encompasses all three of the recognized varieties. Live oak is found in a variety of plant habitats from forest to savanna to grassland. Occasionally it forms extensive pure stands, sometimes sprouting from the root, but more often occurs mixed with other hardwoods and conifers, such as pines and junipers. It is often festooned with Spanish

Occasionally, live oak forms extensive pure stands, sometimes sprouting from the root.

moss, and other epiphytic plants. It is quite adaptable to soil conditions. While growing best on moist, well-drained sandy soils and loams, it can also be found on drier sites, on sites occasionally flooded, and on clay. It is tolerant of salt spray and to a limited extent to salt water in the soil at high tides. Live oak is moderately shade-tolerant, fast-growing and long-lived. Because of its salt tolerance and in the absence of fire, it forms the dominant climax tree in maritime forests.

Reaching a potential 50 ft. (15 m), live oak develops a short, stout trunk supporting several massive, nearly horizontal, wide-spreading limbs forming a broad, dense crown. Its dark brown-gray bark is deeply furrowed into rough scaly ridges. The elliptical leaves are essentially evergreen, to 4 in. (10 cm) long by half as wide, smooth-edged and round-tipped, shining dark green above and gray-green and densely hairy below, shed after new leaves appear in the spring. Flowers and fruit are typically oaklike. The oblong acorns are long-stalked, mature in the first year, and are up to an inch (2.5 cm) long, narrow and half covered by a deep cap. Live oak is thought to be tap-rooted because of its ability to withstand windthrow from hurricane-force winds.

Live oak is a popular and characteristic amenity shade tree in the Southeast, truly noble, majestic and bold in all seasons. It needs room to develop, however, and is best suited to large open places. It isn't susceptible to many diseases or insects unless stressed or damaged by fire. However, a disease called live oak decline is regarded as a potential serious problem, killing thousands of trees annually. It was at one time an important timber tree for building ships, but its commercial use is currently quite limited. Native peoples extracted an oil from the acorn which is said to be equal in quality to olive oil. The acorns themselves are sweet, and are an important food for many birds and mammals. The trees themselves provide valuable protective shelter, and numerous birds nest in it.

Rhamnus purshiana DC.
Rhamnaceae (Buckthorn Family)
Cascara, Cascara Buckthorn, Bearberry, Chittam Bark

Cascara is generally distributed from southwestern British Columbia southward into northern California, primarily west of the Cascades. It can be found sporadically east into northern Idaho and northwestern Montana as well. It is found as an understory plant mixed with other trees and shrubs in several coniferous forest types as well as chaparral, on lower mountain slopes, moist canyons and bottomlands. It is shade-tolerant and moderately long-lived, usually appearing on disturbed sites midway through succession and persisting for some time.

The tiny yellow flowers of cascara are gathered in clusters in the axils of the leaves.

THE WILLOWS (*SALIX*)
Willow Family (*Salicaceae*)

The willows are an extensive genus of some 250 to 300 species, found from the high arctic to lowland temperate regions of the Northern Hemisphere. Seventy-five or so species are native to North America, most of them shrubs. While several regularly attain large tree size, virtually all of them exist as shrubs somewhere within their ranges. This book discusses seven species that to varying extents are tree form, and represent the variety of habitat within which the willows may be found.

Willows prefer moist soils. Most species occur along stream- and riverbanks, some along the shallow edges of lakes or swamps, some in soil that has a high water table, and some where seasonal water runs and groundwater are otherwise plentiful. They are generally very fast-growing, shade-intolerant and short-lived. They tend to colonize water-disturbed sites and form locally pure stands quickly. Barring disturbance, many species are displaced by slower-growing, shade-tolerant, longer-lived trees. Some associated with marshes and swamps tend to persist on the wettest ground because other trees cannot become established under these soil conditions.

As trees, willows vary a good deal in overall habit. Some, like the black willow, develop massive, rugged-barked trunks with wide-spreading, open canopies. Others such as the red willow (as discussed in this book) or pussy willow have slender trunks and more slender crowns. The twigs of willows are slender and often attractively colored, especially in winter. The fine-toothed, simple leaves are arranged in alternate fashion and are variable in shape, from slender and linear to elliptical and oval. Leafy stipules are present at the base of the leafstalk in some species and are usually shed before or soon after the leaf is fully expanded. Leaves are typically deciduous, although those of red willow come very close to being evergreen. Appearing before the leaves unfold, the flowers of willows are tiny, without petals, and unisexual;

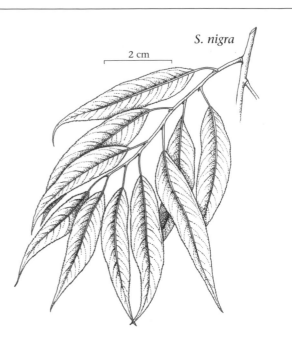

S. nigra

2 cm

Willows generally have narrow elliptical to lance-shaped leaves.

male and female flowers are gathered into same-sex clusters on separate trees. The clusters are catkinlike and erect, a single stem having numerous individual flowers. On female trees the flowers are followed by small, oval, green capsules, densely packed along a somewhat drooping stem. They mature as the leaves are fully grown in early summer, and split open into two, to release their silky, white-haired seeds. The roots of willows are shallow-rooted and very fibrous.

Some of the native tree willows are deliberately grown, or fostered in appropriate settings for attractive catkins or twig color. Many jurisdictions, however, forbid the deliberate cultivation of willows where their roots might interfere with public waterworks or sewers. Except for black willow, whose wood has some minor use, the willows are not economically important for timber. They are probably the easiest tree to propagate from cutting, and this characteristic makes them a mainstay of riparian restoration projects, and slope stabilization in relation to streams and rivers. In wetland habitats they provide useful cover and nesting sites to many birds.

Salix caroliniana MICHX.

Salicaceae (Willow Family)

Coastal Plain Willow, Ward Willow, Southern Willow

Coastal plain willow is actually more widely distributed than its common name suggests. It occurs from southern Pennsylvania south to southern Florida, west to central Texas and north to extreme southeastern Nebraska. Except for along the Atlantic coast and the eastern portion of the Gulf coast its range is fragmented. It may be found in several wetland forest communities along river and streambanks as well as in swamps. It requires soils that are wet most of the time and dependably flooded for at least part of every year. It is shade-intolerant, fast-growing and short-lived. Like most

The bark of coastal plain willow is typically furrowed into flat, wide, and scaly ridges.

willows it roots easily from live twigs that break off during floods and are washed downstream, lodge in flood-exposed soil and become established. It is usually shaded out by larger wetland hardwoods on wetland edges, but wherever it is not overtopped, it reproduces and persists.

Often shrubby, and thicket-forming, coastal plain willow as a tree grows to 30 ft. (9 m) with an oval crown of spreading or somewhat drooping branches and slender, flexible twigs, which are hairy when young. Its smoothish, gray-black bark becomes furrowed into flat, wide, scaly ridges. The narrow elliptical leaves are up to 4 in. (10 cm) long by 0.75 in. (1.9 cm) wide, finely saw-toothed along the edges, very hairy when young, green above, white-green below, with a hairy leafstalk. There is no appreciable fall color. Flowers and fruits are typical of willows, the fruit capsules maturing in late spring or early summer. Coastal plain willow has a shallow, fibrous root system.

Coastal plain willow is a common small tree at lower altitudes in the Southeast and in wetland areas elsewhere in its range. It is not used as an amenity landscape tree, but is useful in wetland restoration projects and streambank stabilization, since live stakes and brush mats can be easily rooted on site. It provides shelter and nesting to many wetland birds.

Salix discolor MUHL.

Salicaceae (Willow Family)

Pussy Willow

Pussy willow ranges from southern Labrador to northern British Columbia, southeast to northeastern Missouri and east to Delaware. Scattered populations occur from North Dakota through Wyoming. It is common in wet meadows, and along rivers and streams, on the shallow shores of lakes and in swamps, particularly in coniferous forest. It is not especially particular about soil type, but requires relatively neutral, permanently very moist to wet soils that are flooded for at least a part of the year. It is shade-intolerant, fast-growing and short-lived. It colonizes sites disturbed by flooding by seeding on the exposed mineral soil, but is eventually shaded

The long narrow leaves of black willow typically have prominent stipules at the base.

Because it roots easily from cuttings, even as posts, it is a very valuable and much-used species for reducing streambank erosion. It also provides valuable habitat for many nesting birds and small mammals, which eat the catkins and fruit as well. Bees visit the flowers, which are an important early source of pollen for bees coming out of hibernation. Black wil-

low is also used as a shade tree especially adjacent to ponds and streams. It makes an interesting and colorful tree in a winter landscape when pollarded to form a brush on a single trunk.

Salix taxifolia KUNTH.
Salicaceae (Willow Family)
Yewleaf Willow

Yewleaf willow is primarily distributed in Mexico, but is found in the United States from southern Texas through southern Arizona. It is essentially a riparian tree, associating with other trees along mountain streams and canyon bottoms where the soil is dependably moist to wet.

KEY FEATURES

Salix nigra

Form:	Crown high, irregular and **wide-spreading**, with **stout** limbs
Trunk:	**Very stout multiple trunks that tend to lean outward**
Bark:	Thick, dark brown-gray to black bark, **deeply furrowed into scaly, forking ridges**
Twig:	Slender, **orange-brown**
Leaves:	Long and narrow, **somewhat curving towards one side**, long-pointed and finely toothed
Flower:	Dioecious, male flowers in fuzzy catkins, female flowers in small green catkins
Fruit:	Stringlike cluster of pointed, oval capsules, splitting open to release cottony seeds

Yewleaf willow has an open crown and fine-textured, pale gray-green foliage.

Reaching to about 50 ft. (15 m), yewleaf willow develops a straight trunk supporting a broad, open crown of branches which tend to droop at the tips. The light gray bark is relatively thick and deeply fissured into broad, flat ridges. Its twigs are finely downy in the first year, becoming purple-brown to light red-brown in the second year. The leaves are narrowly lance-shaped to about 1.25 in. (3.0 cm) long by about 0.1 in. (3 mm) wide, opening covered in soft white hairs that largely disappear as the leaf expands. They are pale gray-green on both surfaces. Very tiny stipules are formed at the base of the leafstalks, but these are quickly shed. Flowers and fruit are typically willowlike. Its root system is fibrous, shallow and wide-spreading.

Yewleaf willow has no commercial importance. Many riparian birds and mammals use it for food, shelter and nesting, however; and like many willows it is valuable in the management of riparian habitats, preventing erosion and contributing to diversity.

Sapindus drummondii HOOK & ARN.
Salicaceae (Willow Family)
Western Soapberry, Wild China Tree, Mexican Soapberry

Often considered a variety of wingleaf soapberry (*Sapindus saponaria*), western soapberry grows from southwestern through southeastern Colorado, into Arizona, east into Texas, adjacent Mexico and Louisiana. It is found in a variety of woodland communities, grasslands and desert scrub communities, most often along rivers and canyon sides, washes, arroyos and dry watercourses in riparian woodlands. It grows best on moist to dry, well-drained, heavy soils derived from limestone, but can be found on other soils as well. Western soapberry is moderately long-lived and is a component of the climax riparian community.

Western soapberry is a medium-sized tree to about 40 ft. (12 m), with a wide-spreading rounded to irregular crown of upright brittle branches. The bark is light gray to red-brown and thin, splitting

Western soapberry has a wide-spreading, rounded to irregular crown of upright branches.

into deep fissures and long narrow scaly plates. Its alternately arranged, pinnately compound leaves are up to 8 in. (20 cm) long, with up to 19 leaflets, each 3 in. (7.5 cm) long by 0.75 in. (1.9 cm) wide, arranged in pairs along a slender mid-vein, the terminal leaflet usually aborting. Leaflets are long-pointed and slightly curved to one side, smooth-edged, short-stalked, yellow-green above, with prominent veins and slightly hairy below, turning a golden yellow in the autumn. A dioecious tree with male and female flowers on separate trees, soapberry has tiny yellow-white flowers in upright clusters about 9 in. (23 cm) long in late spring or early summer. These are followed by yellow to orange, almost transparent, leathery berries to about 0.5 in. (13 mm) in diameter, borne in small clusters,

crown is conical in youth becoming columnar with age. Its red-brown bark is soft, thick and deeply furrowed into wide ridges. The needles are of two kinds. Those on strong-growing shoots and on shoots bearing cones are small, scalelike, pressed towards the shoot and arranged radially around it. All other shoots have longer, narrow needles, 1.75 in. (1.9 cm) long, spreading out to the sides of the shoot. These needles are slightly twisted at the base and run down a short distance along the shoot. They are somewhat stiff and pale green. The male cones are small and globular, shedding their pollen in the spring. The ripened female cones are brown, oblong, to 1.25 in. (3 cm) long, maturing in the autumn of the first year. California redwood develops a root system of deep, wide-spreading laterals.

At maturity, California redwood towers over adjacent trees.

California redwood is among the more important timber trees of California, being very resistant to decay, soft, easily split and worked. It is used for dimension lumber and shingles. Burls of the wood are also used to make table tops, veneers and turned goods. California redwood is used in the restoration of disturbed areas and riparian ecosystems, and is plantation-grown in several other parts of the world, notable New Zealand and Australia. Two small cultivated forms, "nana pendula" and "prostrata," are available commercially and extensively used in landscape applications. In its natural setting, California redwood is valued for the habitat it provides for many birds, mammals, reptiles and amphibians. The old-growth stands are particularly important habitat for the spotted owl, federally designated as threatened, and the marbled murrelet, listed by the state of California as endangered. Both birds nest exclusively in these stands. Pileated woodpeckers cavity-nest in both dead snags and in living trunks.

Sequoiadendron giganteum (LINDL.) BUCHHOLZ
Taxodiaceae (Bald Cypress Family)
Giant Sequoia, Mammoth Tree, Sequoia, Redwood, Bigtree

Highly restricted and fragmented in its distribution, giant sequoia is found in about 75 groves, having a total area of only about 35,607 acres (14,416 ha) along a small section of the western Sierra Nevada in California, from the American River in Placer County to Deer Grove Creek in southern Tulare County. The largest grove is about 2,470 acres (1,000 ha) with 20,000 trees, while the smallest are groves of only 6 trees. Although in a few small areas it approaches forming pure stands, it generally occurs in scattered small groves mixed with other conifers dominated by white fir. Giant sequoia grows best on deep, well-drained, moist and slightly acidic soils derived from granite, although its chief requirements seem to be adequate soil moisture in the dry summer season and temperate winter conditions.

Although shade-intolerant, potentially fast-growing, and long-lived, to about 3,000 years, giant sequoia requires substantial shading as a very young seedling to avoid desiccation and to establish its root system. It does not reproduce naturally from seed very easily, and depends on fire to some extent to renew itself. Given the necessary light levels after it has established its root system, it will form a component in the forest climax forest.

Giant sequoia reaches average heights of about 250 ft. (75 m), although it may grow higher still. The crown is initially conical on a straight trunk, becoming broader with age. Lower limbs are shaded out by upper ones, and for the first century tend to remain dead on the tree. After that the limbs shed

Giant sequoia has red-brown, thick, furrowed, and strongly ridged bark; its leaves are awl-like scales.

after dying and a branch-free tapering trunk develops, often clear up to 100 to 150 ft. (30 to 45 m). The dark brown to red-brown bark is thick, moderately soft, often fluted, furrowed and strongly ridged. Its leaves are awl-like scales, arranged radially around the shoot, forward-pointing, slightly incurved, gray-green, becoming darker and shiny with age, and remaining attached after dying. Male cones are borne at the ends of shoots in the spring. Ripened female cones are green, maturing in the second year. They are oval to 3 in. (7.5 cm) long, and remain closed on the tree after ripening. The root system of giant sequoia is initially a tap root with a few laterals, but after the first several years, lateral root growth predominates and the tap root

Even one of the smaller groves of giant sequoia is an impressive sight.

A very shade-tolerant tree, mountain stewartia is a small understory tree of climax hardwoods.

In the open, mahogany forms a low, rounded, and wide-spreading crown.

oval or elliptical, to 4.5 in. (11 cm) long and half as wide, long-pointed, finely toothed and hairy along the edges. They are smooth dark green above, lighter gray-green below, and turn orange and red in autumn. The waxy white flowers are up to 4 in. (10 cm) in diameter with five unequally sized, wavy-edged petals and numerous yellow-white stamens. They are borne singly in the axil of the leaf in early summer. The brown, hairy fruit is hard, oval but five-angled, with a pointed tip, to 0.75 in. (1.9 cm) long. Mountain stewartia has a deeply penetrating lateral root system.

Mountain stewartia is a popular garden tree or large shrub, valued for its showy flowers, fall foliage color and interesting, multicolored, peeling bark. It can be difficult to transplant as a larger tree, and has specific site requirements of filtered shade and moist acidic soil. But once established it is generally pest- and disease-free. In its native habitat it is not extensively used by wildlife.

Swietenia mahogoni (L.) JACQ.
Meliaceae (Mahogany Family)
Mahogany

Mahogany is an increasingly rare plant in its limited natural range in the United States. It is found only in Dade and Monroe Counties in Florida, where it occurs in subtropical hardwood hammocks. It is

characteristically found on ground with a high water table.

Mahogany becomes a large tree, to about 80 ft. (24 m) on a relatively long, slender trunk, with a high narrow crown in typical forest settings, but lower, rounded and more wide-spreading when open-grown. Its leaves are pinnately compound to 8 in. (20 cm) long by half as wide, with up to 8 leaflets. These are narrowly oval and sharp-pointed, to about 4 in. (10 cm) long. The leaves are dark green above and pale yellow to red-brown below. The flowers are inconspicuous for the most part, borne in small green-white clusters on slender downy stalks in the axils of the leaves. The fruits in contrast are large woody pods to about 5 in. (13 cm) long, maturing in late autumn or winter, splitting open to release 0.75 in. (1.9 cm) long flat, winged seeds.

While the wood of mahogany is very highly valued for furniture, cabinetry and other woodworking, its rarity in North America prevents its commercial use. It is grown, however, as a landscape shade tree for residential use and as a street tree.

Taxodium ascendens BRONGN.
Taxodiaceae (Bald Cypress Family)
Pond Cypress, Pond Bald Cypress

Pond bald cypress is closely related to common bald cypress, and is often considered a variety of it. It

On fast-growing branches, the soft, flat, flexible leaves of pond cypress are arranged in two rows on either side of the twig.

differs in distribution, site preference and some physical characteristics. It ranges from southeastern Virginia to southern Florida to southeastern Louisiana along the coastal plain. It generally prefers shallow ponds, wet depressions and poorly drained, infertile soils, more acidic and less subject to periodic flooding than those preferred by common bald cypress. It is typically found associating with swamp tupelo, as well as other trees that prefer wetland margins. Otherwise, its ecological niche is similar to common bald cypress.

In height and habit pond bald cypress resembles common bald cypress on a somewhat smaller scale, reaching about 70 ft. (21 m) with a more conical and domed crown. Its trunk generally has more rounded ridges on the fluting, and the bark is more coarsely ridged. Its leaves are more scalelike, pressed along and all around the twig. In young trees or on fast-growing branches the leaves are more like the common bald cypress and arranged in two rows to each side of the twig. The cones are also similar to the common bald cypress, as is the root system, except that it is less likely to have knees and they are shorter and more rounded when they do occur.

Pond bald cypress has many of the same uses as common bald cypress. In addition, the ponds and depressions where it is found are the only breeding places for a number of amphibians and are consequently important in maintaining habitat.

Taxodium distichum (L.) RICH.
Taxodiaceae (Bald Cypress Family)
Common Bald Cypress

Common bald cypress ranges along the coastal plain from southern Delaware to southern Florida, and west into central Texas and extreme southeastern Oklahoma. It also occurs up the Mississippi valley to southwestern Indiana. Occupying a variety of wetland forest types, bald cypress commonly occurs along streams, where soil depth and water table may fluctuate considerably over its lifetime, resulting in a variety of different associated trees and shrubs. It prefers flat sites that are typically subject to prolonged and frequent flooding, with either moving

In natural conditions, common bald cypress tends to have a high narrow crown.

Common bald cypress develops a buttressed base to the trunk and characteristic "knees" from the root.

or stagnant water on soil that is fertile. It cannot tolerate salt in the water so is not as common in estuary wetlands. Bald cypress is somewhat shade-tolerant as a sapling, but intolerant with age. It is moderately fast-growing and long-lived. It appears to grow best when colonizing an open site, but it will also take advantage as a shaded sapling to exploit a new gap in the canopy.

Bald cypress grows to about 120 ft. (37 m), or occasionally higher, on a tapering trunk that is often buttressed and fluted at the base. In natural conditions it tends to have a high narrow, rounded crown, but in the open is more wide-spreading and flat-topped. The gray-brown bark fissures shallowly into long, thin, fibrous or scaly ridges that peel off in strips. Its leaves are soft, flat, flexible, deciduous needles, about 0.75 in. (1.9 cm) long, borne feather-like in two crowded rows on a green twig. They are dull light green above, almost white below, turning coppery-brown in the autumn and shed along with the twig that bears them. The male cones are tiny and borne in small clusters. The female cones at maturity are gray, round, to about 1 in. (2.5 cm) in diameter, borne singly or in pairs at the ends of twigs, and shed when ripe. Bald cypress develops a tap root initially, but older trees form several descending roots that provide firm support. In addition, bald cypress forms curious upright, conical roots called knees, which extend above ground to varying heights, up to 12 ft. (3.7 m) in some cases.

The presence and size of knees seems roughly correlated to the average water level of a site, but even cultivated trees will occasionally form small ones.

Bald cypress is widely planted as an ornamental on soils that are permanently moist, wet or even dry. Its striking features are its unusual knees as well as its buttressed trunk and its crown of deciduous branches. The wood of bald cypress has many uses. The heartwood of old-growth trees is highly rot-resistant and has been used for many applications where wood must be in contact with water or high humidity. Second-growth heartwood does not have the same degree of rot resistance, however, and needs to be treated to prevent rot. In its natural setting, bald cypress provides valuable habitat to many species of birds. Woodstorks, eagles and ospreys nest in the tops of old trees, and a number of others nest in cavities in the trunks. The seeds are eaten by squirrels as well as a number of birds, but the principal consumer of these was the now extinct Carolina parakeet. Common bald cypress growing in river swamps also slows water down, spreads it out and increases opportunities for infiltration and sedimentation.

KEY FEATURES

Taxodium distichum

Form:	Wide-spreading and flat-topped in open; narrower and high in dense stands
Trunk:	**Tapering, often buttressed and fluted at the base**
Bark:	Gray-brown, fissuring shallowly into long, thin, fibrous or scaly ridges which peel off in strips
Twig:	Slender, **deciduous with leaves**
Leaves:	Soft, flat, flexible, **deciduous, borne featherlike in two crowded rows on a green twig**
Cones:	Gray, round, borne singly or in pairs at the ends of twigs, and shed when ripe

Taxodium mucronatum TEN.

Taxodiaceae (Bald Cypress Family)

Montezuma Bald Cypress

Widespread through Mexico to Guatemala, Montezuma bald cypress is found in extreme southern Texas near sea level in Cameron and Hidalgo counties. It grows in the same conditions as common bald cypress, preferring the wet soil of streambanks and swamps.

Montezuma bald cypress develops a massive, buttressed trunk supporting a wide-spreading crown of ascending limbs and drooping twigs. Its red-brown bark is smooth to shallowly fissured, shredding in

Montezuma bald cypress develops a magnificent wide-spreading crown of ascending limbs and drooping twigs.

fibrous strips. Its leaves are soft, flat, flexible, evergreen to deciduous needles, about 0.5 in. (13 mm) long, borne featherlike in two crowded rows on a green twig. They are dull light green above, almost white below, turning brown in the autumn and shed along with the twig that bears them when new leaves emerge in the spring. The male cones are tiny and gathered into open drooping clusters. Female cones are brown-gray, round, to about 1 in. (2.5 cm) in diameter, the hard cone-scales shed at maturity to release the seeds. Montezuma bald cypress has a root system similar to that of common bald cypress, sometimes producing small knees from submerged roots.

Montezuma bald cypress has much the same uses as common bald cypress. It becomes a majestic, spectacular tree, usually evergreen. Several particularly large specimens are recorded in Mexico. Those in Chapultepec Park in Mexico City at 165 ft. (50 m) are believed to exceed 600 years old, and to be the oldest cultivated trees in the Americas. Not cold-hardy, Montezuma bald cypress is suitable for only the mild, moist parts of the southern United States.

Taxus brevifolia NUTT.

Taxaceae (Yew Family)

Pacific Yew, Western Yew

Pacific Yew ranges along the Pacific coast from southeastern Alaska southward through western British Columbia, Washington, Oregon and into central California. It also occurs from southeastern British Columbia through northwestern Montana and northern Idaho into eastern Washington and Oregon. It grows as an understory tree in association with other conifers in a number of coniferous forest types. It grows in a variety of cool moist shaded habitats in canyon bottoms, moist flat forested sites near streams and in various upland sites in the dense shade of other trees. It is most commonly found on deep, rich, moist, well-drained, acidic soils derived from a variety of

The needles of Pacific yew are flat and linear, arranged in two rows on either side of the twig.

Thuja occidentalis L.
Cupressaceae (Cypress Family)
Eastern White Cedar, Eastern Arborvitae

A widespread tree of the Great Lakes and St. Lawrence River basin, eastern white cedar ranges from Nova Scotia and Maine west to southeastern Manitoba, southeast around the tip of Lake Michigan and east to New York. It also occurs locally down the Appalachians into North Carolina and Tennessee. Although sometimes found in extensive pure stands, eastern white cedar more commonly is associated with a mix of other conifers and northern hardwoods in several coniferous and mixed forest types. It generally grows best on soils derived from limestone which are

bedrock types. A long-lived, slow-growing tree, Pacific yew is characteristically found in climax and old-growth forests as a dense understory, but also occurs on logging-disturbed sites. It is absent from sites frequently disturbed by fire.

Often shrubby, Pacific yew can attain a height of about 75 ft. (22.5 m) on a single, often contorted trunk, forming a conical open crown with slender drooping branches. Its bark is thin, red-purple and scaly. The needles are flat and linear, to about 1 in. (2.5 cm) long, arranged spirally but flattened to either side of the twig. They are dark green above, lighter yellow-green below and are retained for about five or six years usually. Pacific yew bears its male cones on separate trees from the female cones. The male cones are tiny and produced abundantly every year in spring. Female cones are small, single and greenish. They mature in one year to produce a fleshy red cup about 0.4 in. (1 cm) long, surrounding a single, naked, green or red seed, which is shed in the autumn. The root system of Pacific yew is fibrous, shallow and wide-spreading.

The wood of Pacific yew is valued for its durability, hardness, fine grain, rose-red color and workability. It is used in cabinetry, carving and the manufacture of canoe paddles and bows, for which it is particularly prized. The bark is the source of the anti-cancer agent, taxol. Its needles produce a compound that inhibits the growth of other plants beneath it.

The crown of eastern white cedar is dense and broadly conical, often laden with cones in alternate years.

The foliage of eastern white cedar is arranged in flattened sprays, and the cones are clustered at the ends of twigs.

neutral to slightly alkaline, well-drained, moist, cool, and nutrient-rich. However, it may also be found extensively on well-decomposed organic soils near streams and other wet areas such as swamps and fens that have a strong flow of fairly nutrient-rich water. It may also occur on shallow loams over broken limestone, rich moist soils in old fields, clays, limestone cliffs and sandstone bluffs. Only excessively wet or extremely dry sites do not support it well. It is fairly shade-tolerant, relatively slow-growing and long-lived. Eastern white cedar tends to dominate low-lying, wetland sites in uneven-aged stands as a climax canopy tree, unless fire or some other disturbance opens an area for balsam fir or hardwoods such as black ash. In old fields and in extensively fired or cleared swamps, it dominates in pure even-aged stands.

Eastern white cedar grows to about 70 ft. (21 m) on one to several trunks that are often tapered, and buttressed at the base. Its bark is thin, fissuring shallowly into fibrous, shredding, interconnecting ridges. The crown of eastern white cedar is dense and broadly conical with jointed twigs, much branched and flattened in the horizontal plane. The leaves are small scales arranged in four rows along the twig. The two rows running along the sides of the twigs are strongly keeled, while the one on the top of the twig and the one below are flattened against the twig and have a gland dot in the middle. The leaves are very closely arranged so that the twig itself is not generally visible, and remains on the twig after they have died. The leaves are a rich yellow-green, bronzing strongly in winter. The female cones are borne in clusters, ripen brown and woody, and are egg-shaped when closed. They are somewhat less than half an inch (10 mm) long and open to release several small winged seeds. The root system of eastern white cedar is variable. On drier soils a deep tap root with few laterals develops, but on wet ground a very short tap root is formed and many thick laterals become predominant.

Eastern white cedar is a widely popular evergreen landscape tree that is extensively used in both formal and informal hedging, as well as in windbreaks and visual screens. There are dozens of cultivated forms, varying from dense narrow conical trees to low, rounded mounding shrubs. There are others with varying color hues, those that are golden being very popular, albeit slower-growing. The wood of eastern white cedar is mainly used in lumber and the manufacture of shingles, poles, split-rail fencing, log houses, boats, particularly canoes, and a variety of smaller articles. Cedar boughs are a popular decoration, and cedar oil is distilled from the foliage and used in the manufacture of perfumes

KEY FEATURES

Thuja occidentalis

Form: Dense and broadly conical with jointed twigs, much branched and **flattened in the horizontal plane**

Trunk: One to several, upright to curving outward

Bark: Thin, fissuring shallowly into fibrous, **shredding interconnecting ridges**

Twig: Slender, covered by adpressed leaves

Leaves: Small scales, four-ranked, lateral rows strongly keeled, **fragrant of apple when bruised**

Cones: Borne in clusters, ripen brown and woody, and are **egg-shaped when closed**

and medicines. The foliage and bark are also high in vitamin C, and a tea prepared from the leaves saved Jacques Cartier and his crew from scurvy in 1535 while exploring the St. Lawrence River. Eastern white cedar is also important to wildlife, providing shelter from winter storms, and food in the form of seeds, leaves and inner bark.

Thuja plicata D. DON
Cupressaceae (Cypress Family)
Western Red Cedar, Giant Arborvitae, Pacific Red Cedar,

Western red cedar occurs in three broad ranges in the Pacific Northwest. One is along the Pacific coast,

Western red cedar typically has a conical open crown of rather pendant branches.

With age, the base of the trunk of western red cedar is usually tapered, swollen, and buttressed.

including the Queen Charlotte Islands, from the Alaska Panhandle through into the coastal redwood forests of northern California. Another extends from central Oregon north into southern British Columbia. A third population occurs much farther inland along the west slopes of the Rocky Mountains from Prince George, British Columbia, through northeastern Washington and northern Idaho to western Montana. Western red cedar occurs in a wide variety of coniferous forest habitats as a dominant or co-dominant tree. It is found on a large number of different soil types, but prefers moist, rich soils that are either somewhat acidic, neutral or somewhat alkaline. A slow-growing, shade-tolerant, long-lived tree, western red cedar may be found in all successional phases but tends to persist and dominate in climax forests.

At 100 ft. (30 m), or occasionally more, western red cedar forms a tall, columnar to conical, open crown of rather pendant branches, often layered around the base of the trunk to create a widening circle of clonal trees, although lightning strikes sometimes shatter the leader, resulting in a multicrowned tree. The base of the trunk is usually tapered, swollen and buttressed, and its bark is dark red-brown to somewhat purple-brown, shallowly fissured into shaggy, peeling ridges. Its leaves are small scales arranged in four rows along the branching pendulous twigs. The scales in the two edge rows are keeled outward, while those of the upper and lower twig surface are pressed flat, giving the spray of twigs a flattened, fanlike, slightly drooping appearance. The leaves are lustrous green, turning slightly bronzed in winter. The ripened female cones are brown and woody when mature, pointing upward in clusters towards the ends of twigs, flask-shaped, to about 0.7 in. (1.5 cm) long, consisting of eight to ten scales, and opening in autumn to release several small, winged seeds. The root system of western red cedar is generally extensive, shallow and fibrous, rarely, if at all, forming a tap root.

Western red cedar forms a majestic tree in cultivation and is grown as a landscape ornamental for its combination of drooping branches, flattened sprays of leaves and fibrous bark. It is adaptable to various conditions of soil and shade, and with pruning it makes a superlative formal hedge. There are several cultivated forms available; the slow-growing golden ones are particularly attractive. Western red cedar has a variety of other values as well. Perfumes, insecticides, medicines, veterinary soaps, shoe polishes and deodorants are manufactured from the leaf oil. Various extracts are also used in lead refining, boiler-water additives and glue extenders. Native peoples used western red cedar extensively for a large variety of everyday items ranging from shelters, canoes and fishing nets to clothing. It is currently a commercially important timber tree, its wood being prized for long-lasting

shingles, shakes and siding. It is also used for chests and closets, boats, containers, fencing and utility poles. In its natural setting western red cedar is an important habitat tree for a wide range of wildlife. Larger mammals browse on its lower branches and saplings, while many birds and small mammals eat the seeds. Cavity nesting birds use its trunk for nests, and all animals take refuge from inclement weather beneath it.

KEY FEATURES

Thuja plicata

Form:	Columnar to conical, open crown, **pendant branches** often **layered** around the base of the trunk
Trunk:	**Tall, tapered, swollen and buttressed**
Bark:	Dark red-brown to somewhat purple-brown, shallowly fissured into **shaggy, peeling ridges**
Twig:	Slender, covered by adpressed leaves
Leaves:	Small scales, four-ranked, **lateral rows strongly keeled**
Cones:	Brown and woody when mature, pointing upward in clusters toward the ends of twigs, **flask-shaped**

Tilia americana L.
Tiliaceae (Linden Family)
Basswood, American Linden

Basswood ranges from southern Manitoba east to New Brunswick south into the Appalachians of western North Carolina, west to northeastern Oklahoma. It is generally associated with other deciduous hardwoods, particularly sugar maple, and coniferous trees such as eastern white pine and eastern hemlock in a number of forest types. It rarely occurs in pure stands. While basswood is generally

In the open, the crown of basswood is dense, oval, and quite broad, on a short trunk.

other deciduous hardwoods, and rarely if ever occur in pure stands.

Basswood typically reaches 100 ft. (30 m), usually on a single trunk, although two to several may occur from a stump. The crown is dense, conical to oval, the fine branches often drooping toward the tips. In the open the crown tends to become quite broad, but in crowded stands it is more narrow and columnar. The young bark is brown, smooth and thin, becoming gray-brown and furrowed into slender, flat-topped, tight ridges, typically with horizontal cracks. Its broadly heart-shaped leaves typically reach 6 in. (15 cm) long by almost as wide, and are coarsely toothed along the edge and borne on a long, slender leaf-stalk. They are shiny dark green above, lighter below, and turn a pale yellow to brown in the autumn. The flowers and fruit are borne in typical linden fashion. The individual yellow-white flowers are somewhat more than half an inch (1.2 cm) in diameter and fragrant, opening in early summer. The fruits are elliptical to about 0.4 in. (10 mm) long, hard, nutlike, gray, and somewhat hairy, attached to a long straplike wing by a long, slender stalk, maturing in the autumn and frequently remaining attached well into winter. The root system of basswood is primarily composed of shallow lateral roots that are most well developed in the upper two feet of soil. When cut to the ground, the root system of a healthy tree will sustain the rapid redevelopment of a new multiple-stemmed crown.

The leaf blade of basswood is typically rounded on one side and flat on the other.

associated with moist to dry, sandy to silty loams ranging from fairly acidic to slightly alkaline, it is most common on moist, very slightly acid to slightly alkaline, silty loams. It is shade-tolerant as a sapling, moderately fast-growing and moderately long-lived. On good sites throughout most of its range on good sites it tends to be a self-reproducing dominant or co-dominant canopy tree of the climax forest, capable of replacing itself under the shade of mature trees.

There are two other basswoods some authorities consider varieties of *Tilia americana*. Carolina basswood, or *Tilia caroliniana*, and white basswood, or *Tilia heterophylla* differ only in overall size and some characteristics of the leaf. Like basswood, Carolina and white basswoods are generally associated with

Basswood has a number of economically important uses. Its wood is valued for hand-carving, containers of various kinds, veneer, excelsior and pulp. Its fibrous inner bark, called bast, has provided fiber for woven baskets, ropes, fishing nets and mats. It is also widely planted as a landscape shade tree where space is available. It is a superb tree in flower, and generally provides a good display of autumn color. It also grows relatively quickly, tolerates shade and transplants easily. However, it is sensitive to pollution, salt and soil compaction, as well as prone to a number of diseases and insect problems, especially when environmentally stressed. The combination of shallow fibrous roots and dense canopy usually makes planting beneath the canopy of mature trees a challenge. It is arguably a better tree for large parklike settings than urban ones. Bees are highly attracted to the flowers and produce a fine honey from the nectar. Because the wood tends to rot, many cavity-nesting birds may be found associated with basswood as well.

KEY FEATURES

Tilia americana

Form: Dense, conical to oval, the fine branches often drooping towards the tips

Trunk: One to several, straight

Bark: Smooth, thin becoming gray-brown, furrowed into slender, flat-topped, tight ridges

Twig: Slender, red-brown

Leaves: **Broadly heart-shaped, coarsely toothed on a long, slender leafstalk**

Flower: **Yellow-white, fragrant**, in clusters with **straplike bract**, opening in early summer

Fruit: Elliptical, **hard, nutlike, gray, and somewhat hairy, in clusters**, maturing in the autumn

Torreya californica TORR.

Taxaceae (Yew Family)

California Nutmeg, Stinking Yew, Stinking Nutmeg

Endemic to California in a two-part range, California nutmeg occurs in the Coastal Ranges from southwest Trinity County south to Monterey County, and in the foothills of the Cascades and Sierra Nevada from Shasta County south to Tulare County. It is nowhere abundant, but is not considered rare. It is found in many different plant communities ranging from chaparral to coastal and inland forests. California nutmeg is characteristically found on moist soils at elevations of from 3,000 to 7,000 ft. (915 to 2,135 m) where summers

California nutmeg develops a dense, dark green crown with age.

are hot and dry and winters cool and wet. It occurs on streambanks, shaded slopes, lowland flats, and the floors of canyons. A shade-tolerant, slow-growing, long-lived tree, California nutmeg is typically a tree of late succession and climax communities. It is also fire-adapted and will regenerate from buds on the root crown and trunk base following a fire.

California nutmeg can attain a height of 90 ft. (27 m) with a pyramidal to irregular crown of horizontal spreading branches. Its thin, brown bark is shallowly and irregularly fissured into flat scaly ridges. It has flat, stiff evergreen needles to about 2.75 in. (7 cm) long, spreading in two rows to the sides of the twig, shiny, dark green above, lighter below, with two broad white bands below. When crushed the needles give off a strong, unpleasant, pinelike odor. California nutmeg bears male and female cones on separate trees. The pale yellow male cones are borne at the base of the needles in the spring and are about 0.25 (6 mm) long. The female cones ripen in two years, and are elliptical, to about 1.5 in. (3.7 cm) long, borne singly at the end on a twig. They have a bloomy, dark green, fleshy outer layer marked with purple-red striations and an inner layer that is light red-brown, and thick-walled. The root system of California nutmeg consists of deep laterals.

California nutmeg is sometimes planted as an ornamental tree in cultivated landscapes, but its disagreeable odor when bruised detracts somewhat from its visual aesthetics, particularly as formal hedging where clipping is required. It resembles yew, to which it is related, and provides a useful dark green foil to lighter plantings. Once established, it is generally an easy tree to care for. Currently its wood is not commercially used because of its relative rarity, although it has been used in the past for cabinetry, turnware, fenceposts and fuel. It is a very durable, fine-grained wood with a fragrance said to resemble sandalwood. A high-grade cooking oil may also be extracted from the seeds, which are edible and reported to taste similar to peanuts. The seeds are also consumed by a variety of wildlife.

Torreya taxifolia ARN.
Taxaceae (Yew Family)
Stinking Cedar, Florida Torreya, Polecat Wood, Gopherwood

Stinking cedar has a very restricted distribution, occurring largely on the east side of the Apalachicola River and its tributaries in the extreme southwest of Georgia and adjacent northwest Florida. It is considered endangered at the federal level and threatened at the state level. It grows in widely scattered groups mainly along limestone bluffs, associated with oak, tupelo, cypress and pine. It prefers moist, well-drained, strongly acid to slightly alkaline soils in the shade of the forest canopy. As a seedling it is tolerant of very deep shade and competes best under these conditions. Older trees grow better with full sun, but tend to be less competitive. Stinking cedar

Stinking cedar has flat, stiff, evergreen needles, spreading in two rows to the sides of the twig.

is considered to be an understory plant of late successional and climax forests.

A small tree to 30 ft. (21 m) stinking cedar forms a conical open crown of spreading horizontal branches. Its thin brown bark becomes shallowly and irregularly fissured into broad scaly ridges. It has flat, stiff evergreen needles to about 1.5 in. (4 cm) long, spreading in two rows to the sides of the twig, shiny, dark green above lighter below with two broad, white bands below. When crushed the needles give off a very disagreeable odor. Stinking cedar bears male and female cones on separate trees. The pale yellow male cones are borne at the base of the needles in the spring and are about 0.25 (6 mm) long. The female cones ripen in two years, and are elliptical, to about 1.25 in. (3 cm) long, borne singly at the end on a twig. They have a bloomy, dark green, fleshy outer layer marked with purple, and an inner layer that is light red-brown, and thick-walled. The root system of stinking cedar consists of deep laterals.

THE HEMLOCKS (*TSUGA*)

Pine Family (*Pinaceae*)

Ten species of hemlock are found in the temperate regions of Asia from Japan to the Himalayas as well as in North America, where four species are native. These usually occur mixed with other coniferous trees, or very infrequently in pure stands. They most commonly grow on cool, moist, well-drained and acidic soils, and show a preference for humid montane habitats. The hemlocks are uniformly shade tolerant, rather slow-growing and usually long lived. While they may be present in early successional forests and woods, they are characteristically found in late successional and climax forests that have developed undisturbed. They self-seed in their own shade and tend to acidify the soil.

Hemlocks characteristically develop a broadly conical habit, keeping branches near to the ground when open-growing. The leading shoot also typically nods to one side during the summer and autumn, becoming straight upright late in the winter. The needles are evergreen and resemble spruces in that they are attached via tiny, persistent wooden pegs to the twigs. The needles are notched at the tips, however, and have a distinct and very short leafstalk. The male and female cones are borne on the same tree, the male cones shedding pollen in the spring. The ripened female cones somewhat resemble those of spruces, but are much smaller, with rounded, less stiff cone scales. They ripen, hanging downward, in the

T. canadensis

Hemlocks generally have small, flat needles and small, mature female cones.

autumn of the first year, and when open on the tree resemble small Chinese lanterns.

All four native species of hemlock are grown as landscape amenity trees. They make very graceful evergreen trees and are well adapted to shade. They are used as specimen trees, hedges (both formal and informal), and as a backdrop to set off other trees and shrubs. Cultivars of all four are commercially available, particularly eastern hemlock. In their natural setting hemlocks are rated highly for their aesthetic value as well. The wood of two species is valued commercially, especially for pulp. Hemlocks are important habitat trees to a number of birds and mammals in their natural settings as well.

Tsuga canadensis (L.) CARR.

Pinaceae (Pine Family)

Eastern Hemlock, Canada Hemlock, Hemlock Spruce

Eastern hemlock ranges from Cape Breton Island south through New England and along the Appalachians into northern Georgia and Alabama, and west through southern Ontario to eastern Minnesota. It is commonly found mixed with other deciduous and coniferous trees in a large number of northern forest types. It prefers moist to very moist acidic soils of various textures. In the southern and more westerly parts of its range it prefers cool valleys, northern and eastern slopes, and ravines. In the northern part it may be found on drier and warmer sites. Eastern hemlock is a long-lived, fairly slow-growing, and very shade-tolerant tree. It is able to remain shade-suppressed in the forest understory for up to several hundred years. Eastern hemlock is as a result most often found in late successional and climax forests. It tends to change some soil properties, such as acidity, over time in favor of its own regeneration from seed.

Attaining 70 ft. (21 m) in height, eastern hemlock forms a conical crown of slender spreading horizontal branches, often drooping to the ground. Its leader at the top nods to one side. The bark is thick, red-brown, furrowing deeply into scaly broad ridges. Its narrow needles are up to about 0.6 in. (15 mm) long, round-tipped, with very short leafstalks that attach to minute pegs arranged spirally on the slender twigs. The leaves are pressed into two rows on either side of the twigs, with an occasional smaller leaf pressed upside down and forward along the top of the twig. The leaves are evergreen, dark shiny green above, and paler with two narrow white bands below. The brown elliptical female cones reach about 0.75 in. (1.9 cm) in length, hang downward from short stalks at the ends of twigs, and are composed of several rounded scales. Depending on the soil conditions, eastern hemlock may be shallow-rooted where the water table is high, to rather deeply rooted where drainage is good.

Eastern hemlock forms a conical crown of slender spreading horizontal branches, often drooping to the ground.

Eastern hemlock is a very graceful, well-formed evergreen for landscape applications where soil conditions and climate are appropriate. There are several dwarf forms available, as well as some with golden and variegated foliage. It is one of the few large conifers that will grow well in shade, and may be pruned to form a hedge. It is unfortunately not tolerant of pollution, drought and wind exposure, and consequently performs poorly in urban environments. When stressed it is susceptible to insects and diseases that otherwise it resists. Its wood is brittle and knotty, and is primarily used for pulp, although it has been also used in the past for containers, sub-flooring, roofing, sheathing and light framing. The bark was formally very widely used in tanning. Eastern hemlock has very high value in providing habitat for a variety of birds and mammals. It is regarded as an essential tree for providing winter shelter and bedding for white-tailed deer. Black bears also have a strong preference for this tree, using its hollow trunk for their dens.

Tsuga caroliniana ENGELM.
Pinaceae (Pine Family)
Carolina Hemlock

Carolina hemlock has a very limited distribution, occurring along the slopes of the Appalachians from southwestern Virginia and western North Carolina into northern Georgia and South Carolina. It is considered rare within this range, occurring mixed with deciduous hardwoods and other conifers in several types of forest. It is usually found in very acidic soils on rocky slopes and ridges at elevations from 2,100 to 4,000 ft. (400 to 1,220 m). It is very shade-tolerant and is considered a climax forest tree, seeding itself under the shade of its own canopy.

Although it occasionally reaches well in excess of 70 ft. (21 m), Carolina hemlock is usually shorter, to about 60 ft. (18 m). It forms a narrow, compact, conical crown of drooping branches on a slender trunk. Its leader is very slender and droops. The red-brown bark is scaly and flaky, becoming thick and on older trees deeply furrowed into interconnecting flat scaly ridges. Its narrow needles are up to about 0.75 in. (1.9 cm) long, attached to minute pegs arranged spirally on the slender twigs. The leaves radiate out densely all around the twig, and are evergreen, dark shiny green above, and paler with two narrow white bands below. The brown elliptical female cones reach about 1.4 in. (3.5 cm) in length, hang downward from short stalks at the ends of twigs, and are composed of numerous, widely spreading oblong scales. Depending on the soil conditions, Carolina hemlock has a shallow, wide-spreading root system.

Carolina hemlock is widely used as a landscape amenity tree, tolerating urban conditions better

Carolina hemlock forms a narrow, compact, conical crown of drooping branches on a slender trunk.

than eastern hemlock. It has a handsome, dense, conical form, and is a darker green than eastern hemlock. It is also clipped into formal hedges and used in topiary. While the wood has been used locally for lumber and pulp it is not abundant enough to be commercially important. Although uncommon, Carolina hemlock provides valuable habitat for birds and mammals where it does occur.

Tsuga heterophylla (BONG.) CARR.
Pinaceae (Pine Family)
Western Hemlock, Pacific Hemlock, West Coast Hemlock

Western hemlock occurs in two broad ranges west of the Continental Divide. One range is distributed along the pacific coast from the Kenai Peninsula in Alaska south into Sonoma County, California, with an inland reach along the western and upper eastern slopes of the Cascades in Washington and Oregon. The second range occurs along the western slopes of the northern Rocky Mountains from western Montana and northern Idaho northward to east central British Columbia. Western hemlock is found in several types of coniferous forests, either mixed primarily with other evergreens or relatively dominant. It thrives in humid areas where frequent fog and precipitation occur during the growing season. On the coast it occurs from sea level to about 2,000 ft. (610 m), while inland, where it tends to be drier, it is found at higher elevations, from 1,600 to 4,200 ft. (490 to 1,280 m), at times confined to northerly aspects or

Western hemlock has leaves arranged spirally on slender twigs.

KEY FEATURES	

KEY FEATURES

Tsuga heterophylla

Form:	Narrow, with horizontal or slightly drooping slender branches, **nodding leader**
Trunk:	**Slender, becoming fluted at the base as it matures**
Bark:	**Thin** at all ages, scaly when young, becoming furrowed into wide, flat ridges
Twig:	Slender
Leaves:	Narrow, flat needles, round-tipped, **widely parted below, but more erect above the shoot**
Cones:	Oval, **hanging downward from short stalks at the ends of twigs**

moist bottoms along streams. It performs best on rich, moist, well-drained, strongly acid soils. Western hemlock is intolerant of drought, but very tolerant of shade, long-lived, and fairly slow-growing. Like other hemlocks it is regarded as a characteristic tree of late successional and climax forests, able to seed itself in the shade of its own canopy on favorable sites.

While it is not uncommon to find western hemlock up to 200 ft. (61 m), the usual height is 150 ft. (46 m). The trunk is slender, becoming fluted at the base as it matures while the crown is narrow, with horizontal or slightly drooping slender branches. Its bark is thin at all ages, scaly when young, becoming furrowed into wide, flat ridges. The narrow, flat needles are variable in length, round-tipped, with very short leafstalks that attach to minute pegs arranged spirally on the slender twigs. The leaves are widely parted below, but more erect above the shoot, dark, shiny green above, paler with two white bands below. Female cones are oval to about 0.75 in. (1.9 cm) long, hang downward from short stalks at the ends of twigs, and are composed of several rounded scales. The root system of western hemlock is shallow, wide-spreading and fibrous.

The wood of western hemlock is valued as an all-purpose wood. It is the major source of alpha-cellulose fiber, which is used in the making of rayon, cellophane and many plastics. It is also used extensively in the manufacture of paper and pulp products. As lumber, the wood is used for interior finishes, containers, kitchen cabinets, flooring and veneer. As a landscape tree, western hemlock is particularly valued as a graceful, tall-growing specimen, but is useful in groups as well for visual and wind screening. Because of its dark foliage and tendency to retain lower branches it is good for providing a background for other plants. Younger trees may also be sheared to create excellent large formal hedges. In its natural setting many birds and mammals, including grizzly bears, make use of western hemlock for habitat and food.

Tsuga mertensiana (BONG.) CARR.
Pinaceae (Pine Family)
Mountain Hemlock, Alpine Hemlock, Black Hemlock

Mountain hemlock, as its name suggests, occurs in montane habitats primarily along the west coast from southeastern Alaska to Tulare County in California. It also occurs in the Rocky Mountains of southeastern British Columbia, northern Idaho and

Found at high altitude on loose, coarse-textured soils, mountain hemlock has a slender conical crown.

Narrow crown, branches to the ground and slightly nodding tip characterize mountain hemlock.

western Montana. Commonly occurring as either a dominant tree or co-dominant with other conifers in high-elevation alpine or sub-alpine forests in cold, snowy topography, mountain hemlock grows best on loose, coarse-textured, acidic, moist but well-drained soils. It is long-lived, slow-growing and shade-tolerant, becoming, like other hemlocks, a dominant or co-dominant climax tree on suitable sites.

Variable in form depending on the conditions, mountain hemlock usually tops out at 100 ft. (30 m) forming a slender crown. In the open the trunk is strongly tapered, with a narrow, conical crown, nodding leader and branches nearly to the ground. In denser stands, the taper is less pronounced and the lower half of the trunk is generally free of branches. The bark is rough and broken on young trees and becomes thick and deeply furrowed into scaly plates with age. Its narrow needles are up to about 0.75 in. (1.9 cm) long, notched at the tip, attached to minute pegs arranged spirally on the slender twigs. The leaves radiate all around the twig, and are evergreen, dark shiny green above, and paler with two narrow white bands below. The brown elliptical female cones hang downward from short stalks at the ends of twigs, and are composed of numerous, widely spreading scales. Mountain hemlock has a shallow, wide-spreading root system.

Mountain hemlock is highly valued in the Pacific Northwest as a landscape tree on account of its dense foliage, compact conical form when open-grown and slow growth rate. This hemlock as well as others were important in the mythology of the Thompson and Lillooet Interior Salish of British Columbia, who regarded them as having supernatural powers. The timber of mountain hemlock is only occasionally harvested when occurring at lower altitudes and is sold and used as western hemlock. It is also an important tree for watershed protection, capturing and delaying snowmelt in the spring. Stands of mountain hemlock also provide thermal cover and habitat to a number of large and small mammals and birds.

THE ELMS (*ULMUS*)

Elm Family (*Ulmaceae*)

There are about 18 species of elms in the temperate regions of the Northern Hemisphere. Of these, six are native to North America. The remainder are distributed in Europe and Asia. The native elms are usually found associating with other deciduous trees, and are characteristically found on moist, well-drained soils, often along stream and river valleys, although some also occur on rocky upland sites. Generally somewhat shade-tolerant as saplings, elms are intolerant at maturity. Some species tolerate brief flooding in the spring while others are less adaptable. They are also relatively fast-growing and moderately long-lived. They often appear on disturbed sites and are able to persist into the climax plant community.

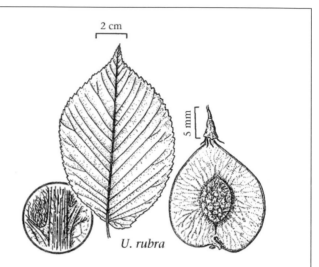

The leaves of elms are tooth-edged and oval, with the base of the blade uneven to either side of the leafstalk. The fruit is always flat and dry, with a disk-like wing.

The native elms are medium to large trees, having a single trunk and a large crown. A few of them are potentially majestic trees. Their leaves are arranged alternately along the twigs, usually in two rows to either side of the twig. Elms have a characteristic shape to the base of the leaf-blade. To one side the base is broadly curved, but on the other side it is slightly stepped and sharply angled forward. The leaves are otherwise oval in shape with teeth along the edges, and usually sharp-pointed at the tip. The flowers and fruit of elms are also characteristic, with minor differences between the species. The flowers are tiny, without petals, both male and female parts in each flower. They are gathered into clusters which, with one exception, emerge early in the spring before the leaves. The fruit that ripens in late spring in all but one native species is a small flattened disk with a papery wing all around, often notched at the tip, and having an overall shape that is round to elliptical depending on the species. Elms have a root system that tends to run deep if the soil and water table permit; otherwise, the roots are shallow and extensive.

The native elms are variably prone to Dutch elm disease, which is caused by a fungus that blocks the water-carrying vessels of the sapwood. The fungus is transported by beetles that burrow under the bark. American elm has been particularly devastated, but other species have been affected as well. As a result, elms are not used in landscape applications to any extent now. Particular fine specimens are maintained disease-free in many cities and arboreta at considerable cost. In the past they were used mostly as shade and street trees. The wood of a few species is used in furniture and several other products. In their natural setting the native elms provide shelter and nesting to a number of birds, including cavity-nesting ones. The fruit is also eaten by birds and small mammals.

Ulmus alata MICHX.
Ulmaceae (Elm Family)
Winged Elm

Winged elm ranges through the Southeast, from southern Virginia to central Florida, west into central Texas and north into central Missouri. It is rare in the lower Mississippi Valley and much of the Gulf Coast. It forms a component of several hardwood forest types throughout its range, and is generally associated with intermittent streams and moist lower slopes, although it colonizes old fields and dry sites as well. While found on a variety of soils, winged elm prefers rich moist well-drained soils. It is tolerant of minor flooding and some shade, particularly as a seedling and sapling, but requires full sun at maturity. It grows quickly and is moderately long-lived. It generally colonizes disturbed sites and abandoned fields early, and persists for some time before being replaced by more shade-tolerant hardwoods.

A medium-sized tree, winged elm reaches about 80 ft. (24 m) on a single, short trunk, forming a wide, open crown with twigs that often have two broad corky wings. Its thin, light brown bark is unevenly furrowed. The leaves are typically elm-shaped, to about 2.5 in. (6 cm) long and arranged in two rows along the twigs. They are firm, thick, smooth dark green above and softly hairy below, turning yellow to red in the autumn. The fruit of winged elm ripens in early spring and is typical of elms, reddish and

hairy, having a narrow wing with two curved points at the tip, about 0.4 in. (10 mm) long.

Winged elm is not commonly used in landscape applications, although it deserves wider application for its smaller form, winged twigs and red autumn foliage. It is, however, prone to the fungus causing Dutch elm disease and to elm phloem necrosis, both of which render the tree susceptible to many insect pests. Its wood is occasionally sold as Hard Elm and similarly used, particularly for bent furniture and hockey sticks. A sturdy rope was at one time made from the fibrous inner bark. The fruit is generally produced in abundance and is consumed by birds and mammals.

Ulmus americana L.
Ulmaceae (Elm Family)
American Elm, White Elm, Gray Elm, Water Elm, Swamp Elm

Found throughout eastern North America, American elm ranges from Cape Breton west into southeastern Saskatchewan, southward to central Texas, and east to south-central Florida. It is found in a large number of different forest types throughout its

Winged elm forms a wide, open crown of winged twigs and dense foliage, which generally turns red in autumn.

The national champion American elm in Louisville, Kansas, displays the massive outward arching main limbs typical of the species.

American elm has leaves typical of elms: arranged in two rows along the twig, sharply toothed, and uneven at the base of the blade.

range, usually in association with bottomlands, streams, waterways, and swamp margins. While it grows best and is found reaching maximum size on rich, well-drained soils, American elm is also common on sandy soils with high water tables and on silty clays. It is fairly shade-tolerant, particularly as a young sapling, grows quickly and lives relatively long. It colonizes disturbed sites and may persist in the understory until released by an open gap in the canopy. Once it attains maturity it will persist in the canopy into the climax community, but over time is generally replaced by more shade-tolerant hardwood trees, such as sugar maple.

American elm reaches a height of 100 ft. (30 m) but in dense forests can reach higher still. On wetter or drier sites it tends to be smaller. It generally forms a single trunk that in dense forest may be free of branches for 50 to 60 ft. (15 to 18 m). In the open it generally forks at about 20 ft. (6 m) into several large outward arching limbs that support somewhat pendulous branches and fine twigs. Its bark is light gray, and furrowed into tight, broad, forking, scaly ridges. Its leaves are typically elm-shaped, to 6 in. (15 cm) long, arranged in two rows along the twig. They are dark green, and either smooth or stiffly and lightly hairy above, but paler with soft hairs below, turning yellow in the autumn. Flowers and fruits are also typical of elms. The fruits are shed in spring, and are about 0.5 in.

(13 mm) long, hairy along the edges of the wing, and notched at the tip with two incurved points. On good sites the roots are wide and deep-spreading laterals; however, this tends to vary with the soil type and depth.

At one time highly valued as a street and shade tree, American elm has been ravaged by Dutch elm disease, which is caused by a fungus carried by both introduced and native bark beetles. This disease was introduced about 1930 and has largely eliminated American elm as an urban tree and throughout most of its range. Weakened trees become more susceptible to insects as well. Programs to maintain healthy trees are available but expensive. In addition, there appears to be variable genetic resistance to the disease and efforts are being taken to breed this resistance into future stocks. American elm wood is used in making containers, furniture, agricultural implements and caskets as well as veneer, but is not very durable. The fruits are heavily produced and eaten by many birds and small mammals; many cavity-nesting birds use the trunks as well.

KEY FEATURES

Ulmus americana

Form:	Open, high, **vase-shaped crown with drooping branches**
Trunk:	Single, straight
Bark:	Light gray, and furrowed into tight, broad, forking, scaly ridges
Twig:	Slender, **slightly zigzagging**
Leaves:	Elliptical, **unequal at the base**, arranged in two rows along the twig, either smooth, or stiffly hairy
Flower:	Tiny, in small clusters before the leaves in mid-spring
Fruit:	A flat samara, wing all around, **hairy along the edges**, notched at the tip with **two incurved points**

Ulmus crassifolia NUTT.

Ulmaceae (Elm Family)

Cedar Elm, Red Elm, Basket Elm, Southern Rock Elm

Cedar elm occurs from northeastern Mexico through eastern Texas into Arkansas, Louisiana and western Mississippi. One isolated population is located in northern Florida. Usually found mixed with other bottomland hardwoods on moist limestone soils along watercourses, cedar elm also occurs on drier limestone hills. However, it grows best on deep rich soils. It is moderately tolerant of shade as a sapling, rapidly growing and fairly long-lived. It is found in late successional and climax hardwood forests on preferred sites.

Reaching to about 80 ft. (24 m) under good conditions, cedar elm forms a short-trunked tree with a wide-spreading, open, rounded crown of somewhat drooping branches and hairy twigs often having corky wings. Its light brown bark is furrowed into scaly broad ridges. Cedar elm has the smallest leaves of any native elm, to about 2 in. (5 cm) long and half as wide, shaped in typical elm fashion. They are coarsely saw-toothed, somewhat leathery, thick, dark green and rough above, paler and softly hairy below, turning bright yellow in the autumn. Flowers and fruit are likewise typical of elms. However, cedar elm flowers in late summer with the fruit maturing in the autumn. The fruit is about 0.5 in. (13 mm) long,

Cedar elm, with its wide-spreading crown of somewhat drooping branches, makes a good shade tree.

white-hairy, having a narrow wing with a deep notch and two curved points at the tip. The root system of cedar elm tends to be wide-spreading and shallow.

Cedar elm is planted locally as a shade tree. It is susceptible to Dutch elm disease, but not to the extent that American elm is. Its pollen is thought to either cause or complicate summer hayfever, however, so its use should probably be tempered in heavily populated areas. Its wood is strong and shock-resistant and is used as a substitute for rock elm. The leaves of cedar elm are very sensitive to air pollution and have been used as indicators of the severity of pollution in urban environments.

Ulmus rubra MUHL.

Ulmaceae (Elm Family)

Slippery Elm, Red Elm, Gras Elm, Moose Elm

Slippery elm has an extensive distribution throughout eastern North America, from southwestern Maine, through extreme southwestern Quebec, and southern Ontario westward into southeastern North Dakota, southward to central Texas, and east into northwestern Florida. It is most abundant in the Great Lakes Basin and the cornbelt of the Midwest, and rare on the Gulf and southern Atlantic coastal plains. Slippery elm is found in a large number of forest types over its range, and may associate with more than 60 different deciduous tree species in a variety of topographical conditions, ranging from floodplains to lower slopes to upland sites. It reaches its maximum size on moist rich soils of lower slopes, streambanks and bottomlands, but it is also found on drier soils of limestone origin. It is somewhat flood-tolerant for brief periods in the spring, but will not survive prolonged flooding. It is a moderately shade-tolerant, fast-growing, moderately long-lived tree, which on favorable sites will perpetuate itself in the climax forest, most often as a component of the subcanopy.

A medium-sized tree, slippery elm attains an average height of about 70 ft. (21 m), but is often less on drier sites, and may grow to twice this height in

Slippery elm forms a single straight trunk supporting an open crown of wide-spreading branches.

the most favorable conditions. It forms a single trunk supporting a broad, flat-topped, open crown of widely spreading branches. The dark brown bark is deeply furrowed with a very slippery, gummy inner bark. Its typically formed elmlike leaves are up to 7 in. (18 cm) long by 3 in. (7.5 cm) wide, arranged in two rows along the stout hairy twigs. They are doubly saw-toothed, thick, dark green and very rough above, and densely but softly hairy below, turning a dull yellow in the autumn. The typically elmlike fruit is nearly circular, about 0.75 in. (1.9 cm) in diameter, barely notched at the tip, hairless and shed in the spring. Its flower is also typical of elms.

The wood of slippery elm is sold and used as American elm, although it is generally considered inferior. The inner mucilaginous bark, besides being useful in identification, is fragrant and edible. It can

be dried and remoistened for use as a poultice or cough remedy. It is not widely planted as a landscape amenity tree, although it once was. It is unfortunately prone to Dutch elm disease and several other conditions that weaken the tree and make it prone to insect pests. Its seeds are a valuable food source to many birds and mammals

Ulmus serotina SARG.
Ulmaceae (Elm Family)
September Elm, Red Elm

September elm has a fairly localized and scattered distribution from Kentucky southward into northwestern Georgia and westward into eastern Oklahoma. It is found very sporadically in several forest types mixed with other hardwoods on flat to moderately sloping ground, and is most abundant in Arkansas and Tennessee. Generally preferring moderately to well-drained, moist soils ranging from clay loams to sandy loams, September elm may also occur on rocky, dry soils derived from limestone. It is fairly shade-tolerant and may persist under the forest canopy as a sapling until released by a gap appearing in the overstory. On sites to which it is well adapted it will perpetuate itself in this way into the climax plant community.

Somewhat reminiscent of American elm in form, September elm is smaller, reaching about 70 ft. (21 m). The trunk is single, supporting a broad vaselike crown of wide-spreading branches and slender brown twigs that often have corky wings and droop towards the tips. The thin, brown bark is shallowly fissured into scaly, broad ridges. Its leaves are elmlike in shape, to about 3.5 in. (9 cm) in length and about half as wide, and arranged in two rows along the twig. They are coarsely and doubly toothed, shiny green above, paler and finely hairy on the veins beneath, turning yellow in the autumn. Its flowers and fruit are typically elmlike, but the flowers appear in early autumn and are followed later by the fruit. This is elliptical in shape, to 0.5 in. (12 mm) long, fringed along the edge of the wing with white hairs, and deeply notched at the tip.

With a broad vaselike crown of wide-spreading branches, September elm makes a graceful landscape tree.

While making an attractive landscape amenity tree for shade, September elm is susceptible to Dutch elm disease in all life stages. It is also reported to be a host of American mistletoe. Its hard wood is graded, sold and used as rock elm. In its natural setting, the fruit of September elm provides forage for many birds and small mammals, and the twigs and buds are occasionally browsed by deer.

Ulmus thomasii SARG.
Ulmaceae (Elm Family)
Rock Elm, Cork Elm

Found in east central North America, rock elm ranges from extreme southwestern Quebec, west-ward through southern Ontario to Minnesota, southward through extreme northeastern Kansas to northern Arkansas, and east to southwestern Virginia. It is generally found mixed with other hardwoods, notably bur oak, chinquapin oak and basswood, in a few hardwood forest types, usually on moist flatlands, but often also on rocky ridges, limestone outcroppings and streambanks. It is most common on moist but well-drained loam soils. It is not tolerant of more than minimal flooding in the spring, but is quite shade-tolerant as a sapling, and can remain in the forest understory for a long time waiting for a gap in the canopy to appear, after which it rapidly grows and becomes a relatively shade-intolerant canopy tree. On sites to which it is best adapted it can perpetuate itself in this fashion into the climax plant community.

Rock elm can attain a height of 100 ft. (30 m) on good sites, but is often only half that height on drier, rockier terrain. It develops a single trunk that penetrates high into the narrow, cylindrical crown of short, drooping branches and irregularly corky twigs. Its gray bark is deeply furrowed into scaly broad ridges. Leaves are elmlike, to about 3.5 in. (9.0 cm) long by 2.0 in. (5.0 cm) wide, with a doubly saw-toothed margin. They are shiny dark green above, paler and softly hairy below, and turning a bright yellow in the autumn. Flowers and fruit follow the elm pattern, with the fruit being wide-winged, elliptical, to about 0.75 in. (1.9 mm) long, finely hairy and notched at the tips and maturing in the spring.

Rock elm typically has prominent corky wings on its twigs.

Severely over cut in some areas, rock elm is highly prized for its hard, strong, flexible, shock-resistant wood, which is used for bentwood elements in furniture, for crates, containers, and agricultural implements and as a base for veneers. It is not used extensively as a landscape amenity tree, and like other elms is susceptible to Dutch elm disease. Although the full extent to which rock elm is affected is unknown, it has been very severely reduced in numbers. If unaffected by spring frosts, it produces abundant fruit, which is relished by a large variety of birds and mammals. The seeds are also palatable to humans, and apparently have a filbertlike flavor.

Umbellularia californica (HOOK. & ARN.) NUTT.
Lauraceae (Laurel Family)

California Laurel, California Bay, Oregon Myrtle, Spice tree, Pepperwood

California laurel occurs from the Umpqua River Valley in Douglas County, Oregon, south to San Diego County in California, eastward to the foothills of the Cascade Range in Oregon and California and into the western Sierra Nevada for its full length. It can be found most often mixed with other coniferous and deciduous trees in several types of forests, although it occurs infrequently in pure stands. California laurel occupies a variety of topographical locations and different kinds of soils if moisture conditions are favorable. Best development happens on deep, well-drained soils along valley bottoms subject to infrequent inundation. It is a shade-tolerant, long-lived tree that on favorable, undisturbed sites is able to reproduce from seed in its own shade, thus persisting over time in the climax forest community.

The height attained by California laurel is strongly influenced by site. Under ideal conditions it reaches

California laurel is a potentially large tree, often forming a dense crown that is wider than it is high.

100 ft. (30 m), but may occasionally exceed this. It often is multistemmed, and forms a crown that is often wider than it is high. The bark is thin, and the leaves evergreen, elliptical, to about 3 in. (7.5 cm) long. The yellow flowers are produced from an early age, and are about 0.5 in. (12 mm) in diameter and are borne in clusters in the axils of the leaves of the previous season, just before the current year's leaves emerge. These are followed by the large fruits which are yellow-green to purple drupes containing a thin-shelled, nutlike seed. They are borne in clusters of up to three and ripen in one year. The root system of California laurel is fleshy, deep and wide-spreading, although there are some exceptions.

California laurel is widely used in landscaping for evergreen, broadleaved hedges, windbreaks and ornament. The leaves, seeds, and wood are used in food seasoning and for medicinal purposes. Its richly grained and colored wood is highly prized for wood carving and marketed as myrtlewood. It is also used for woodenware, interior trim, furniture, paneling, veneer and gunstocks. In its natural environment the seeds are eaten by a wide variety of birds and mammals, and deer and domestic goats eat the new leaves and twigs.

Crown Shapes of Trees

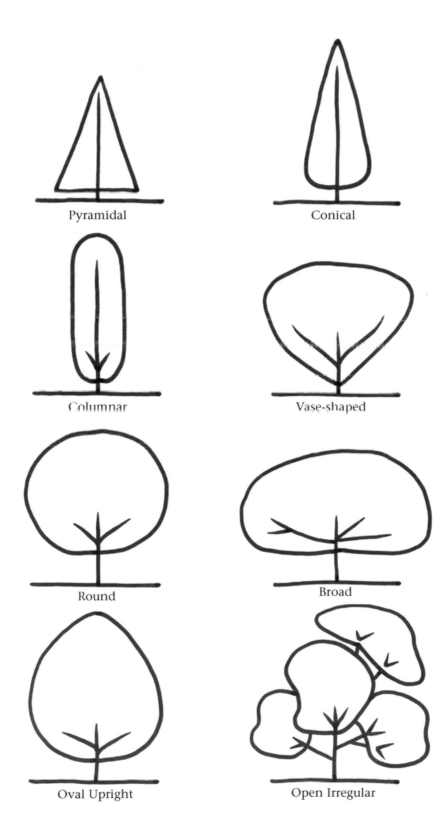

Pyramidal

Conical

Columnar

Vase-shaped

Round

Broad

Oval Upright

Open Irregular

Tree Hardiness Zones

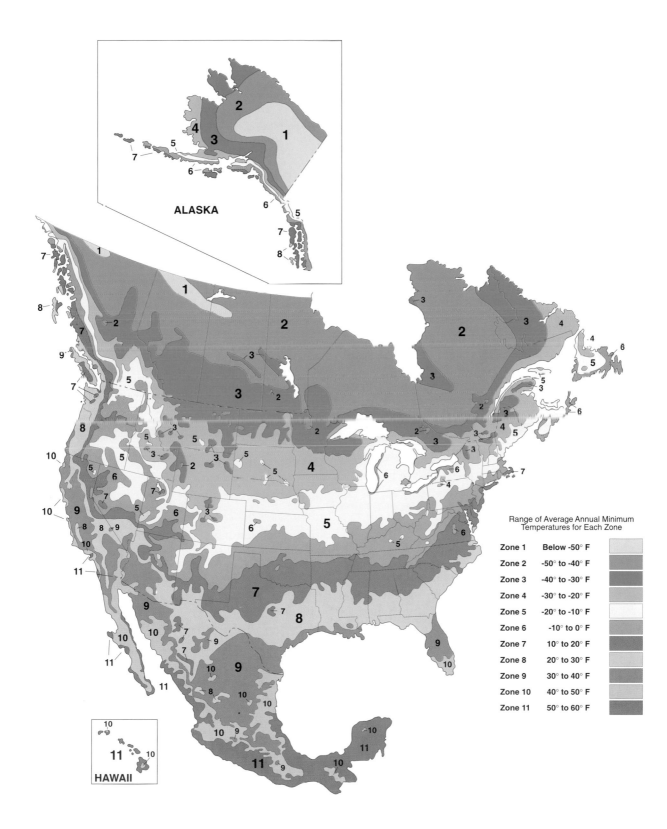

ALASKA

HAWAII

Range of Average Annual Minimum
Temperatures for Each Zone

Zone 1	Below -50° F
Zone 2	-50° to -40° F
Zone 3	-40° to -30° F
Zone 4	-30° to -20° F
Zone 5	-20° to -10° F
Zone 6	-10° to 0° F
Zone 7	10° to 20° F
Zone 8	20° to 30° F
Zone 9	30° to 40° F
Zone 10	40° to 50° F
Zone 11	50° to 60° F

Tree Hardiness Zones

The following listing of zone hardiness is based upon the rating developed by the United States Department of Agriculture (USDA). The numbers for each zone correspond to the **average** minimum winter temperature as measured in 10 degree Fahrenheit increments. As shown below, the smaller the number, the colder the average minimum winter temperature that occurs within that zone. Knowing your local average minimum winter temperature allows you to select your local zone. The listing below indicates the coldest (**C**) and warmest (**W**) zone for each tree discussed in this book, where such information is available. Knowing your local zone and the zone ranges for any particular tree, allows you to determine if it might survive your local winter. Bracketed zones for some trees indicate there is some possibility of growing it in those zones, if care is taken to place the tree in a warmer (or cooler) winter microclimate. Blanks throughout the chart indicate that the extent of a species' hardiness is unavailable. Zone hardiness is intended to be a guide in selecting and situating trees and other plants. It is not the sole consideration upon which to base such choices. But it is a useful starting point. Ideally, some knowledge of the habitat within which the tree or plant naturally occurs should be used as well.

Zone Number	Ave. Min. Winter Temperature Range (F°)	Ave. Min. Winter Temperature Range (C°)
1	–50 and below	–45.5 and below
2	–40 to –50	–40 to –45.5
3	–30 to –40	–34.5 to –40
4	–20 to –30	–29 to –34.5
5	–10 to –20	–23 to –29
6	0 to –10	–17.5 to –23
7	10 to 0	–12 to –17.5
8	20 to 10	–6.5 to –12
9	30 to 20	–1 to –6.5
10	40 to 30	4.5 to –1

Tree Name	C	W	Tree Name	C	W
Abies amabilis	(5)6	9	Alnus rhombifolia	5	9
Abies balsamea	3	5(6)	Alnus rubra	5	9
Abies bracteata	7	9(10)	Alnus rugosa	4	8
Abies concolor	3	7(8)	Amelanchier arborea	4	9
Abies fraseri	4	7	Amelanchier laevis	4	7
Abies grandis	5	9	Arbutus arizonica	7	9
Abies lasiocarpa	2	9	Arbutus menziesii	7	9
Abies magnifica	(5)6	9	Arbutus xalapensis		
Abies procera	5	9	Asimina triloba	5	8
Acer glabrum	3	9	Avicennia germinans		
Acer macrophyllum	7	9	Betula alleghaniensis	3	6
Acer negundo	2	9	Betula lenta	3	6
Acer pensylvanicum	3	4	Betula nigra	4	9
Acer rubrum	3	9	Betula occidentalis	3	9
Acer saccharinum	3	9	Betula papyrifera	2	9
Acer saccharum	3	8	Betula populifolia	3	6(7)
Aesculus californica	6	9(10)	Betula uber	6	
Aesculus flava	3	8	Bursera simaruba		
Aesculus georgiana			Calocedrus decurrens	5	8
Aesculus glabra	3	9	Carpinus caroliniana	2	9
Aesculus pavia	4	8	Carya aquatica		

Tree Name	C	W	Tree Name	C	W
Carya carolinae-septentrionalis			Fraxinus latifolia	7	9
Carya cordiformis	(3)4	9	Fraxinus nigra	2	7
Carya floridana			Fraxinus pennsylvanica	3	9
Carya glabra	4	9	Fraxinus profunda	5	8
Carya illinoensis	5	9	Fraxinus quadrangulata	4	7
Carya laciniosa	5	8	Fraxinus texensis		
Carya ovata	5	8	Fraxinus velutina	7	9
Carya tomentosa	4	9	Gleditsia aquatica		
Carya ovalis			Gleditsia triacanthos	3	9
Carya pallida			Gordonia lasianthus		
Carya texana			Gymnocladus dioicus	3	8(9)
Castanea dentata	4	8	Halesia carolina	4	8
Catalpa bignonioides	5	9	Halesia monticola	5	
Catalpa speciosa	4	8	Hamamelis virginiana	3	8
Celtis laevigata	5	9	Ilex opaca	(5)6	9
Celtis occidentalis	2	9	Juglans californica	9	
Celtis tenuifolia			Juglans cinerea	3	7
Cercis canadensis	(3)4	9	Juglans elaeopyren		
Chamaecyparis lawsoniana	(5)6	7(9)	Juglans nigra	4	8
Chamaecyparis nootkatensis	4		Juniperus californica	9	
Chamaecyparis thyoides	3	8	Juniperus erythrocarpa	8	
Chionanthus virginicus	3	9	Juniperus flaccida	8	
Chrysolepis chrysophylla			Juniperus occidentalis	7	
Cladrastis lutea	3	8	Juniperus osteosperma	(3)6	9
Cornus alternifolia	3	7	Juniperus scopulorum	3	9
Cornus florida	5	9	Juniperus silicicola	9	
Cornus nuttallii	7	9	Juniperus virginiana	(2)3	9
Crataegus crus-galli	3	7	Laguncularia racemosa		
Crataegus douglasii	3	9	Larix laricina	(1)2	4(5)
Crataegus phaenopyrum	3	8	Larix lyallii	3	
Cupressus abramsiana	7		Larix occidentalis	4	9
Cupressus arizonica	7	10	Liquidambar styraciflua	5	9
Cupressus forbsii	8		Liriodendron tulipifera	4	9
Cupressus glabra	7		Lyonothamnus floribundus		
Cupressus goveniana	8		Lysiloma latisiliquum		
Cupressus macnabiana	8		Maclura pomifera	4	9
Cupressus macrocarpa	7	9	Magnolia acuminata	3	8
Cupressus sargentii	9		Magnolia fraseri	5	8(9)
Diospyros virginiana	4	9	Magnolia grandiflora	6	9
Fagus grandifolia	3	9	Magnolia macrophylla	5	8
Franklinia alatamaha	5	8(9)	Magnolia pyramidata		
Fraxinus americana	3	9	Magnolia tripetala	4	8
Fraxinus berlandieriana			Magnolia virginiana	5	9
Fraxinus caroliniana			Malus angustifolia		

Tree Name	C	W	Tree Name	C	W
Malus coronaria			*Pinus muricata*	8	9
Malus fusca			*Pinus palustris*	7	9
Malus ioensis	4	8	*Pinus ponderosa*	(3)4	9
Mastichodendron foetidissimum			*Pinus pungens*	7	
Metopium toxiferum			*Pinus quadrifolia*	7	9
Morus rubra	4	8	*Pinus radiata*	8	9
Nyssa aquatica			*Pinus resinosa*	(2)3	5
Nyssa biflora			*Pinus rigida*	4	7
Nyssa ogeche	7		*Pinus sabiniana*	8	9
Nyssa sylvatica	3	9	*Pinus serotina*	8	
Osmanthus americanus	6		*Pinus strobiformis*	(5)6	9
Ostrya virginiana	3	9	*Pinus strobus*	3	8
Oxydendrum arboreum	4	9	*Pinus taeda*	(6)7	9
Persea borbonia			*Pinus torreyana*	9	
Persea palustris			*Pinus virginiana*	(4)5	8
Picea breweriana	5		*Pinus washoensis*	6	
Picea engelmannii	3	9	*Planera aquatica*		
Picea glauca	2	7	*Platanus occidentalis*	4	9
Picea mariana	2	7	*Platanus racemosa*	9	
Picea pungens	(2)3	7	*Platanus wrightii*	7	9
Picea rubens	3	6	*Populus angustifolia*	3	9
Picea sitchensis	6	8	*Populus balsamifera*	2	9
Pinus albicaulis	(2)4	9	*Populus deltoides*	2	9
Pinus aristata	(4)5	9	*Populus fremontii*	4	9
Pinus arizonica	6		*Populus grandidentata*	3	9
Pinus attenuata	7		*Populus heterophylla*		
Pinus balfouriana	6	9	*Populus tremuloides*	1	9
Pinus banksiana	2	6	*Populus trichocarpa*	3	9
Pinus cembroides	7		*Prunus americana*	2	8
Pinus chihuahuana	7		*Prunus caroliniana*		
Pinus clausa	7		*Prunus nigra*		
Pinus contorta	(4)5	9	*Prunus pensylvanica*	2	
Pinus coulteri	8	9	*Prunus serotina*	3	9
Pinus echinata	(6)7	9	*Prunus virginiana*	2	7
Pinus edulis	(5)8	9	*Pseudotsuga macrocarpa*	7	
Pinus elliottii	(8)9	10	*Pseudotsuga menziesii*	(4)5	8
Pinus engelmannii	8	9	*Ptelea trifoliata*	3	9
Pinus flexilis	4	9	*Quercus alba*	3	9
Pinus glabra	9		*Quercus austrina*		
Pinus jeffreyi	(5)6	9	*Quercus bicolor*	3	8
Pinus lambertiana	(5)7	9	*Quercus chrysolepis*	(7)8	9
Pinus longaeva	(4)5	9	*Quercus coccinea*	4	9
Pinus monophylla	(5)8	9	*Quercus douglasii*	9	
Pinus monticola	(4)7	9	*Quercus ellipsoidalis*		

Tree Name	C	W	Tree Name	C	W
Quercus engelmannii	9		Salix nigra	3	8
Quercus falcata	7	9	Salix taxifolia		
Quercus garryana	7	9	Sapindus saponaria	(5)6	9
Quercus hemisphaerica			Sassafras albidum	4	8
Quercus imbricaria	4	8	Sequoia sempervirens	7	9
Quercus incana			Sequoiadendron giganteum	(5)6	9
Quercus kelloggii	6	9	Sorbus americana	(2)3	6
Quercus laevis			Stewartia ovata	5	9
Quercus laurifolia	6	9	Swietenia mahogoni		
Quercus lobata			Taxodium ascendens	7	9
Quercus lyrata	5	10	Taxodium distichum	5	9
Quercus macrocarpa	2	8	Taxodium mucronatum	8	
Quercus marilandica			Taxus brevifolia	4	9
Quercus michauxii			Thuja occidentalis	2	8
Quercus muhlenbergii	5		Thuja plicata	5	7
Quercus nigra	6	9	Tilia americana	2	8
Quercus pagoda			Tilia caroliniana		
Quercus palustris	4	8(9)	Tilia heterophylla		
Quercus phellos	5	9	Torreya californica	8	9
Quercus prinus	4	8	Torreya taxifolia	8	
Quercus rubra	4	8	Tsuga canadensis	(3)4	7(8)
Quercus stellata	5	8	Tsuga caroliniana	4	7
Quercus tomentella			Tsuga heterophylla	6	9
Quercus velutina	3	9	Tsuga mertensiana	(4)5	9
Quercus virginiana	7	10	Ulmus alata	6	9
Rhamnus purshiana	5	9	Ulmus americana	2	9
Rhizophora mangle			Ulmus crassifolia	7	9
Robinia pseudoacacia	3	8(9)	Ulmus rubra	3	9
Salix caroliniana			Ulmus serotina	5	
Salix discolor			Ulmus thomasii	(2)3	8
Salix lucida			Umbellularia californica	7	9

Glossary

acorn: the fruit of oaks; a thick-walled nut with a woody cup-like base.

acute: having an apex taper to a point.

alternate: having leaves or other organs not opposite or whorled, but situated one at a node, as leaves on a stem.

anther: pollen-bearing part of the stamen.

apetalous: without petals

apex: the tip or end of a structure.

apical: pertaining to the apex.

aromatic: fragrantly scented.

axil: belonging to the axis; the angle between the axis and a leaf.

axillary: in the axil.

axis: the main stem or support of a plant.

bark: the dead, outer, protective tissue of woody plants; often includes all tissue from the vascular cambium outwards.

berry: a fleshy, multi-seeded fruit.

blade: the expanded part of the leaf or petal.

bloom: a waxy coating found on stems, leaves, flowers, and fruits, usually of greyish cast and easily removed.

bract: a much reduced leaf, often scalelike and usually associated with a flower or inflorescence.

bud: a structure of young tissues, which will become a leaf, a flower or both, or a new shoot; especially the stage in which a growing point spends the dormant season; may be naked or enclosed in scales.

bud scale: a modified leaf or stipule (there may be one, several, or many) protective of the young tissue of the bud.

bud scale scar: the mark left by the sloughing off of the bud scale.

calyx: the outer part of a flower, usually green in colour and smaller than the petals.

capsule: a dry, dehiscent fruit (e.g., the fruit of a catalpa).

catkin: a spike-like inflorescence composed of scaly bracts subtending one-sexed, somewhat pendulous flowers. The inflorescences of willows and poplars are also catkins.

chambered: of pith; divided into empty horizontal chambers by cross partitions.

climax: a more-or-less self-perpetuating plant community and associated animals on a site resulting from succession; the climax community is not static: changes to its composition are gradual and highly localized. For example, when a canopy tree dies, understory plants respond to the higher light intensities.

clone: plants derived vegetatively from one parent plant, identical to each other and the parent.

clustered: crowded leaves, so as not to be clearly alternate or opposite.

compound leaf: a leaf of two or more leaflets; in some cases (eastern redbud) the lateral leaflets may have been lost and only the terminal leaflet remains; **ternately compound** when the leaflets are in 3s (hoptree); **palmately compound** when three or more leaflets arise from a common point (buckeyes); **pinnately compound** when arranged along a common stalk, or if only three leaflets are present at least the terminal leaflet is petioled; **odd-pinnate** if a terminal leaflet is present and the total number of leaflets for the leaf is odd-numbered (hickories); **even-pinnate** if no terminal leaf is present and the total is an even number (Kentucky coffee tree).

cordate: heart-shaped, with a sinus and rounded lobes (e.g., the base of the leafblade of red mulberry).

corolla: the petals of the flower.

crown: the upper mass, or head of a tree.

cultivar: a cultivated variety or clone.

deciduous: falling off, as leaves from a tree.

dehiscent: splitting open.

dentate: having marginal teeth whose tips are perpendicular to the margin and do not point forward.

dioecious: said of a species having unisexual flowers, each sex confined to a separate plant.

drupe: a fleshy fruit, whose seed is enclosed in a stony endocarp (e.g., plums and cherries).

endemic: found naturally only in a small geographic area.

entire: having a margin without teeth.

epidermis: the outer superficial layer of cells.

exfoliate: peeling in shreds or thin layers, as bark from a tree.

exotic: foreign; not natural.

exserted: projecting beyond, as the bracts of the douglas fir cone.

fastigiate: branches erect and close together.

fibrous: having long narrow shreds or flakes.

filament: the stalk of a stamen.

flower: the reproductive organ of a plant.

form: a subdivision of a species which occurs occasionally in the wild, seldom breeds true, and does not develop a natural population or distribution.

fruit: a ripened ovary from the female part of the flower and any attached parts.

genus: a group of related species possessing fundamental traits in common but different in other lesser characteristics.

glaucous: covered with a waxy bloom or whitish material that rubs off easily (e.g., the bloom and stems of box elder).

habit: the general mode of plant growth.

habitat: the type of surrounding in which a plant grows.

herbaceous: having no persistent woody stem above ground.

hybrid: a plant resulting from a cross between two or more other plants at the rank of species or higher.

imbricate: overlapping, as the shingles of a roof.

inflorescence: the method of flower bearing; the position of the flowers on a stem.

internode: that part of an axis between two successive nodes.

introduced: brought intentionally from another region for cultivation.

involucre: one or more small leaves or bracts that are below a flower or inflorescence (e.g., the cap of an acorn).

juvenile: an early phase of plant growth, usually characterized by non-flowering, vigorous increase in size. Juvenile plants often have thorns and leaves that are simple and/or entire which, in woody, deciduous species, are retained dead on the plant through winter.

key: a small one-seeded fruit with a wing; a samara (e.g., the fruit of maples and elms).

lanceolate: much longer than wide, broadest below the middle and tapering to a point.

lateral: borne on the side of a stem, as flowers, buds or branches.

lateral bud: a bud borne in the axis of the previous season's leaf.

leader: the primary shoot of a tree.

leaf: the whole organ of photosynthesis, characterized by an axillary bud most of the year at its point of attachment to the branch or twig.

leaflet: an element of a compound leaf.

leaf scar: the mark remaining on a twig after the leaf has fallen off.

legume: a dry fruit splitting open along two edges (e.g., black locust).

lenticel: a small corky spot on young bark.

margin: the edge of a leaf.

mature: a later phase of growth characterized by flowering, a reduced rate of increase in size, a development of leaf lobing, and a loss of thorniness.

monoecious: said of a species having unisexual flowers, with both sexes on the same plant.

multiple buds: a terminal or lateral bud crowded by many accessory buds (e.g., silver maple).

multiple fruit: one formed from several flowers into a single structure having a common stem (e.g., red mulberry).

mutation: a sudden change in genetic material resulting in an altered individual.

native: original to an area; naturally adapted over time to a specific set of biotic and abiotic environmental conditions.

naturalized: thoroughly established in an environment but originating in another environment in some way(s) similar, elsewhere.

node: a joint on a stem, represented by a point of origin of a leaf or bud; sometimes discernable externally by a constricting or swollen ring, or by a distinct leaf and/or stipule scars, or by thorns.

nut: a dry, one-celled, one-seeded fruit having a hard inner portion of the ovary wall; the outer parts may be fibrous or fleshy (e.g., walnuts).

nutlet: a small nutlike fruit (e.g., musclewood).

opposite: two at a node, as leaves.

ovary: the ovule bearing part of the pistil.

ovule: the egg-containing unit of the ovary, which after fertilization becomes the seed.

palmate: digitate, radiating fan-like from a common point, as leaflets of a palmately compound leaf.

panicle: an inflorescence whose primary axis bears branches of stalked flowers.

parallel: especially of veins, running side by side from base to tip.

pedicel: the stalk of a flower or fruit when in a cluster.

peduncle: the stalk of a flower cluster or a single flower when it is solitary.

perennial: of three or more seasons duration.

persistent: adhering to a position instead of falling, whether alive or dead.

petal: one unit of the corolla, usually colored and more-or-less showy.

petaloid: said of a structure that is not a petal but is the colour and shape of a petal.

petiole: leaf stalk joining blade to node.

petiolule: leaflet stalk.

pinna: the leaflet of a pinnately compound leaf.

pinnate: compounded, or lobed, with the leaflets along each side of a common axis.

pinnule: the secondary leaflet of a twice compound leaf.

pistil: the female part of a flower.

pith: the central part of a twig, usually lighter or darker than the wood, and softer.

pod: a general term for a dry, dehiscent fruit.

pollen: dustlike, male reproductive cells contained within the anther.

pome: a type of fleshy fruit represented by crabapples, and related genera.

pseudo-terminal bud: the apparent terminal bud of a twig, but actually the uppermost lateral bud with its associated leaf scar on one side and the scar of the aborted terminal bud often visible on the opposite side (e.g., elms).

rachis: stem bearing leaflets; the primary stem of an inflorescence.

receptacle: the distal end of the flower-bearing axis, usually more-or-less enlarged, flattened or cuplike.

reflexed: bent abruptly backwards or downwards.

root: the descending axis of a plant, with specialized structures and anatomy, usually below ground.

scar: a mark left from a former attachment.

seed: the fertilized, ripened ovule that contains the embryo.

sepal: one of the units comprising the calyx; a usually green, leafy element below the corolla.

shrub: a woody plant that is not tree-like in habit and that regularly produces branches or shoots from or near the ground.

simple: said of a leaf that is not compound.

sinus: the space between two lobes of a leaf.

species: the smallest, inter-breeding population that is consistently and persistently unique and distinguishable by ordinary means.

stamen: the male part of a flower; the pollen-bearing organ of a seed plant.

stem: the primary axis of a plant having foliage and flowers and/or organs derived from them.

stigma: the furthest end of the pistil that receives the pollen, variously textured and shaped, usually sticky when receptive.

stipule: the basal, usually leafy appendage found at the node of some plants, such as willows. The leaf usually has one stipule on each of its sides, but they tend to fall off as it grows.

sucker: a shoot arising from the roots or from beneath the surface of the ground.

succession: the gradual replacement of one community of plants and associated animals by another on the same site.

taxonomy: the study, identification, and classification of the genetic and evolutionary relationships between plants.

terminal: at the tip or distal end.

thicket: a dense growth of shrubs and trees.

thorn: a modified twig, which has tiny leaf scars and buds (e.g., hawthorns, which have single or branched thorns; honey locust, whose thorns are also a modified stipule; and black locust).

toothed: the margin of the leaf broken up into small, rather irregular segments.

tree: a woody plant with one to three (sometimes five) main stems, usually at least 12 ft. (4 m) tall, and having a distinct crown.

twig: the shoot of a woody plant representing growth of the current season.

variety: a naturally occurring sub-set population of a species with a distinct geographic range, marked by distinct differences which breed true within that population.

vein: the vascular rib of a leaf.

whorl: three or more structures arising from a single node.

Places and Organizations

Hopefully the reader at some point in using this book will want to see some of the trees discussed and shown here. The kinds of places where this is possible and the organizations that can help are many. In general, many larger urban centers have arboreta or botanical gardens that maintain collections of local native trees (as well as many other plants). National forests, national and state (or provincial) parks and municipal parks are also worth exploring. Local horticultural societies and field naturalist societies are active self-organizing groups that offer a range of programs and information services geared to the local environment. State organizations also worth contacting are state forestry services and horticulture extensions, as well as colleges and universities with departments of agriculture, horticulture, landscape architecture or forestry.

Below is a list of some more notable places to see locally native trees.

Adkins Arboretum
12610 Eveland Road, P.O. Box 100, Ridgely, MD 21660 USA; 443-634-2847
http://www.hort.vt.edu/vthg/

Alaska Botanical Garden
P.O. Box 202202, Anchorage, AK 99520 USA; 907-265-3165

Alfred B. Maclay State Gardens
3540 Thomasville Road, Tallahassee, FL 32308 USA; 850-487-4115

Arboretum
University of Central Florida, c/o Dept. of Biology, Orlando, FL 32816-2368 USA; 407-823-2978

Arboretum at Arizona State University
Facilities Management/Department Grounds, Tempe, AZ 85287-3305 USA; 602-965-8137
http://www.fm.asu.edu/arboretum.htm

Arboretum at Flagstaff
P.O. Box 670, Flagstaff, AZ 86002 USA; 520-774-1442
http://www.thearb.org/

Arboretum of Los Angeles County
301 N. Baldwin Avenue, Arcadia, CA 91007-2697 USA; 626-821-3234
http://www.aabga.org/memberpages/losangeles/

Arboretum, University of Guelph,
Guelph, ON N1G 2W1 Canada; 519-824-4120
http://www.uoguelph.ca/~arboretu/

Arizona-Sonora Desert Museum
2021 N. Kinney Road, Tucson, AZ 85743-8918 USA; 520-883-1380
http://www.desertmuseum.org/

Arnold Arboretum
c/o Harvard University, 125 Arborway, Jamaica Plain, MA 02130-3500 USA; 617-524-1718
http://www.arboretum.harvard.edu/

Atlanta Botanical Garden
P.O. Box 77246, Atlanta, GA 30357 USA; 404-876-5859
http://www.atlantabotanicalgarden.org/

Beal Botanical Garden

Division of Campus Park & Planning, 412 Olds Hall, Office, East Lansing, MI 48824-1047 USA; 517-355-9582

http://beal.cpp.msu.edu:80/beal/

Beardsley Zoological Gardens

1875 Noble Avenue, Bridgeport, CT 06610 USA; 203-394-6569

http://www.BeardsleyZoo.org/

Bernheim Arboretum and Research Forest

Hwy. 245, Clermont, KY 40110 USA; 502-955-8512

http://www.win.net/bernheim/

Berry Botanic Garden

11505 SW Summerville Avenue, Portland, OR 97219-8309 USA; 503-636-4112

http://www.berrybot.org/

Betty Ford Alpine Gardens

183 Gore Creek Drive, Vail, CO 81657 USA; 970-476-0103

http://www.vail.net/alpinegarden/

Biltmore Estate

One N. Pack Square, Asheville, NC 28801 USA; 828-274-6202

http://www.biltmore.com/

Birmingham Botanical Gardens

2612 Lane Park Road, Birmingham, AL 35223 USA; 205-879-1227

http://www.biltmore.com/

Botanica, The Wichita Gardens

701 N. Amidon, Wichita, KS 67203 USA; 316-264-0448

http://www.botanica.org/

Boyce Thompson Southwestern Arboretum

37615 U.S. 60, Superior, AZ 85273-5100 USA; 520-689-2723

http://Ag.Arizona.Edu/BTA/

Brooklyn Botanic Garden

1000 Washington Avenue, Brooklyn, NY 11225-1099 USA; 718-622-4433

http://www.bbg.org/

Cape Fear Botanical Garden

P.O. Box 53485, Fayetteville, NC 28305 USA; 910-486-0221

Cedar Valley Arboretum & Botanic Gardens

P.O. Box 1833, Waterloo, IA 50704 USA; 319-296-9297

http://www.cedarnet.org/gardens/

Cheekwood Botanical Garden

1200 Forrest Park Drive, Nashville, TN 37205 USA; 615-353-2148

http://www.aabga.org/memberpages/cheekwood/

Cheyenne Botanic Garden

710 S. Lions Park Drive, Cheyenne, WY 82001 USA; 307-637-6458

http://www.botanic.org/

Chicago Botanic Garden

1000 Lake Cook Road, Glencoe, IL 60022 USA; 847-835-5440

http://www.chicago-botanic.org/

Cincinnati Zoo and Botanical Garden

3400 Vine Street, Cincinnati, OH 45220 USA; 513-559-7734

http://www.cincyzoo.org/

Cleveland Botanical Garden

11030 East Blvd., Cleveland, OH 44106 USA; 216-721-1600

Crosby Arboretum, Mississippi State University

P.O. Box 1639, Picayune, MS 39466 USA; 601-799-2311

Dawes Arboretum

7770 Jacksontown Road, SE, Newark, OH 43056-9380 USA; 740-323-2355

http://www.dawesarb.org/

Denver Botanic Gardens
909 York Street, Denver, CO 80206 USA;
303-331-4000
http://www.botanicgardens.org/

Desert Botanical Garden
1201 N. Galvin Pkwy., Phoenix, AZ 85008 USA;
602-941-1225
http://www.dbg.org/

Dothan Area Botanical Gardens
P.O. Box 5971, Dothan, AL 36302 USA;
334-793-3224
http://www.dabg.com/

Dyck Arboretum of the Plains
Hesston College, P.O. Box 3000, Hesston, KS
67062 USA; 316-327-8127
http://erb.hesston.edu/arbor/

Florida Botanical Gardens
12175 125th Street North, Largo, FL 33774 USA;
727-582-2100

Forest Lawn Cemetery & Arboretum
4000 Pilots Lane, Richmond, VA 23222 USA;
804-321-7655

Fullerton Arboretum
c/o California State University, P.O. Box 6850,
Fullerton, CA 92834-6850 USA; 714-278-3579
http://arboretum.fullerton.edu/home.htm

Garfield Park Botanical Conservatory
2505 Conservatory Drive, Indianapolis, IN 46203
USA; 317-327-7184

Georgia Southern Botanical Garden
Georgia Southern University, P.O. Box 8039,
The Botanical Gardens, Statesboro, GA 30460-8039
USA; 912-871-1114
http://www2.gasou.edu/garden/

Gifford Arboretum
University of Miami, Dept. of Biology, Cox Science
Center, Room 215, 1301 Memorial Drive, Coral
Gables, FL 33146 USA; 305-284-5364
http://fig.cox.miami.edu/Arboretum/gifford.html

Graver Arboretum of Muhlenberg College
Biology Dept., 2400 Chew Street, Allentown, PA
18104-5586 USA; 610-821-3258
http://www.muhlenberg.edu/

Green Bay Botanical Garden
2600 Larsen Road, P.O. Box 12644, Green Bay, WI
54307-2644 USA; 920-490-9457
http://www.uwm.edu/Dept/Biology/domes/

Haverford College Arboretum
Haverford College, 370 Lancaster Avenue,
Haverford, PA 19041 USA; 610-896-1101
http://www.haverford.edu/

Hayes Regional Arboretum
801 Elks Road, Richmond, IN 47374 USA;
765-962-3745
http://www.infocom.com/hayes/

Highland Botanical Park
180 Reservoir Avenue, Rochester, NY 14620 USA;
716-244-9023

Highstead Arboretum
P.O. Box 1097, Redding, CT 06875 USA;
203-938-8809

Hoyt Arboretum
Bureau of Parks, 4000 SW Fairview Blvd., Portland,
OR 97221 USA; 503-228-8733

Iowa Arboretum
1875 Peach Avenue, Madrid, IA 50156 USA;
515-795-3216

J.C. Raulston Arboretum
P.O. Box 7609, Dept. of Horticultural Science,
North Carolina State University, Raleigh, NC
27695-7609 USA; 919-515-1192

James Madison University Arboretum
MSU 6901, James Madison University,
Harrisonburg, VA 22807 USA; 540-568-3194

Jardin Botanique de Montreal
4101, rue Sherbrooke Est, Montreal, PQ H1X 2B2
Canada; 514-872-1452

Leach Botanical Garden

6704 SE 122nd Avenue, Portland, OR 97236 USA;
503-761-9503

Lockerly Arboretum

1534 Irwinton Road, Milledgeville, GA 31061 USA;
912-452-2112

Marie Selby Botanical Gardens

811 S. Palm Avenue, Sarasota, FL 34236 USA;
941-366-5731
http://www.selby.org/

Mary Grace Burns Arboretum

Georgian Court College, 900 Lakewood Avenue,
Lakewood, NJ 08701 USA; 732-364-2200
http://www.Georgian.edu/bi_arbor/bi_arb.htm

Marywood University Arboretum

2300 Adams Avenue, Scranton, PA 18509 USA;
717-348-6265

Matthaei Botanical Gardens

University of Michigan, 1800 N. Dixboro Road,
Ann Arbor, MI 48105 USA; 734-998-7061
http://www.lsa.umich.edu/mbg/

**Memorial University of Newfoundland
Botanical Garden**

Memorial University of Newfoundland,
306 Mt. Scio Road, St. Johns, NF A1C 557 Canada;
709-737-8590
http://www.mun.ca/botgarden/

Memphis Botanic Garden

750 Cherry Road, Memphis, TN 38117-4699 USA;
901-685-1566
http://www.aabga.org/memberpages/memphis/

Mendocino Coast Botanical Gardens

18220 N. Hwy. 1, Fort Bragg, CA 95437 USA;
707-964-4352
http://www.fortbragg.com/gardens.htm

Mercer Arboretum & Botanic Gardens

22306 Aldine-Westfield Road, Humble, TX
77338-1071 USA; 281-443-8731
http://www.cechouston.org/groups/memberguide.html

Minnesota Landscape Arboretum

University of Minnesota, 3675 Arboretum Drive,
Box 39, Chanhassen, MN 55317
USA; 612-443-2460
http://www.arboretum.umn.edu/fall_index.htm

Missouri Botanical Garden

P.O. Box 299, St. Louis, MO 63166-0299 USA;
314-577-5111
http://www.mobot.org/

**Morris Arboretum of the
University of Pennsylvania**

9414 Meadowbrook Avenue, Philadelphia, PA
19118 USA; 215-247-5777
http://www.upenn.edu/morris/

Morton Arboretum

4100 Illinois Rte. 53, Lisle, IL 60532-1293 USA;
630-968-0074
http://www.mortonarb.org/

Mount Auburn Cemetery

580 Mt. Auburn Street, Cambridge, MA 02138 USA;
617-547-7105

Mount Pisgah Arboretum

33735 Seavey Loop Road, Eugene, OR 97405-9602
USA; 541-747-3817
http://www.efn.org/~mtpisgah/

Mounts Botanical Garden

531 N. Military Trail, West Palm Beach, FL
33415-1395 USA; 561-233-1749
http://www.mounts.org/

Myriad Botanical Gardens

100 Myriad Gardens, Oklahoma City, OK 73102
USA; 405-297-3995
http://www.okccvb.org/myrgard/myrgard.html

Nebraska Statewide Arboretum

P.O. Box 830715, University of Nebraska, Lincoln,
NE 68583-0715 USA; 402-472-2971
http://www.ianr.unl.edu/nsa/

New Orleans Botanical Garden

1 Palm Drive, New Orleans, LA 70124 USA;
504-483-9386

New York Botanical Garden

200 Street & Kazimiroff Blvd., Bronx, NY
10458-5126 USA; 718-817-8700
http://www.nybg.org/

Niagara Parks Botanical Gardens

P.O. Box 150, Niagara Falls, ON L2E 6T2 Canada;
905-356-8554
http://www.niagaraparks.com/

Nichols Arboretum

University of Michigan, Dana Bldg., 430 E.
University, Ann Arbor, MI 48109-1115 USA;
734-763-4033
http://www.umich.edu/~snrewww/arb/

Norfolk Botanical Garden

6700 Azalea Garden Road, Norfolk, VA
23518-5337 USA; 757-441-5830

North Carolina Arboretum

100 Frederick Law Olmsted Way, Asheville, NC
28806-9315 USA; 828-665-2492

North Carolina Botanical Garden

University of North Carolina at Chapel Hill, CB
3375, Totten Center, Chapel Hill, NC 27599-3375
USA; 919-962-0522
http://www.unc.edu/depts/ncbg/

Ohio State University Chadwick Arboretum

2001 Fyffe Court, Columbus, OH 43210 USA;
614-292-4678

Oklahoma Botanical Garden & Arboretum

OK State University, Hort. & L.A., 360 Agriculture
Hall, Stillwater, OK 74078-6027 USA; 405-744-5414

Omaha Botanical Gardens

P.O. Box 24089, Omaha, NE 68124 USA;
402-346-4002

Orland E. White Arboretum

State Arboretum of Virginia, Rt. 2, Box 210, Boyce,
VA 22620 USA; 540-837-1758
http://www.virginia.edu/~blandy/

**Overland Park Arboretum
& Botanical Garden**

8500 Santa Fe, Overland Park, KS 66212 USA;
913-685-3604

Red Butte Garden and Arboretum

University of Utah, 18A deTrobriand Street, Salt
Lake City, UT 84113-5044 USA; 801-581-4747
http://www.utah.edu/redbutte/

Reeves-Reed Arboretum

165 Hobart Avenue, Summit, NJ 07901 USA;
908-273-8787
http://www.reeves-reedarboretum.org/

**Reflection Riding Arboretum
and Botanical Garden**

400 Garden Road, Chattanooga, TN 37419 USA;
423-821-9582
http://www.chattanooga.net/rriding/

Reiman Gardens

Iowa State University, 1407 Elwood Drive, Ames,
IA 50011 USA; 515-294-3718

Royal Botanical Gardens

P.O. Box 399, Hamilton, ON L8N 3H8 Canada;
905-527-1158
http://www.rbg.ca/

Salisbury State University Arboretum

1101 Camden Avenue, Salisbury, MD 21801 USA;
443-543-6323
http://www.ssu.edu/

San Antonio Botanical Gardens

555 Funston Place, San Antonio, TX 78209 USA;
210-207-3255
http://www.sabot.org/

Santa Barbara Botanic Garden

1212 Mission Canyon Road, Santa Barbara, CA
93105 USA; 805-682-4726
http://www.sbbg.org/

Santa Fe Botanical Garden

P.O. Box 23343, Santa Fe, NM 87502-3343 USA;
505-428-1684

Sarah P. Duke Gardens
Duke University, Box 90341, Durham, NC
27708-0341 USA; 919-684-3698
http://www.hr.duke.edu/dukegardens/
dukegardens.html

Scott Arboretum of Swarthmore College
500 College Avenue, Swarthmore, PA 19081-1397
USA; 610-328-8025

Secrest Arboretum
OARDC/OSU, 1680 Madison Avenue, Wooster, OH
44691 USA; 330-263-3761

Sherwood Fox Arboretum
Staging Bldg., University of Western Ontario,
London, ON N6A 5B7 Canada; 519-679-2111

Slayton Arboretum of Hillsdale College
Dept. of Biology, Hillsdale, MI 49242 USA;
517-437-7341
http://www.aabga.org/memberpages/slayton/

South Carolina Botanical Garden
130 Lehotsky Hall, Clemson University, Public
Service & Agriculture, Clemson, SC 29634-0375
USA; 864-656-3405
http://virtual.clemson.edu/groups/scbg/

State Botanical Garden of Georgia
University of Georgia, 2450 S. Milledge Avenue,
Athens, GA 30605 USA; 706-542-1244
http://www.uga.edu/~botgarden/

State Fair Park Arboretum
Nebraska State Board of Agriculture, P.O. Box
81223, Lincoln, NE 68501 USA; 402-474-5371

Stranahan Arboretum
Dept. of Biology, The University of Toledo, Toledo,
OH 43606-3390 USA; 419-882-6806

Strybing Arboretum & Botanical Gardens
9th Avenue & Lincoln Way, San Francisco, CA
94122 USA; 415-661-1316
http://www.strybing.org/

Taylor Memorial Arboretum
10 Ridley Drive, Wallingford, PA 19086 USA;
610-876-2649
http://www.aabga.org/memberpages/taylor/

Toledo Botanical Garden
5403 Elmer Drive, Toledo, OH 43615 USA;
419-936-2986

Toronto Zoo
361A Old Finch Avenue, Scarborough, ON
M1B 5K7 Canada; 416-392-5973
http://www.torontozoo.com/

Tucson Botanical Gardens
2150 N. Alvernon Way, Tucson, AZ 85712 USA;
520-326-9686
http://www.azstarnet.com/~tbg/

Tyler Arboretum
515 Painter Road, Media, PA 19063 USA;
610-566-9134

U. S. Botanic Garden
Administrative Office, 245 First Street, SW,
Washington, DC 20024 USA; 202-225-8333

UC Davis Arboretum
University of California, One Shields Avenue,
Davis, CA 95616 USA; 530-752-2498

UCI Arboretum
North Campus, UC Irvine, Irvine, CA 92697-1450
USA; 949-824-5833

United States National Arboretum
3501 New York Avenue, NE, Washington, DC
20002-1958 USA; 202-245-2726

**University of Alberta Devonian
Botanic Garden,**
Edmonton, AB T6G 2E1 Canada; 403-987-3054

**University of British Columbia
Botanical Garden**
6804 SW Marine Drive, Vancouver, BC V6T 1Z4
Canada; 604-822-3928
http://www.hedgerows.com/

University of California Botanical Garden
200 Centennial Drive, #5045, Berkeley, CA
94720-5045 USA; 510-642-0849

**University of California
Santa Cruz Arboretum**
Arboretum UCSC, 1156 High Street, Santa Cruz,
CA 95064 USA; 381-427-2998

**University of California-Riverside
Botanic Garden,**
Riverside, CA 92521-0124 USA; 909-787-4650

University of Delaware Botanic Gardens
Dept. of Plant & Soil Science, University of
Delaware, Newark, DE 19717 USA; 302-831-1388

**University of Idaho Arboretum &
Botanical Garden**
109-110 Alumni Center, Moscow, ID 83844-3226
USA; 208-885-6250

University of Illinois Arboretum
205 Swanlund Administration Bldg., 601 E. John
Street, Champaign, IL 61820 USA; 217-333-8846

University of Kentucky Arboretum
University of Kentucky, Room 8, Gillis Bldg.,
Lexington, KY 40506-0033 USA; 606-257-6955
http://www.uky.edu/OtherOrgs/Arboretum/

**University of NE-Lincoln Botanical
Garden & Arboretum**
1340 N. 17th Street, Lincoln, NE 68588-0609 USA;
402-472-2679
http://www.unl.edu/unlbga/

University of Wisconsin Arboretum
1207 Seminole Hwy., Madison, WI 53711 USA;
608-262-2746

VanDusen Botanical Garden
5251 Oak Street, Vancouver, BC V6M 4H1 Canada;
604-257-8666

Washington Park Arboretum
University of Washington, P.O. Box 358010,
Seattle, WA 98195-8010 USA; 206-543-8800

Further Reading

Many sources of information have gone into the preparation of this book. The following are some that the reader may wish to consult to further understand a particular tree or group. The list is intended to provide a means for the reader to start investigating. To this end the readings have been grouped by topic area. Books are listed first, followed by Internet sites.

Trees: General

An Illustrated Manual of Pacific Coast Trees. H.E. McMinn and E. Maino, University of California Press, Berkeley, CA, 1967.

A Natural History of Trees of East and Central North America. D.C. Peattie, Houghton Mifflin Co., Boston, MA., 1977.

Atlas of United States Trees. Vol. 1. Conifers and Important Hardwoods. E.L. Little. USDA Forest Service, Washington, DC, 1971.

Atlas of United States Trees. Vol. 3. Minor Western Hardwoods. E.L. Little. USDA Forest Service, Washington, DC, 1976.

Atlas of United States Trees. Vol. 4. Minor Eastern Hardwoods. E.L. Little. USDA Forest Service, Washington, DC, 1977.

Atlas of United States Trees. Vol.6. Supplement. E.L. Little. USDA Forest Service, Washington, DC, 1981.

Field Guide to North America Trees, revised edition. T.S. Elias, Grolier Books Clubs Inc., Danbury, CT, 1989.

Plants of Coastal British Columbia, including Washington, Oregon and Alaska. J. Pojar and A. MacKinnon, eds., Lone Pine, Vancouver, BC, 1994.

Textbook of Dendrology: Covering the Important Trees of the United States and Canada, seventh edition. W.M. Harlow, E.S. Harrar, J.W. Hardin, and F.M. White, McGraw-Hill, New York, NY, 1991.

Trees in Canada. J.L. Farrar, Fitzhenry and Whiteside and the Canadian Forest Service, Ottawa, ON, 1995.

Trees: Specific

Conifers. K.D. Rushforth, Facts on File, New York, NY, 1987.

Maples of the World. D.M. van Gelderen, P.C. de Jong, H.J. Oterdoom, Timber Press, Portland, OR, 1994.

Native and Cultivated Conifers of Northeastern North America. E.A. Cope, Cornell University Press, Ithaca, NY, 1986.

The Cultivated Hemlocks. J.C. Swartley, Timber Press, Beaverton, OR, 1985.

Taxonomic

An Integrated System of Classification of Flowering Plants, A.J. Cronquist, Columbia University Press, New York, NY, 1981.

The Evolution and Classification of Flowering Plants, second edition. A.J. Cronquist, New York Botanical Garden, New York, NY, 1988.

Checklist of United States Trees, Agricultural Handbook 541. E.L. Little, USDA, Washington, DC, 1979.

Flora of North America North of Mexico Volume 2: Pteridophytes and Gymnosperms. Edited by Flora of North America Editorial Committee Convening Editor: Nancy R. Morin, Oxford University Press, New York, NY, 1993.

Flora of North America North of Mexico Volume 3: Magnoliophyta: Magnoliidae and Hamamelidae. Edited by Flora of North America Editorial Committee Convening Editor: Nancy R. Morin, Oxford University Press, New York, NY, 1997.

Landscape

Manual of Woody Landscape Plants. M.A. Dirr, Stipes Publ., New York, NY, 1988.

Native Trees, Shrubs and Vines for Urban and Rural America. G.L. Hightshoe, Van Nostrand Reinhold: New York, NY, 1988.

The Audubon Society Field Guide to North American Trees. E. Little, Alfred A. Knopf, New York, NY, 1980.

The Hillier Manual of Trees and Shrubs, sixth edition. Hillier Nurseries, David & Charles, United Kingdom, 1991.

Internet Sites

http://danr.ucop.edu/ihrmp/oaks.html

University of California Integrated Hardwood Range Management Program: California's Rangeland Oak Species

http://eco.bio.lmu.edu/socal_nat_hist/plants/plants.htm

Southern California Natural History, a Multimedia Textbook: Southern California Natural History, Terrestrial plants

http://plants.usda.gov/plantproj/plants/index.html

USDA PLANTS National Database

http://willow.ncfes.umn.edu/silvics_manual/volume_1/vol1_Table_o f_contents.htm

Volume 1 of Silvics of North America

http://willow.ncfes.umn.edu/silvics_manual/volume_2/vol2_Table_o f_contents.htm

Volume 2 of Silvics of North America

http://www.fl-ag.com/forest/treeid.htm#Forward

Forest Trees of Florida, Florida Department of Agriculture and Consumer Services, 17th edition.

http://www.fs.fed.us/database/feis/

UDSA Forest Service: Fire Effects Information

Index

Photo Credits

Frederick D. Atwood
pp. 30, 96 (r), 97, 117, 118 (l), 140, 162(r)
Bill Beatty
pp. 109 (r), 113, 125(r), 137 (l), 153 (r), 154, 230, 243, 244 (l), 246 (l)
Whit Bronaugh
pp. 6 (Ponderosa pine), 8 (Bigleaf maple), 12 (Subalpine larch), 14 (Engelmann spruce), 17 (American chestnut), 42 (l), 87 (r), 106, 108 (l), 100, 118 (r), 176, 215(l), 224, 248, 249 (r), 269 (r)
Brother Alfred Brousseau
pp. 25, 78, 79, 87 (l), 90 (l), 112, 138, 160 (l), 160 (r), 161, 174, 237 (r), 242 (r), 261
Calflora
p. 31, 85 (l), 187 (l)
Jeannie Couch
pp.63 (l), 119, 158 (r), 178, 190 (r), 194 (l), 196 (r), 210 (l), 249 (l), cover
Rob Curtis/The Early Birders
pp. 153 (l), 183, 257, 270
Katherine and Julian Dunster
p. 73
George M. Ferguson
pp. 159, 169 (l), 244 (r), 294 (Arizona pine)
Edward F. Gilman
pp. 137 (l), 229 (r)
Susan M. Glascock
pp.59 (r), 47 (l), 62, 67 (l), 93, 94 (l), 101 (l), 175 (l), 181 (r), 184, 188, 217, 222 (r), 253 (l), 266 (l)
L. J. Grauke
pp. 60, 65, 66
Horticopia (all photographs by Edward F. Gilman)
pp. 58, 76, 88, 98 (r), 102, 108(l), 116, 120 (r), 129 (r), 131, 139 (r), 148, 165, 170, 177 (r), 182, 211, 218R, 221, 222, 223, 225 (l), 227, 229 (l), 235, 245, 255, 265, 269(l), 182, 273 (l)
Horticultural Photography
pp. 144, 236, 252 (l)
Charlie Houder
pp. 103 (r), 142, 187 (r), 182 (l), 227
Alex Inselberg
p. 24 (l)
Bill Johnson
pp. 26 (l), 38, 44 (l), 67 (r), 69 (r), 77 (r), 104 (l), 134 (r), 226, 282 (Quaking aspen)
Byron Jorjorian
p. 10 (Baldcypress), 20 (Eastern redbud), 254
KAC Productions
pp. 51, 133, 135, 147
Leslie Landrum
pp. 44 (r)
David Liebman
pp. 39 (r), 61 (r), 72 (r), 100, 126, 141 (r), 146, 171 (r), 203
Glen P. Lumis
pp. 24 (r), 37 (r), 47 (r), 57, 80L, 84, 85 (r), 94 (r), 96 (l), 101 (r), 104 (r), 107, 108 (r), 145, 152L, 162L, 202, 207, 210 (r), 212, 214, 219, 220, 228, 231, 232, 234, 246 (r), 258, 260, 272, 273 (r)

Malak Photographs Ltd.
pp. 35, 139 (l), 242 (l), 250, 251
George K. Peck
pp. 33L, 47 (l), 89, 129 (l), 155
Lee Rentz
pp. 125 (l), 173 (l), 198, 256 (l), 267
Royal Botanical Gardens
pp. 42 (l), 137 (r)
Rob and Ann Simpson
pp. 26 (r), 33 (r), 43, 64, 63 (l), 72 (r), 74, 77 (l), 110, 121, 163 (l), 168, 186, 189, 195, 238
Richard Shiell
pp. 41, 50 (r), 92 (r), 128, 132 (r), 134 (l), 166 (r), 181 (l), 193, 200, 201, 205, 213, 215 (r), 216, 271
John Span
pp. 2 (White spruce), 34, 35 (r), 50 (l), 52 (r), 59 (l), 69 (l), 75, 99, 123, 127, 143 (l), 152 (l), 173 (r), 182 (r), 204, 206 (r), 233, 264
Scott T. Smith
pp. 32, 52 (l), 120 (l), 158 (l), 167, 169 (r), 171 (l), 172, 177 (l), 192, 206 (l)
Charles D. Steinmetz
pp. 122, 141 (l)
Ned Therrien
pp. 53, 56, 179, 180, 185, 225 (r)
Connie Toops
pp. 72, 80 (r), 143 (r), 163 (r), 166 (l), 175 (r), 237 (l), 239, 252 (r), 253, 262
Mark Turner
pp. 27, 81, 82, 91, 124, 151, 164, 190 (r), 194 (r), 218 (l), 276 (Mountain hemlock)
Visuals Unlimited
Walt Anderson: p. 37 (l), 103 (l); Norris Blake: p. 55 (r); Gerald and Buff Corsi: p. 92 (l); John D. Cunningham: p. 28 (r); Derrick Ditchburn: p. 45; Mark Epstein: p. 105; W.M. Grenfell: p. 98 (l); Mark Henley: p. 274; Robert E. Lyons: p. 55 (l), 79 (r); Glen Oliver: p. 14L; Nada Pecnik: p. 48, John Serrao: p. 54; John Sholden: p. 256 (r); Gilbert Twelst: p. 39L; Kenneth D. Whitney: p. 90 (r); Peter K. Ziminski: p. 29
Illustrations
Dorothy Siemens
pp. 29, 36, 83, 95, 136, 191, 199, 240, 275
Flora of North America Association
Bobbi Angell: 115, 149; Laurie Klingensmith: 23, 86, 263; Laurie Lange: 156; John K. Meyers: 49, 57, 70, 111, 130, 208, 268; Yevonn Wilson-Ramsey: 40
Reviews
Key Porter Books thanks the following people for their help reviewing the information in this book:
Dr. John D. Ambrose, Curator of Botany, Metropolitan Toronto Zoo
George A. Meyers
David Ward, Sir Sanford Fleming College
Hardiness Zone Map on page 277 illustrated by Pat Dunlavey and reprinted with permission from The Herb Gardener: A Guide for All Seasons by Susan McClure, published by Garden Way Publishing, Pownal, VT.